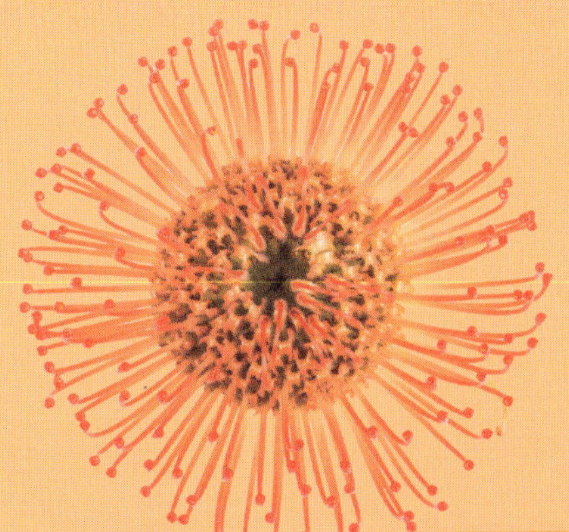

NSW Targeting Maths

Year 5

Garda Turner

PASCAL
PRESS

Contents

Term 1

Unit	Topic	Page
1	Hundred Thousands	2
2	Addition	5
3	Subtraction	10
4	Factors and Multiples	14
5	Fractions	19
6	Chance	25
	Investigation 1 Games Day Carnival	28
Revision		30
7	Patterns and Algebra	32
8	Length	35
9	Angles	40
10	Data	44
Term 1 Revision		48

Term 2

Unit	Topic	Page
NAPLAN* Practice		50
11	Place Value	58
12	Addition	63
13	Division	66
14	Fractions, Decimals and Percentages	70
15	Operations in Decimals	75
	Investigation 2 NewTime	80
Revision		82
16	Area and Perimeter	84
17	Volume and Capacity	89
18	Time	93
19	Position	97
20	Data	100
Term 2 Revision		104

Term 3

Unit	Topic	Page
21	Addition and Subtraction	106
22	Multiplication	109
23	Division	114
24	Fractions	119
25	Patterns and Algebra	123
	Investigation 3 Playground Marking	128
Revision		130
26	Perimeter and Area	132
27	Mass	134
28	3D Objects	138
29	2D Space	141
30	Angles	145
31	Data	148
Term 3 Revision		152

Term 4

Unit	Topic	Page
32	Division	154
33	Operations	159
34	Fractions	165
35	Fractions and Decimals	168
36	Measurement	172
37	Multiplication Strategies	176
	Investigation 4 All the Fun of the Fair	180
Revision		182
38	3D Objects	184
39	Transformation	187
40	Data and Chance	192
Term 4 Revision		198

New Edition

Targeting Maths Australia's Favourite Maths Program

Australian Curriculum/ NSW Alignment

This NEW Edition fully aligns each student page with both the new NSW Syllabus (2024) and the new Australian Curriculum: Mathematics F-10 version 9.0. The NSW Syllabus outcome codes and content groups appear with the Australian Curriculum strand and code on each student page.

iPad Apps

With an app for each year, from Foundation/Kindergarten to Year 6, the Targeting Maths Apps include all the essential maths content that children need to know in an amazing app that makes learning maths fun, motivating and full of rewards. Look for it in Apple's App Store today! Made especially for the iPad and aligned to each student page in this book.

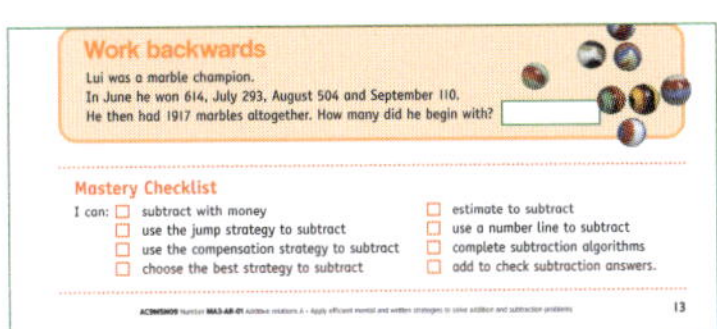

Work backwards

Lui was a marble champion.
In June he won 614, July 293, August 504 and September 110.
He then had 1917 marbles altogether. How many did he begin with?

Mastery Checklist

I can:
- subtract with money
- use the jump strategy to subtract
- use the compensation strategy to subtract
- choose the best strategy to subtract
- estimate to subtract
- use a number line to subtract
- complete subtraction algorithms
- add to check subtraction answers.

13

Mastery Checklists

Each unit has a Mastery Checklist. These checklists engage students in visible learning as they recognise and reflect on the specific maths skills learnt in each unit.

Integrated Problem-solving Program

Includes an integrated problem-solving program that actively builds students' problem solving capabilities.

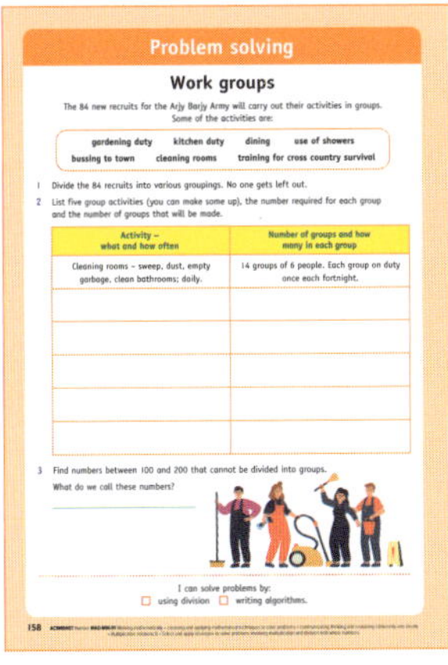

Problem solving

Work groups

gardening duty	kitchen duty	dining	use of showers
bussing to town	cleaning rooms	training for cross country survival	

1 Divide the 84 recruits into various groupings. No one gets left out.

2 List five group activities (you can make some up), the number required for each group and the number of groups that will be made.

Activity – what and how often	Number of groups and how many in each group
Cleaning rooms – sweep, dust, empty garbage, clean bathrooms; daily.	14 groups of 6 people. Each group on duty once each fortnight.

3 Find numbers between 100 and 200 that cannot be divided into groups. What do we call these numbers?

I can solve problems by:
- using division
- writing algorithms.

158

In-stage Topic Alignment for Composite Classes

Great for composite classes too, the contents of each book in one stage, eg Year 5 and Year 6, match topic by topic.

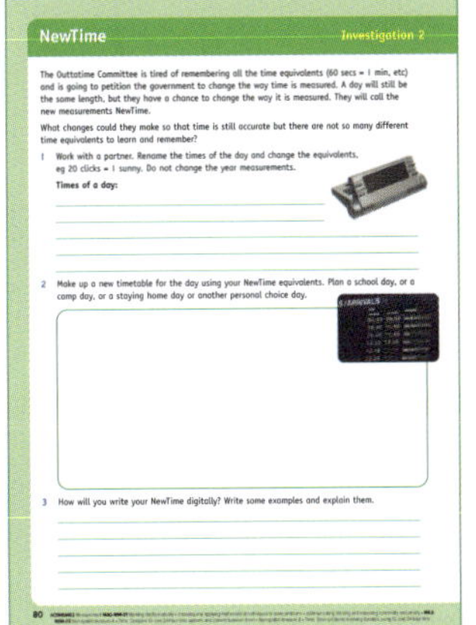

NewTime — Investigation 2

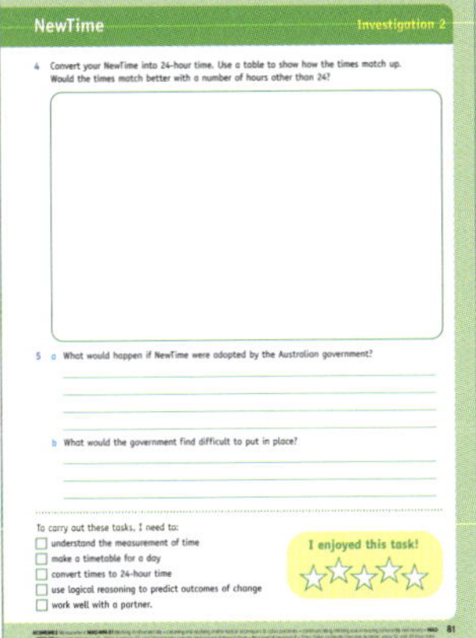

NewTime — Investigation 2

I enjoyed this task!

Term Investigations

Each term includes an investigation that will get students planning and working through an extended problem.

Regular Revision

Revision pages appear both at mid term and at the end of each term to revise key concepts.

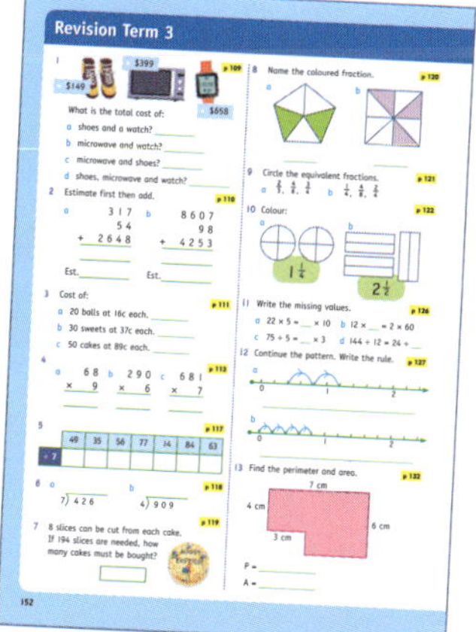

Revision Term 3

Hands-on Activities

Various hands-on activities are included in each term, asking students to measure and make, count and compare, using objects from around the classroom or home.

Year 5 Outcomes

Strand	NSW Syllabus Outcomes	Student pages
Working Mathematically	**MA1-WM-01** develops understanding and fluency in mathematics through exploring and connecting mathematical concepts	2–184
Working Mathematically	**MA1-WM-01** develops understanding and fluency in mathematics through choosing and applying mathematical techniques to solve problems	9, 24, 28, 29, 39, 69, 80, 81, 96, 113, 118, 122, 128, 129, 137, 158, 163, 164, 180, 181
Working Mathematically	**MA1-WM-01** evelops understanding and fluency in mathematics through communicating their thinking and reasoning coherently and clearly	9, 28, 29, 69, 80, 81, 96, 128, 129, 158, 163, 164, 180, 181
Number and Algebra	**Representing whole numbers**	
Number and Algebra	**MA3-RN-01** applies an understanding of place value and the role of zero to represent the properties of numbers	2, 3, 4, 58, 59, 62
Number and Algebra	**MA3-RN-02** compares and orders decimals up to 3 decimal places	21, 60, 61, 70, 75, 76, 170
Number and Algebra	**MA3-RN-03** determines percentages of quantities, and finds equivalent fractions and decimals for benchmark percentage values	71, 72, 73, 74
Number and Algebra	**Additive relations**	
Number and Algebra	**MA3-AR-01** selects and applies appropriate strategies to solve addition and subtraction problems	5, 6, 7, 8, 9, 10, 11, 12, 13, 33, 34, 63, 64, 65, 75, 77, 78, 106, 107, 108, 113, 117, 123, 159, 160, 162, 164, 180
Number and Algebra	**Multiplicative relations**	
Number and Algebra	**MA3-MR-01** selects and applies appropriate strategies to solve multiplication and division problems	14, 15, 16, 17, 18, 28, 33, 34, 66, 67, 68, 69, 79, 109, 110, 111, 112, 113, 114, 115, 116, 117, 118, 123, 124, 125, 126, 127, 154, 155, 156, 157, 158, 161, 162, 163, 164, 171, 176, 177, 178, 179, 180
Number and Algebra	**MA3-MR-02** constructs and completes number sentences involving multiplicative relations, applying the order of operations to calculations	32
Number and Algebra	**Fractions**	
Number and Algebra	**MA3-RQF-01** compares and orders fractions with denominators of 2, 3, 4, 5, 6, 8 and 10	19, 20, 21, 24, 119, 120, 121, 122, 165, 166, 167, 168, 169
Number and Algebra	**MA3-RQF-02** determines $\frac{1}{2}$, $\frac{1}{4}$, $\frac{1}{5}$ and $\frac{1}{10}$ of measures and quantities	20, 22, 23, 24
Measurement and Space	**Geometric measure**	
Measurement and Space	**MA3-GM-01** locates and describes points on a coordinate plane	97, 98, 99
Measurement and Space	**MA3-GM-02** selects and uses the appropriate unit and device to measure lengths and distances including perimeters	35, 36, 37, 38, 39, 84, 85, 132, 133, 173, 174
Measurement and Space	**MA3-GM-03** measures and constructs angles, and identifies the relationships between angles on a straight line and angles at a point	40, 41, 42, 43, 145, 146, 147
Measurement and Space	**Two-dimensional (2D) spatial structure**	
Measurement and Space	**MA3-2DS-01** investigates and classifies two-dimensional shapes, including triangles and quadrilaterals based on their properties	128, 141, 142, 143, 144, 145, 187, 188, 189, 190, 191
Measurement and Space	**MA3-2DS-02** selects and uses the appropriate unit to calculate areas, including areas of rectangles	84, 85, 86, 87, 128, 132, 133
Measurement and Space	**MA3-2DS-03** combines, splits and rearranges shapes to determine the area of parallelograms and triangles	88
Measurement and Space	**Three-dimensional (3D) spatial structure**	
Measurement and Space	**MA3-3DS-01** visualises, sketches and constructs three-dimensional objects, including prisms and pyramids, making connections to two-dimensional representations	91, 138, 139, 140, 184, 185, 186
Measurement and Space	**MA3-3DS-02** selects and uses the appropriate unit to estimate, measure and calculate volumes and capacities	89, 90, 92
Measurement and Space	**Non-spatial measure**	
Measurement and Space	**MA3-NSM-01** selects and uses the appropriate unit and device to measure the masses of objects	95, 134, 135, 136, 137, 175
Measurement and Space	**MA3-NSM-02** measures and compares duration, using 12- and 24-hour time and am and pm notation	80, 93, 94, 96, 172
Statistics & Probability	**Data and Chance**	
Statistics & Probability	**MA3-DATA-01** constructs graphs using many-to-one scales	45, 46, 47, 101, 102, 103, 195, 196
Statistics & Probability	**MA3-DATA-02** interprets data displays, including timelines and line graphs	44, 46, 47, 100, 148, 149, 150, 151, 194, 195, 197
Statistics & Probability	**MA3-CHAN-01** conducts chance experiments and quantifies the probability	25, 26, 27, 192, 193

Strand	Australian Curriculum Content Descriptions *Students learn to:*	Student pages
Number and Algebra	**Number**	
Number and Algebra	**AC9M5N01** interpret, compare and order numbers with more than 2 decimal places, including numbers greater than one, using place value understanding; represent these on a number line	21, 22, 60, 61, 70, 75, 76, 77, 78, 79, 170, 171
Number and Algebra	**AC9M5N02** express natural numbers as products of their factors, recognise multiples and determine if one number is divisible by another	14, 15, 18, 28, 66, 67, 68, 69, 155, 157
Number and Algebra	**AC9M5N03** compare and order fractions with the same and related denominators including mixed numerals, applying knowledge of factors and multiples; represent these fractions on a number line	19, 20, 21, 119, 120, 121, 122, 165, 166, 167, 176
Number and Algebra	**AC9M5N04** recognise that 100% represents the complete whole and use percentages to describe, represent and compare relative size; connect familiar percentages to their decimal and fraction equivalents	23, 71, 72, 73
Number and Algebra	**AC9M5N05** solve problems involving addition and subtraction of fractions with the same or related denominators, using different strategies	19, 24, 121, 122, 168, 169, 176
Number and Algebra	**AC9M5N06** solve problems involving multiplication of larger numbers by one- or two-digit numbers, choosing efficient calculation strategies and using digital tools where appropriate; check the reasonableness of answers	17, 79, 109, 110, 111, 112, 115, 117, 161, 177, 178, 179
Number and Algebra	**AC9M5N07** solve problems involving division, choosing efficient strategies and using digital tools where appropriate; interpret any remainder according to the context and express results as a whole number, decimal or fraction	20, 22, 28, 66, 67, 69, 72, 113, 114, 116, 118, 154, 156, 157, 158, 162, 163
Number and Algebra	**AC9M5N08** check and explain the reasonableness of solutions to problems including financial contexts using estimation strategies appropriate to the context	5, 7, 8, 10, 11, 39, 63, 64, 65, 108, 116, 118, 156, 160, 180
Number and Algebra	**AC9M5N09** use mathematical modelling to solve practical problems involving additive and multiplicative situations including financial contexts; formulate the problems, choosing operations and efficient calculation strategies, using digital tools where appropriate; interpret and communicate solutions in terms of the situation	5, 6, 7, 8, 9, 10, 11, 12, 13, 63, 64, 106, 107, 108, 109, 110, 113, 123, 124, 125, 159, 160, 161, 164, 177, 178, 179
Number and Algebra	**AC9M5N10** create and use algorithms involving a sequence of steps and decisions and digital tools to experiment with factors, multiples and divisibility; identify, interpret and describe emerging patterns	15, 16, 32, 65, 126, 127
Number and Algebra	**Algebra**	
Number and Algebra	**AC9M5A01** recognise and explain the connection between multiplication and division as inverse operations and use this to develop families of number facts	33, 34, 155
Number and Algebra	**AC9M5A02** find unknown values in numerical equations involving multiplication and division using the properties of numbers and operations	33, 34, 123, 124, 125
Measurement and Geometry	**Measurement**	
Measurement and Geometry	**AC9M5M01** choose appropriate metric units when measuring the length, mass and capacity of objects; use smaller units or a combination of units to obtain a more accurate measure	35, 36, 37, 38, 39, 88, 89, 90, 91, 92, 128, 134, 135, 136, 137, 141, 173, 175
Measurement and Geometry	**AC9M5M02** solve practical problems involving the perimeter and area of regular and irregular shapes using appropriate metric units	38, 84, 85, 86, 87, 128, 132, 133, 174
Measurement and Geometry	**AC9M5M03** compare 12- and 24-hour time systems and solve practical problems involving the conversion between them	80, 93, 94, 96, 172
Measurement and Geometry	**AC9M5M04** estimate, construct and measure angles in degrees, using appropriate tools including a protractor, and relate these measures to angle names	40, 41, 42, 43, 142, 145, 146, 147
Measurement and Geometry	**Space**	
Measurement and Geometry	**AC9M5SP01** connect objects to their nets and build objects from their nets using spatial and geometric reasoning	138, 139, 140, 184, 185, 186
Measurement and Geometry	**AC9M5SP02** construct a grid coordinate system that uses coordinates to locate positions within a space; use coordinates and directional language to describe position and movement	97, 98, 99, 194, 195, 196
Measurement and Geometry	**AC9M5SP03** describe and perform translations, reflections and rotations of shapes, using dynamic geometric software where appropriate; recognise what changes and what remains the same, and identify any symmetries	143, 187, 188, 191
Statistics and Probability	**Statistics**	
Statistics and Probability	**AC9M5ST01** acquire, validate and represent data for nominal and ordinal categorical and discrete numerical variables to address a question of interest or purpose using software including spreadsheets; discuss and report on data distributions in terms of highest frequency (mode) and shape, in the context of the data	44, 45, 46, 47, 100, 101, 102, 103, 197
Statistics and Probability	**AC9M5ST02** interpret line graphs representing change over time; discuss the relationships that are represented and conclusions that can be made	148, 149, 150, 151
Statistics and Probability	**AC9M5ST03** plan and conduct statistical investigations by posing questions or identifying a problem and collecting relevant data; choose appropriate displays and interpret the data; communicate findings within the context of the investigation	102, 103
Statistics and Probability	**Probability**	
Statistics and Probability	**AC9M5P01** list the possible outcomes of chance experiments involving equally likely outcomes and compare to those which are not equally likely	25, 26, 27, 192, 193
Statistics and Probability	**AC9M5P02** conduct repeated chance experiments including those with and without equally likely outcomes, observe and record the results ; use frequency to compare outcomes and estimate their likelihoods	26, 192, 193

How to Solve a Problem

Read • Plan • Work • Check

Read the problem carefully. Read it again. Underline important words.

Plan what you are going to do — add, subtract, multiply or divide.

Work Write the steps you take to work out the answer. Write your answer in full.

Check your answer! Make sure that your answer makes sense and that you answered the question.

Draw a diagram

Draw a simple picture.
Use symbols if you can.

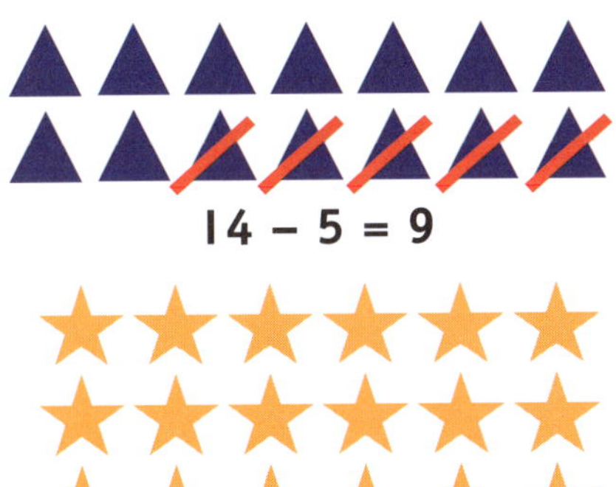

3 × 6 = 18

Trial and Error

Make a guess and write it down. Check if it is right. If not, work out if your guess should be higher or lower. Make another guess and write it down. Check if it's right. Keep going until you have the correct answer.

Look for patterns

Study the numbers in the problem.
Write them down in a list.
Can you see a pattern?
What comes next in the pattern.
Write it as your answer.

Cindy cycles 3 km, then 6 km, then 9 km on 3 days. How far should she cycle on the 4th day to keep to her pattern?

3, 6, 9, ? *3, 6, 9, 12*

Cindy should cycle 12 km.

Use a table

Put the information from the problem in columns. Can you see the pattern? The information is clearer in a table.

Use this to work out the answer.

Jerry	5 mins	10 cakes	2 in 1 min.
Cam	4 mins	8 cakes	2 in 1 min.
Tilly	3 mins	9 cakes	3 in 1 min.

Who eats the fastest?

Answer: Tilly eats fastest.

Work backwards

Read the problem all the way through. Find one piece of information. Write it down. Find another piece of information that relates and put them together. Write it down. Keep working backwards until you solve all the pieces of the problem.

Kell has $2 more than Matt, who has $3 less than Jan. Jan has $10. How much do they each have?

Jan = $10

Matt = $10 – $3 = $7

Kell = $7 + $2 = $9

Dictionary

angle

The amount of turning between two straight lines that meet at a point.

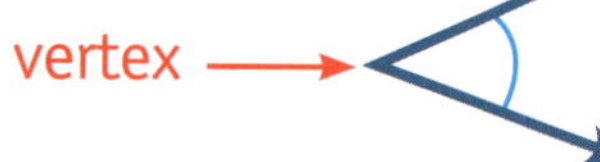

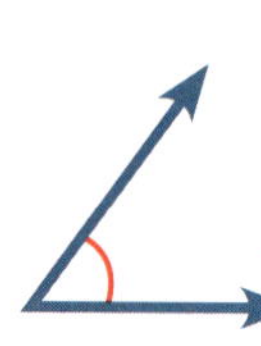

Acute angles are less than 90°.

Straight angles are 180°.

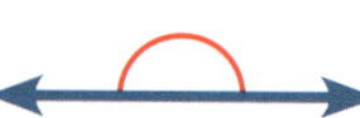

Obtuse angles are larger than 90° but less than 180°.

Reflex angles are larger than 180° but less than 360°.

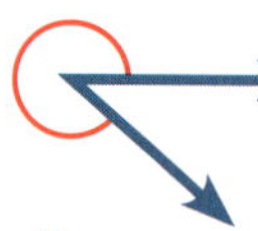

Revolutions are 360°.

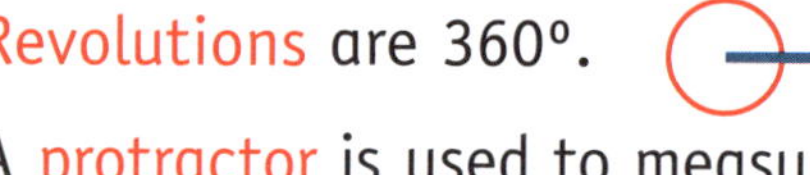

A protractor is used to measure angles.

area

Area is the size of the surface.
It is measured in square units.
square centimetres (cm^2)
square metres (m^2)
hectares (ha) (1 ha = 10 000 m^2)
square kilometres (km^2)

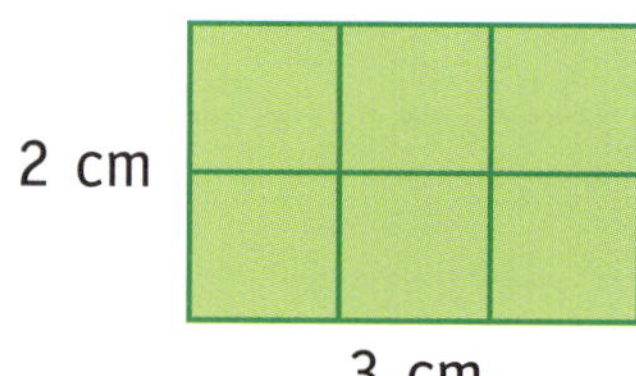

Area = 2 cm × 3 cm
= 6 cm^2

average

Average = sum of scores ÷ number of scores

average of 7, 9, 12, 16 = $\frac{7 + 9 + 12 + 16}{4}$
= 11

capacity

The amount a container can hold.

The capacity of this bottle is 1 litre.

coordinates

A pair of numbers or letters that tell position.

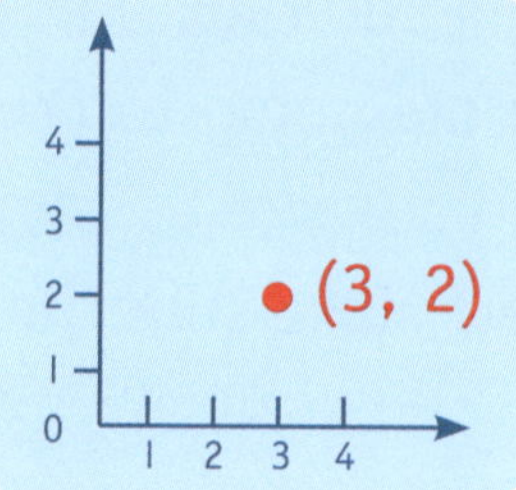

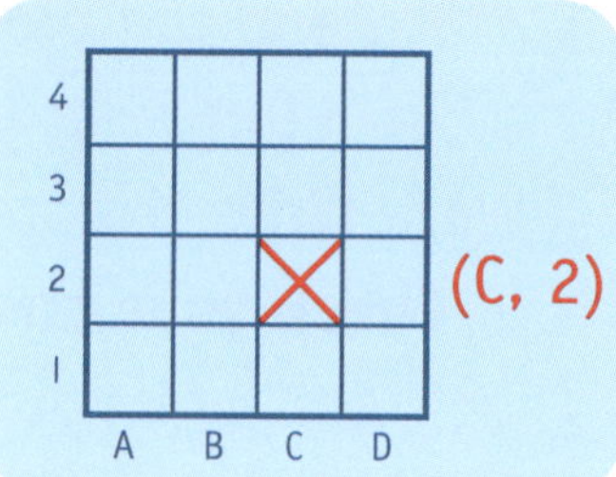

The bottom number or letter always comes first.

cross-section

The surface that is seen when a solid shape is cut through.

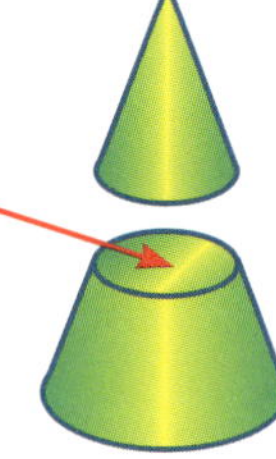

data

A collection of information.

Favourite sports		
Sport	**Votes**	**Total**
Soccer	𝍸 𝍸 ǁ	**12**
Netball	𝍸 |	**6**
Football	𝍸 |||	**8**
Chess	𝍸 𝍸 |	**11**

edge/face/vertex

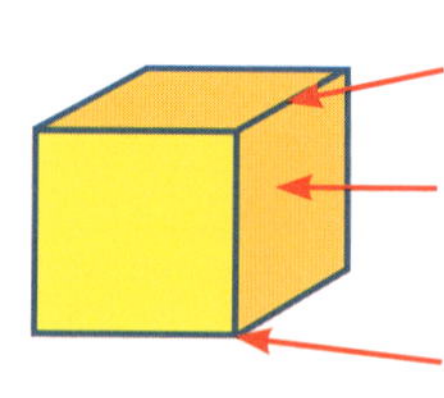

An edge is where two flat surfaces meet.

A face is the flat surface of a solid shape.

A vertex is where the edges meet to make a corner.

factor

A whole number that can be divided exactly into another number.

6 is a factor of 42.

Dictionary

fraction

Any part of a group or whole.

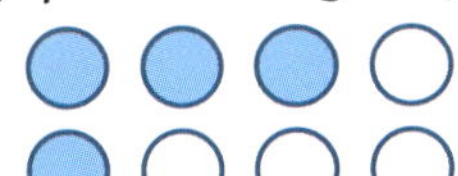

$\frac{4}{8}$ ← numerator ← denominator

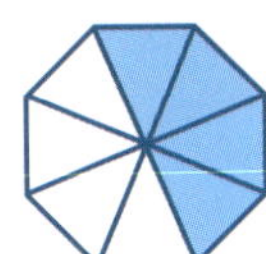

$\frac{4}{8} = \frac{1}{2}$

Equivalent fractions are fractions that have the same value, eg $\frac{4}{8} = \frac{1}{2}$.

Decimal fractions are ones written using a decimal point to show the tenths, hundredths etc. eg 3·63.

Mixed numbers have a whole number and a fraction, eg $4\frac{1}{2}$

graphs

A diagram that shows a collection of data.

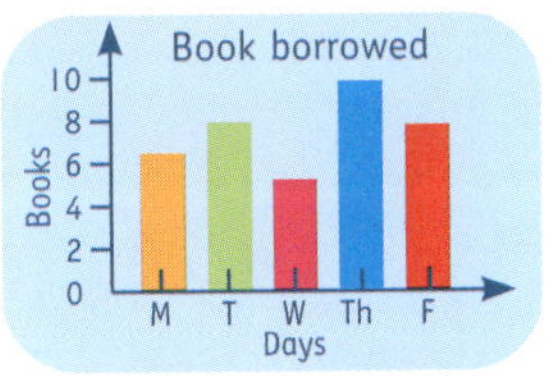

column graph

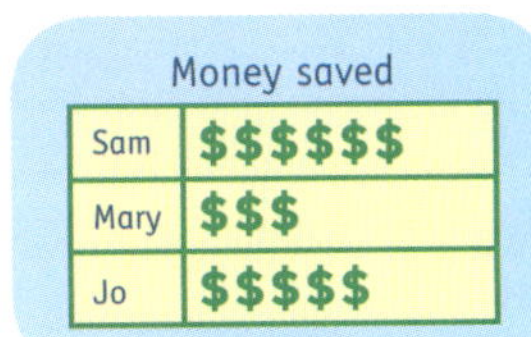

picture graph

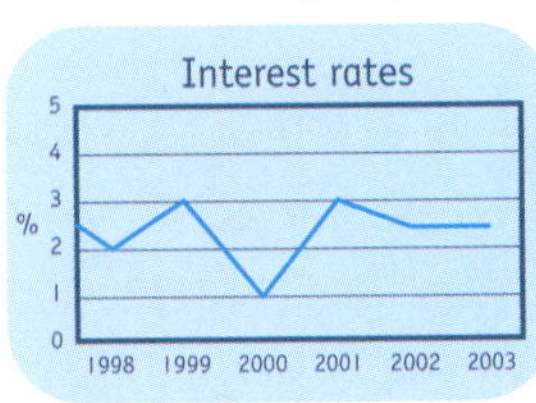

line graph

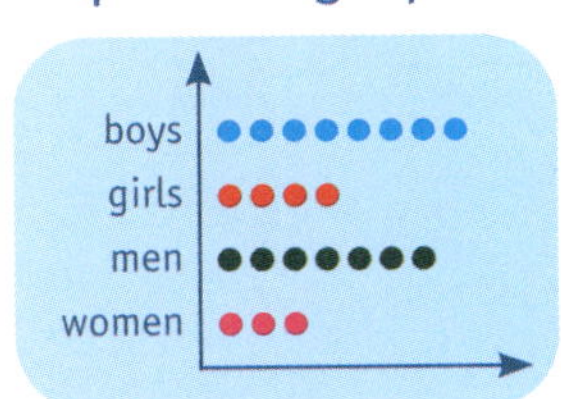

dot plot

highest common factor

The HCF is the highest number which is a factor of two or more numbers, eg the HCF of 9 and 15 is 3.

length

The distance from one end to another. Length is measured in millimetres (mm), centimetres (cm), metres (m) and kilometres (km).

10 mm = 1 cm   100 cm = 1 m
1000 m = 1 km

lines

Parallel lines never meet.

Perpendicular lines are at right angles.

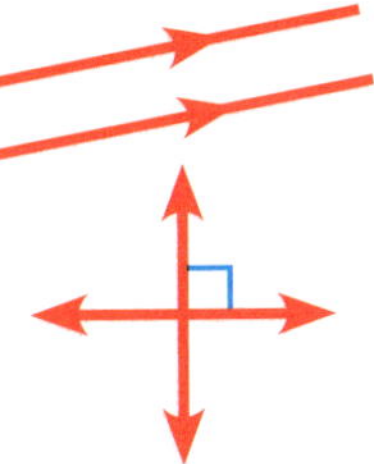

lowest common multiple

The LCM is the lowest number which is a multiple of two or more numbers, eg LCM of 4 and 3 is 12.

mass

Mass is measured in grams (g), kilograms (kg) and tonnes (t).

1000 g = 1 kg   1000 kg = 1 t

mean

Mean is the average of a set of scores.

Scores: 4, 6, 2, 4, 5, 3, 5
Mean: $29 \div 7 = 4\frac{1}{7}$

multiple

The product of two or more factors.

$3 \times 2 \times 4 = 24$

24 is a multiple of 2, 3 and 4.

outcome

A result of an experiment or trial eg rolling a die has 6 outcomes:

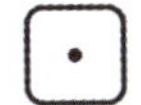

percent

An amount out of one hundred (%).

$\frac{53}{100}$ fraction

0·53 decimal

53% percentage

perimeter

The length of the outside boundary of a shape.

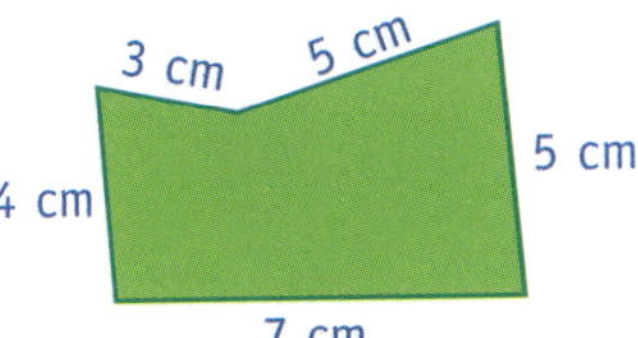

P = 4 cm + 3 cm + 5 cm + 5 cm + 7 cm
P = 24 cm

Dictionary

place value

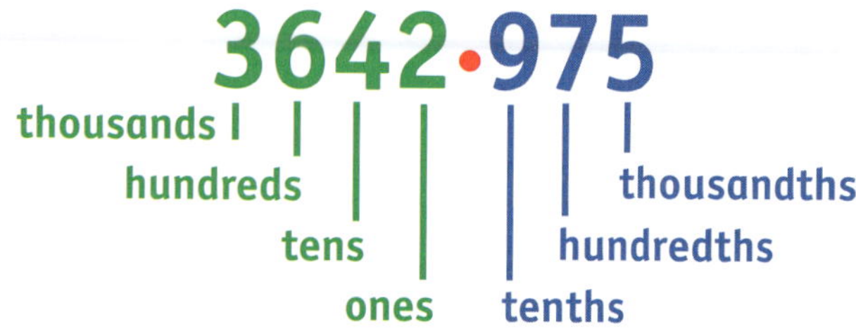

prime number
A number which has only two factors – itself and one.

2 has factors 2 and 1.
19 has factors 19 and 1.
2 and 19 are prime numbers.

Numbers with more than two factors are composite numbers.

probability
The chance of something happening. Probability can be described in:

words: certain, impossible, likely, unlikely.

decimals from 0 to 1: 0·5, 0·75

percentages: 10% chance, 50% chance

spreadsheet
A table used to organise data into rows and columns

	A	B	C	D	E
1	5	6	11		
2	6	7	13		
3	7	8	15		
4	8	9	17		

A1 + B1 = C1

surface
The flat or curved outside layer of a olid shape.

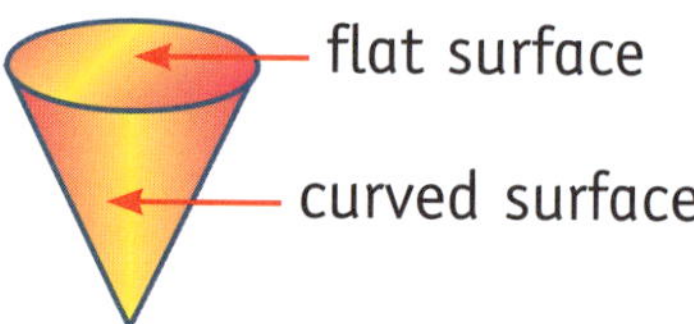

symmetry
A shape has line symmetry if both halves match exactly when it is folded on the axis of symmetry.

axis of symmetry

A shape has rotational symmetry when a tracing of the shape matches the original as it rotates around its centre.

tally
A mark made to represent an item when counting. Four vertical marks are made and crossed horizontally with the fifth to keep them in bundles of fives.

卌 卌 ||| = 13

three-dimensional (3D) objects
A 3D object has length, width and height. They include:

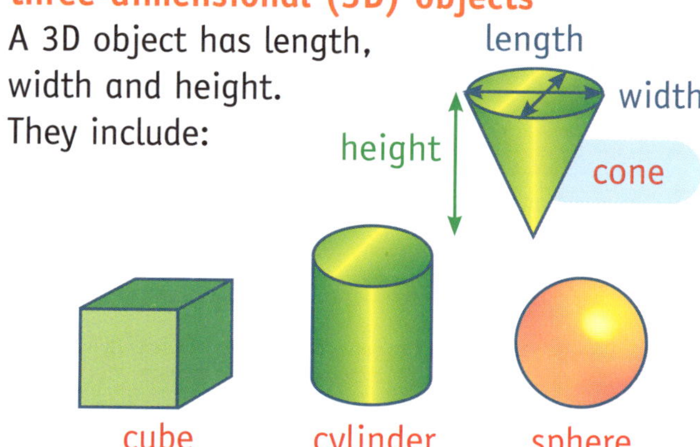

prisms – Objects which have a uniform cross-section, two end faces which give a prism its name and all other faces are rectangles.

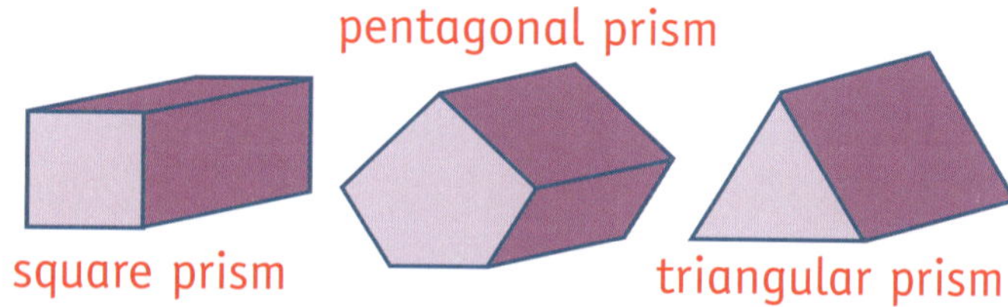

pyramids – Objects which have polygons as a base and all other sides are triangles.

Dictionary

time
Time can be displayed in 12-hour or 24-hour form.

analogue

digital

1 hour = 60 minutes
1 minute = 60 seconds

transformations
The three types of transformations are:

Translation: slide a 2D shape without changing it in any way

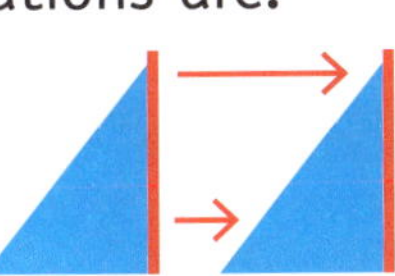

Reflection: flip a shape over to make a mirror image

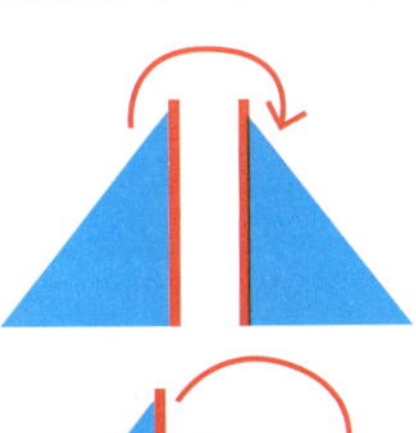

Rotation: turn a shape around a fixed point.

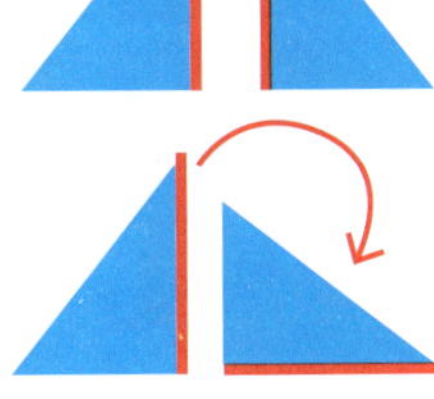

triangle
A polygon with three angles and three sides. There are 4 types of triangles.

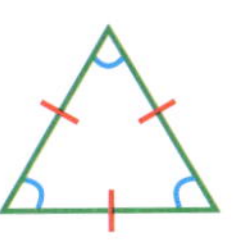

equilateral — All sides are equal. All angles are equal.

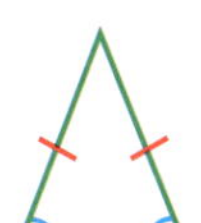

isosceles — Two sides are equal. Two angles are equal.

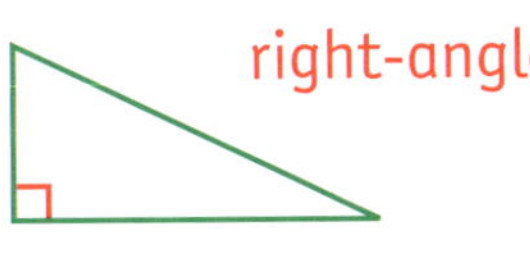

right-angled — One angle is a right angle (90°).

scalene — Each side is a different length.

two-dimensional (2D) shapes
Shapes that have only two dimensions — length and width. They include:

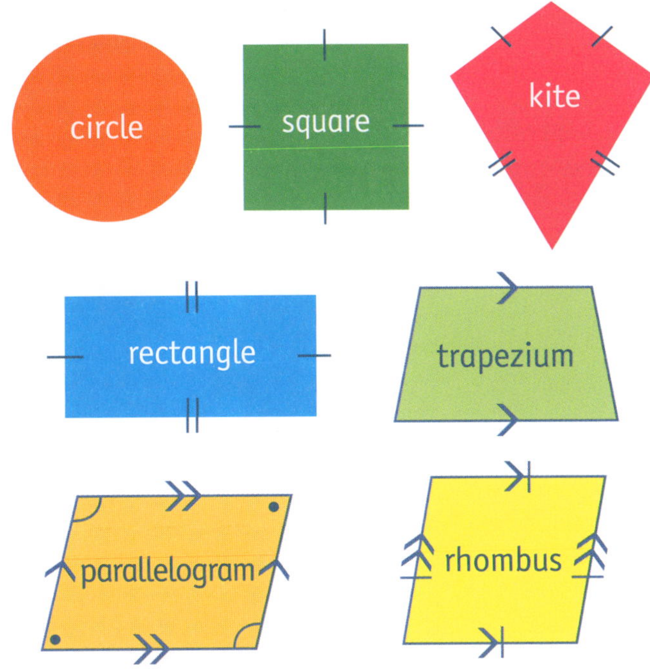

polygons: 5 sides – pentagon
6 sides – hexagon
7 sides – heptagon
8 sides – octagon
9 sides – nonagon
10 sides – decagon

regular polygons – All sides are equal and all angles are equal.

volume
The amount of space a solid object takes up.

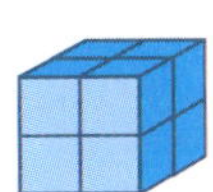

Volume = 2 × 2 × 2
= 8 cubic units

Units of volume:
cubic centimetres (cm^3)
cubic metres (m^3)

Unit 1 Hundred thousands

HOUSES FOR SALE

BUDAROO
REAL ESTATE
is selling these houses.

1 What does K mean in the price? ______________________

____

2 Why would a real estate agent use K in the price of a house? ______________________

3 Write the price of each house in full.

A ________ B ________ C ________ D ________

E ________ F ________ G ________

4 Write the houses in order from least expensive to most expensive.

____

5 Write the prices of these houses in words.

A ______________________

C ______________________

F ______________________

Unit 1 Place value

Place value

1 Write these numbers in their correct places.

	Hundred thousands	Ten thousands	Thousands	Hundreds	Tens	Ones
a 64 329						
b 906						
c 528 045						
d 80 961						
e 439 200						
f 6030						
g 700 358						

2 Write the value of each green numeral.

a 7651 __________ b 8139 __________

c 15 384 __________ d 769 128 __________

e 934 058 __________ f 60 573 __________

g 26 290 __________ h 517 846 __________

Digit value

8794

8 is in the thousands place and has a value of 8000.

3 Write in ascending order the numbers in question 2 that are less than 500 000.

____

4 Write in expanded notation the numbers in question 2 that are more than 500 000.

a 517 846 = 500 000 + 10 000 + ______ + ______ + ______ + ______

b ______ = __________________

c ______ = __________________

Look at page 2.

5 Round each house price to the nearest ten thousand dollars.

A ______ B ______ C ______ D ______

E ______ F ______ G ______

6 Draw a line to match each object to its price.

a 

b 

c 

d $99.00

Unit 1 Hundred thousands

Partition numbers

To add large numbers mentally, pull them apart and put them together differently.

eg 138 900 + 180 000 can be worked as 120 000 + 18 900 + 180 000. Add 120 000 and 180 000 to get 300 000, then add 18 900. The answer is 318 900.

1 Write two ways that these numbers can be partitioned.

a 426 __________ __________

b 769 __________ __________

c 1560 __________ __________

d 2486 __________ __________

e 13 900 __________ __________

f 78 950 __________ __________

g 245 600 __________ __________

h 845 300 __________ __________

2 Partition these numbers and add them mentally. Show how you reached your answer.

a 680 + 125 __________

b 709 + 345 __________

c 5690 + 756 __________

d 89 000 + 43 250 __________

e 74 262 + 56 840 __________

f 236 050 + 190 050 __________

3 A car driver reads **106 479·6** on the odometer.
Which digit will change when she has driven another:

a 1 km? __________ b 100 km? __________

c 10 000 km? __________ d 10 km? __________

e 100 000 km? __________ f 100 m? __________

4 What will the odometer read after travelling:

a 40 km? __________ b 50 000 km? __________

c 10·2 km? __________ d 3000 km? __________

e 200 000 km? __________

Mastery Checklist I can:

- ☐ use place value to hundred thousands
- ☐ partition numbers to hundred thousands
- ☐ partition to add.

Unit 2 Two-digit addition

CHERRY PIPPING COMPETITION

Sam

97

Mary

56

Terry

49

Jill

78

Ahmed

80

Suzie

65

1 In the cherry pipping competition who:

a did the most? ________ b did the least? ________

2 Add the totals.

a Sam + Mary ____ b Terry + Ahmed ____ c Suzie + Jill ____

d Mary + Jill ____ e Ahmed + Sam ____ f Terry + Suzie ____

3 Which two children together pipped:

a 146? ______ b 158? ______ c 162? ______

4 a Add the three highest scores. ______

b Add the three lowest scores. ______

5 Which three children pipped a total of:

a 233? ________ b 223? ________

6 a Estimate how many cherries were pipped altogether. ______

b Use a calculator to find the exact total. ______

Unit 2 Addition facts

Strategies +

Near doubles
15 + 16 = 15 + 15 + 1
27 + 25 = 27 + 27 − 2

Quick practice.

1 Use doubles and near doubles.

a 9 + 8 = ______ b 11 + 12 = ______ c 15 + 16 = ______ d 25 + 24 = ______
e 17 + 18 = ______ f 35 + 34 = ______ g 43 + 44 = ______ h 56 + 57 = ______
i 16 + 11 + 16 = ______ j 23 + 17 + 17 = ______ k 92 + 92 + 83 = ______

2 Use the split strategy.

Split strategy
67 + 32 = 60 + 30 + 7 + 2 = 99
54 + 87 = 50 + 80 + 4 + 7 = 141

a 43 + 34 = ______ b 65 + 24 = ______
c 81 + 17 = ______ d 38 + 27 = ______
e 55 + 38 = ______ f 68 + 49 = ______
g 85 + 27 = ______ h 39 + 49 = ______ i 76 + 67 = ______ j 46 + 79 = ______

3 Use the compensation strategy.

a 27 + 41 = ______ b 45 + 29 = ______
c 83 + 38 = ______ d 57 + 42 = ______
e 56 + 39 = ______ f 74 + 81 = ______
g 98 + 73 = ______ h 66 + 52 = ______

Compensation strategy
38 + 42 = 38 + 40 + 2
= 78 + 2
= 80
53 + 39 = 53 + 40 − 1
= 93 − 1
= 92

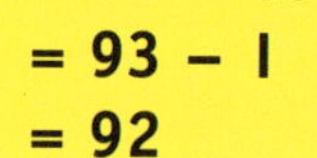

4 Use the jump strategy.

a 46 + 38 = ______ b 72 + 27 = ______
c 39 + 55 = ______ d 23 + 69 = ______
e 68 + 64 = ______ f 19 + 77 = ______
g 57 + 83 = ______ h 84 + 97 = ______ i 28 + 69 = ______

Jump strategy
53 + 38
53 + 30 = 83
83 + 8 = 91

5

a 38 sheep. 43 cows. 27 horses. How many animals altogether? ☐

b I spent 17c on an apple, 46c on a peach, 85c on a mango. How much did I spend? ☐

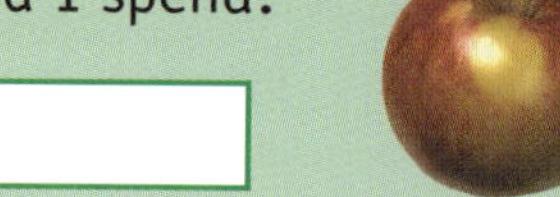

c 49 red pens. 38 blue pens. 64 black pens. How many pens altogether? ☐

Challenge! Work these out mentally. Name the strategies you used.

	Strategies
a 68 + 47 + 48 =	
b 93 + 17 + 76 =	
c 46 + 59 + 37 =	

Unit 2 Addition algorithms

1

a	b	c	d	e
37	58	72	55	80
64	19	16	94	39
28	20	85	78	69
+ 43	+ 64	+ 57	+ 46	+ 63
____	____	____	____	____

2

a	b	c	d	e
342	216	206	374	158
+ 113	+ 453	+ 345	+ 518	+ 629
____	____	____	____	____

f	g	h
407	634	255
+ 287	+ 279	+ 463
____	____	____

Don't forget to add the extra tens and hundreds.

i	j	k
193	264	323
+ 754	+ 584	+ 597
____	____	____

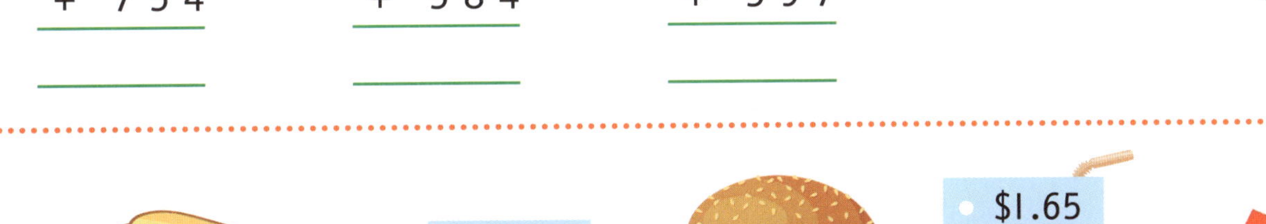

3 Calculate mentally the price of:

a a sandwich and a drink. ________

b a hamburger and a fruit salad. ________

c a pie and a drink. ________

d a sandwich and a pie. ________

e a hamburger and a sandwich. ________

f a drink and a fruit salad. ________

4 Write algorithms for the cost of:

a a pie, a sandwich and a fruit salad.

b 3 hamburgers.

Challenge!

What is the total cost of buying 2 of each item for a family picnic?

Unit 2 Number lines

Strategies +

1 Use the number lines.

a 723 + 254 = ________

b 618 + 176 = ________

c 375 + 481 = ________

d 546 + 363 = ________

2 Estimate first.

a
```
   6 8
   4 9
   8 1
+  2 6
------
```
Est. ________

b
```
   7 5
   1 8
   5 4
+  3 7
------
```
Est. ________

c
```
   2 6 5
+  5 7 8
--------
```
Est. ________

d
```
   4 0 8
+  3 9 5
--------
```
Est. ________

What a lot of adding.

3 Work the above examples using number lines.

a = ________

b = ________

c = ________

d = ________

4 What strategies could you use for question 2, c and d?

________________________________ ________________________________

5 a Which method was easiest? ________________________________

b Why? ________________________________

Mastery Checklist

I can:

- ☐ compare and add numbers
- ☐ estimate to add
- ☐ use near doubles to add
- ☐ use the split strategy to add
- ☐ use the compensation strategy to add
- ☐ use the jump strategy to add
- ☐ use a number line to add
- ☐ choose the best strategy to add
- ☐ complete addition algorithms.

AC9M5N08 • AC9M5N09 Number **MA3-AR-01** Additive relations A • Apply efficient mental and written strategies to solve addition and subtraction problems • Use estimation and place value understanding to determine the reasonableness of solutions

Problem solving

Digit shuffling

1 Using the digits 1, 4, 6, 7, 9, form a three-digit and a two-digit number to:

a give the largest sum possible.

Largest sum = ____

b give the smallest sum possible.

Smallest sum = ____

c What different strategies can you use to make these sums?

2 a Make a one-digit and 2 two-digit numbers that add to the greatest sum.

b Make the same large sum by rearranging these digits.

3 What strategies helped to solve these problems? Explain.

1 4 6 7 9 1 4 6 7 9 1 4 6 7 9

I can solve problems by:

☐ adding numbers ☐ using different strategies.

Unit 3 Subtraction of money

Yesterday's cakes CHEAP!

Apple tart
$1.75

Cherry tart
$1.90

Chocolate bear
$0.95

Cherry danish
$1.65

Fruit tart
$2.10

Gingerbread man
$1.20

Orange tart
$1.70

Peanut slice
$0.60

The kids in Jones Street love buying the stale cakes.

1 Pete has $2.

a What cake can't he buy? ____________________

b How much change will he get if he buys:

a peanut slice? ________ a cherry danish? ________ a gingerbread man? ________

2 Terri has $3. What did she buy if her change is:

a $2.05? __________ **b** $1.10? __________ **c** $1.80? __________

3 Louis has $5. How much change will he get if he buys:

a an apple tart? ________ **b** an orange tart? ________ **c** a cherry danish? ________

4 Dale will get $2.90 change if she buys the most expensive cake.

a How much change would she get if she buys the cheapest cake? ________

b Could she buy any three cakes? ________ Why? ______________________________

____

Unit 3 Subtraction strategies

1 Use the jump strategy.

a 29 − 18 = ____ b 36 − 17 = ____ c 54 − 25 = ____

d 71 − 46 = ____ e 66 − 39 = ____ f 87 − 55 = ____

g 90 − 34 = ____ h 45 − 23 = ____ i 91 − 68 = ____

2 Use the compensation strategy.

a 43 − 19 = ____ b 85 − 31 = ____ c 54 − 22 = ____

d 79 − 18 = ____ e 72 − 28 = ____ f 37 − 19 = ____

Jump strategy

54 − 37: 54 − 30 = 24
24 − 7 = 17

Compensation strategy

65 − 28: 65 − 30 = 35
35 + 2 = 37

60 − 41: 60 − 40 = 20
20 − 1 = 19

3 Choose a strategy.

a 65 − 37 = ____

b What strategy did you use? ________________________

c Why? ________________________

4 a 53 − 29 = ____

b What strategy did you use? ________________________

c Why? ________________________

5 Complete.

a

−	31	84	68	42	96	75	53	27
19								

b

−	41	79	50	37	74	90	63	82
29								

6 Estimate the answers.

a 124 + 73 ____ b 97 + 201 ____ c 42 + 81 ____ d 311 + 38 ____

e 117 + 61 ____ f 229 + 54 ____ g 309 + 102 ____ h 156 + 27 ____

7 Now work the answers for question 6 using a calculator.

a ____ b ____ c ____ d ____

e ____ f ____ g ____ h ____

8 How do you rate your estimating skills? Poor — Fair — Good — Excellent

Challenge!

a Estimate. 174 + 203 + 98 + 156 ____

b Use a calculator for the exact answer. ____

c Was your estimate a good one? ____

Unit 3 Subtraction methods

Number lines

You choose whether to take big jumps or small jumps. Both are correct.

1 Use the number lines.

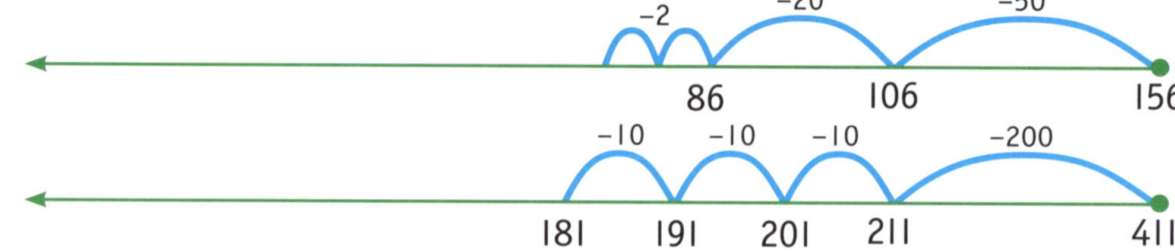

a 156 − 72 = _____

b 411 − 238 = _____

c 235 − 116 = _____

d 369 − 247 = _____

e 753 − 488 = _____

f 614 − 375 = _____

2 Trade in the tens.

Remember!
71 is the same as 60 + 11.

a $\begin{array}{r} 471 \\ -\ 237 \\ \hline \end{array}$ b $\begin{array}{r} 583 \\ -\ 165 \\ \hline \end{array}$ c $\begin{array}{r} 637 \\ -\ 418 \\ \hline \end{array}$

d $\begin{array}{r} 990 \\ -\ 726 \\ \hline \end{array}$ e $\begin{array}{r} 556 \\ -\ 339 \\ \hline \end{array}$ f $\begin{array}{r} 782 \\ -\ 537 \\ \hline \end{array}$ g $\begin{array}{r} 894 \\ -\ 547 \\ \hline \end{array}$

3 Trade in the hundreds.

a $\begin{array}{r} 736 \\ -\ 264 \\ \hline \end{array}$ b $\begin{array}{r} 885 \\ -\ 691 \\ \hline \end{array}$ c $\begin{array}{r} 614 \\ -\ 330 \\ \hline \end{array}$ d $\begin{array}{r} 577 \\ -\ 185 \\ \hline \end{array}$ e $\begin{array}{r} 949 \\ -\ 492 \\ \hline \end{array}$

f $\begin{array}{r} 428 \\ -\ 156 \\ \hline \end{array}$ g $\begin{array}{r} 653 \\ -\ 470 \\ \hline \end{array}$ h $\begin{array}{r} 862 \\ -\ 581 \\ \hline \end{array}$ i $\begin{array}{r} 716 \\ -\ 455 \\ \hline \end{array}$ j $\begin{array}{r} 537 \\ -\ 391 \\ \hline \end{array}$

4 a $\begin{array}{r} 725 \\ -\ 247 \\ \hline \end{array}$ b $\begin{array}{r} 348 \\ -\ 186 \\ \hline \end{array}$ c $\begin{array}{r} 693 \\ -\ 389 \\ \hline \end{array}$ d $\begin{array}{r} 857 \\ -\ 278 \\ \hline \end{array}$ e $\begin{array}{r} 906 \\ -\ 618 \\ \hline \end{array}$

Unit 3 Checking answers

1 Work the algorithms, then add to check your answers.

a
$$\begin{array}{r} 627 \\ -\ 263 \\ \hline \end{array}$$

b
$$\begin{array}{r} 835 \\ -\ 548 \\ \hline \end{array}$$

c
$$\begin{array}{r} 410 \\ -\ 168 \\ \hline \end{array}$$

d
$$\begin{array}{r} 727 \\ -\ 590 \\ \hline \end{array}$$

Check.

a
$$\begin{array}{r} 263 \\ +\ \\ \hline \end{array}$$

b
$$\begin{array}{r} 548 \\ +\ \\ \hline \end{array}$$

c ______ +

d ______ +

Checking
Use + to check subtraction.

$$\begin{array}{r} 815 \\ -\ 278 \\ \hline 537 \end{array}$$

Check
$$\begin{array}{r} 537 \\ +\ 278 \\ \hline 815 \end{array}$$

2 The trucks are all carrying cartons to Sam's Super Seconds shop. What are the differences in the numbers of cartons they are carrying? Write the subtractions using the letters.

a **A** – **B** = ______ b **A** – **C** = ______ c ______ d ______

e ______ f ______ g ______ h ______

i ______ j ______

k Why can you not work **A** – **E** or **C** – **D**?

______

3 Complete the path, then work backwards to check.

Work backwards

Lui was a marble champion.
In June he won 614, July 293, August 504 and September 110.
He then had 1917 marbles altogether. How many did he begin with? ______

Mastery Checklist

I can:
- ☐ subtract with money
- ☐ use the jump strategy to subtract
- ☐ use the compensation strategy to subtract
- ☐ choose the best strategy to subtract
- ☐ estimate to subtract
- ☐ use a number line to subtract
- ☐ complete subtraction algorithms
- ☐ add to check subtraction answers.

Unit 4 Factors

The leaves are factors. Write the leaf numbers on the tree they belong to.

Some leaves will go on more than one tree. Circle the common factors of 60 and 72.

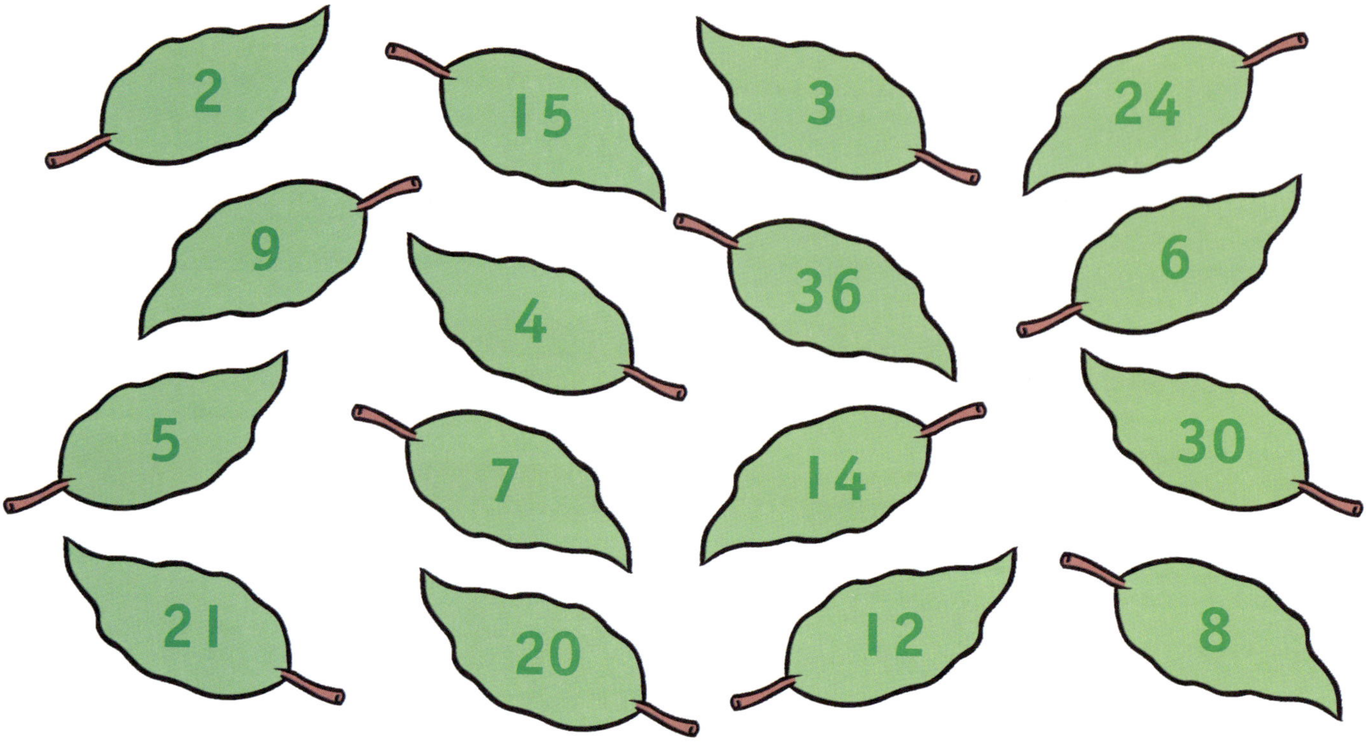

2 15 3 24

9 4 36 6

5 7 14 30

21 20 12 8

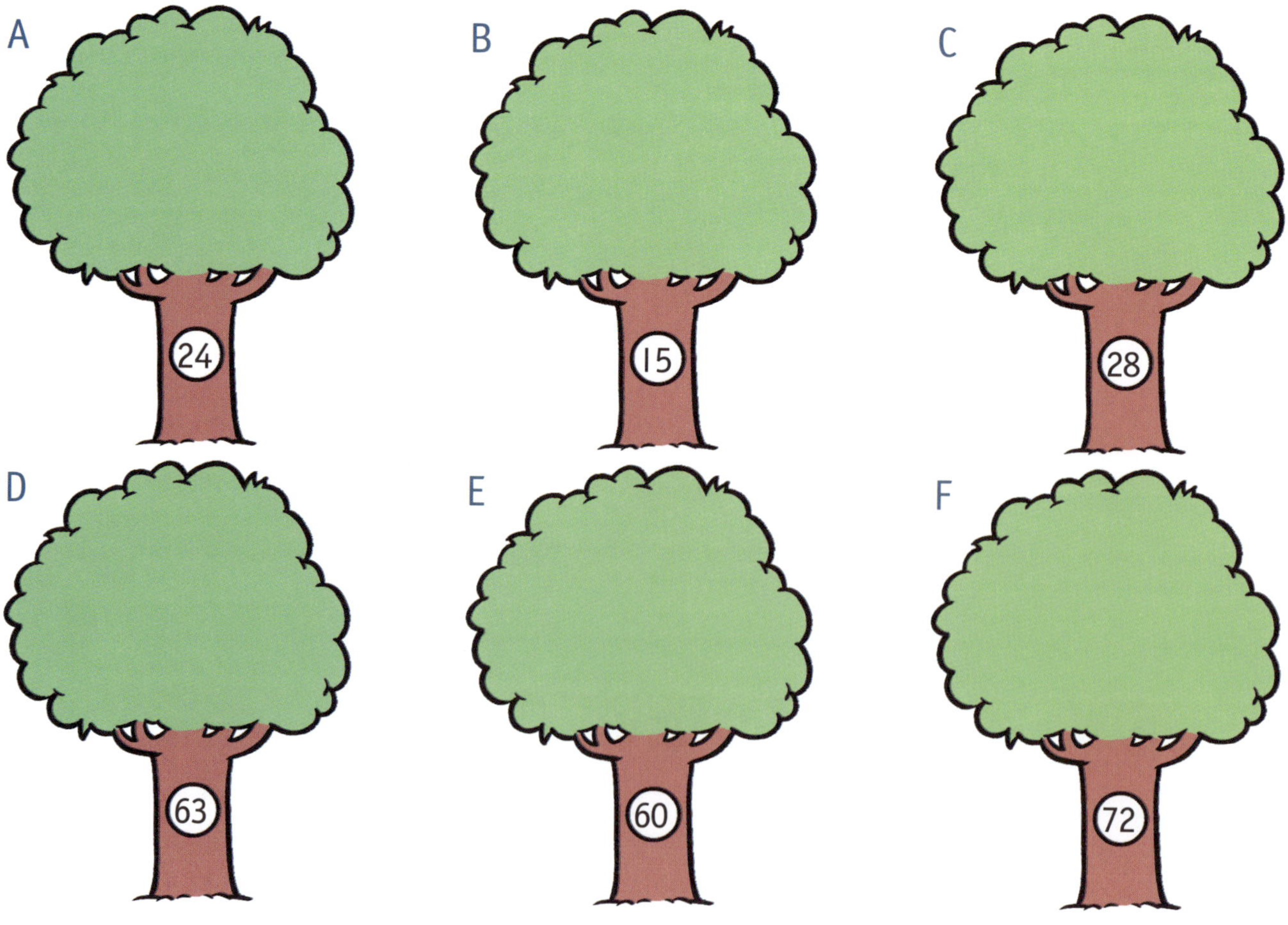

A 24

B 15

C 28

D 63

E 60

F 72

Unit 4 Multiples

1 Write the first 5 multiples of:

a 4. ______ ______ ______ ______ ______

b 7. ______ ______ ______ ______ ______

c 9. ______ ______ ______ ______ ______

d 11. ______ ______ ______ ______ ______

e 20. ______ ______ ______ ______ ______

Product is the answer when numbers are multiplied.
eg 7 × 3 = 21
21 is the product.

Multiple is the product of two factors.
eg 3 × 4 = 12
12 is a multiple of 3.
12 is a multiple of 4.

2 Complete.

Factor	7	6		5		10		7
Factor	7		8		10	16	4	
Product		54	24	35	60		80	56

3 Put these multiples in their correct boxes. Some will go in more than one box.

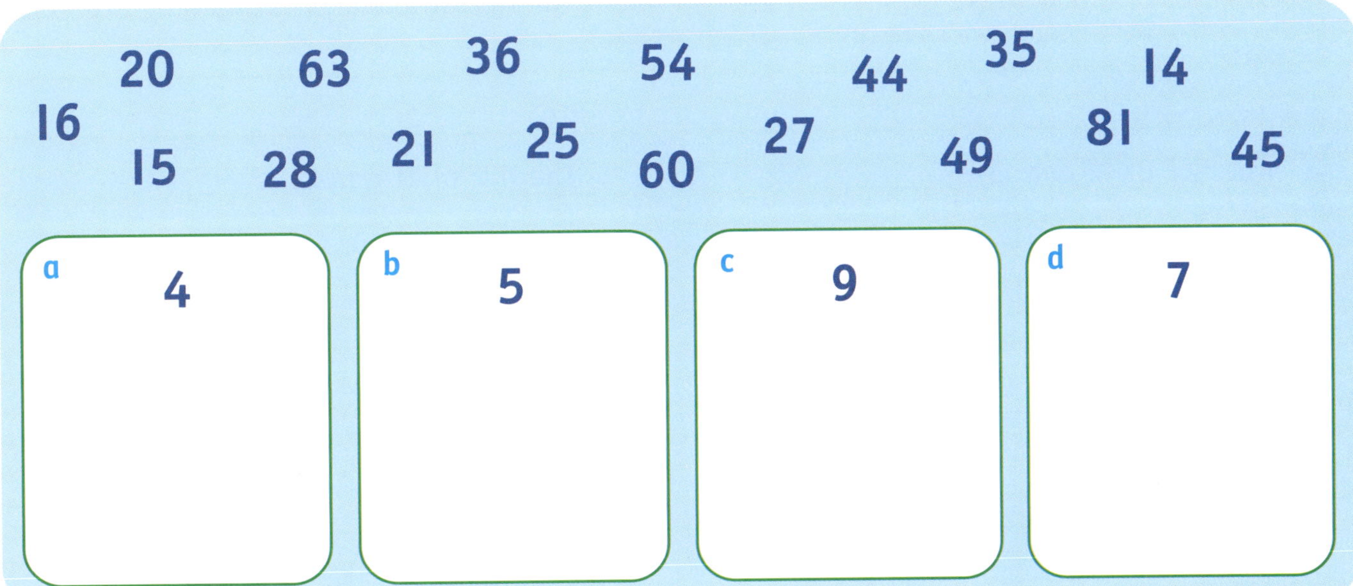

4 Multiply by 2 (double).

a 14 ______ b 19 ______ c 23 ______ d 35 ______ e 67 ______

5 Multiply by 4 (double, double).

a 8 ______ b 12 ______ c 24 ______ d 42 ______ e 71 ______

6 Multiply by 8 (double, double, double).

a 6 ______ b 12 ______ c 15 ______ d 27 ______ e 63 ______

Challenge! Use doubles to multiply these numbers by 32.

a 3 [ ] b 5 [ ] c 9 [ ] d 20 [ ]

Unit 4 Common factors and multiples

HCF stands for **Highest Common Factor.**

The HCF of two numbers is the highest number that is a factor of both numbers.

What is the HCF of 30 and 45?

Factors of 30: 1, 2, 3, 5, 6, 10, (15), 30

Factors of 45: 1, 3, 5, (15), 45

15 is the HCF of 30 and 45.

LCM stands for **Lowest Common Multiple.**

The LCM of two numbers is the lowest number that is a multiple of both numbers.

What is the LCM of 8 and 12?

Multiples of 8: 8, 16, (24), 32, 40

Multiples of 12: 12, (24), 36, 48

24 is the LCM of 30 and 45.

1 What is the HCF?

a 8: ________________

10: ________________

The HCF of 8 and 10 is _____.

b 9: ________________

27: ________________

The HCF of 9 and 27 is _____.

c 12: ________________

15: ________________

The HCF of 12 and 15 is _____.

d 21: ________________

24: ________________

The HCF of 21 and 24 is _____.

e 20: ________________

36: ________________

The HCF of 20 and 36 is _____.

f 35: ________________

42: ________________

The HCF of 35 and 42 is _____.

2 What is the LCM?

a 3: ________________

5: ________________

The LCM of 3 and 5 is _____.

b 3: ________________

4: ________________

The LCM of 3 and 4 is _____.

c 2: ________________

10: ________________

The LCM of 2 and 10 is _____.

d 4: ________________

6: ________________

The LCM of 4 and 6 is _____.

e 6: ________________

7: ________________

The LCM of 6 and 7 is _____.

f 5: ________________

8: ________________

The LCM of 5 and 8 is _____.

Challenge! Find the LCM of 7, 11 and 13. ________

Unit 4 Multiplication

1 Work each one mentally. Then write how you did it.

a $16 \times 8 =$ ______

______

______

b $82 \times 5 =$ ______

______

______

c $62 \times 20 =$ ______

______

d $106 \times 4 =$ ______

______

e $78 \times 20 =$ ______

______

Some tricks

× 10	add a zero 16 × 10 = 160
× 2	double
× 4	double, double
× 8	double, double, double
× 5	×10 then halve 16 × 5 = 160 ÷ 2

2 This multiplication square contains mistakes.

a Colour each square that has an error.

×	7	4	8	6	9	0	5	3
8	54	30	64	48	78	8	45	28
4	28	16	24	24	34	0	20	12
7	49	28	56	46	62	7	37	20
3	23	10	32	20	27	0	15	6
9	61	36	72	54	81	0	45	12
6	40	26	46	34	15	6	35	16

b How many squares are coloured? ______

c Fix the errors.

Challenge!

Use these digit cards to write eight different multiplications for the red cards.

Unit 4 Using factors

Factors

1 Mentally calculate the following using factors.

a 13 × 6 = ________ b 19 × 6 = ________

c 29 × 4 = ________ d 23 × 9 = ________

e 32 × 9 = ________ f 12 × 15 = ________

g 32 × 12 = ________ h 17 × 12 = ________

i 22 × 15 = ________ j 56 × 16 = ________

17 × 6 Factors of 6 are 2 and 3. To multiply by 6, multiply by 2 and then by 3.

17 × 2 = 34

34 × 3 = 90 + 12 = 102

2 Mentally calculate the following using factors.

a 72 ÷ 18 = ________ b 84 ÷ 14 = ________

c 120 ÷ 8 = ________ d 96 ÷ 16 = ________

e 144 ÷ 6 = ________ f 276 ÷ 12 = ________

96 ÷ 12 Factors of 12 are 3 and 4. To divide by 12, divide by 3 and then by 4.

96 ÷ 3 = 32

32 ÷ 4 = 8

3

a Teams of 16 children are needed to run a relay. How many teams will 128 children make?

____

b Each bag of gummies contains 75 gummies. How many gummies will there be in 8 bags?

____

c How many fortnights are there in 126 days?

____

d How many hours are there in 17 days?

____

Mastery Checklist I can:

- ☐ recognise factors
- ☐ find common factors and multiples
- ☐ recognise multiples
- ☐ use doubles to multiply
- ☐ use factors to multiple and divide.

 AC9M5N02 Number **MA3-MR-01** Multiplicative relations A • Determine products and factors • Select and apply mental and written strategies to multiply 2- and 3-digit numbers by 2-digit numbers • Multiplicative relations B • Select and apply strategies to solve problems involving multiplication and division with whole numbers

Unit 5 Equivalent fractions

$\frac{1}{2}$	$\frac{1}{2}$

$\frac{1}{3}$	$\frac{1}{3}$	$\frac{1}{3}$

$\frac{1}{4}$	$\frac{1}{4}$	$\frac{1}{4}$	$\frac{1}{4}$

$\frac{1}{5}$	$\frac{1}{5}$	$\frac{1}{5}$	$\frac{1}{5}$	$\frac{1}{5}$

$\frac{1}{6}$	$\frac{1}{6}$	$\frac{1}{6}$	$\frac{1}{6}$	$\frac{1}{6}$	$\frac{1}{6}$

$\frac{1}{8}$	$\frac{1}{8}$	$\frac{1}{8}$	$\frac{1}{8}$	$\frac{1}{8}$	$\frac{1}{8}$	$\frac{1}{8}$	$\frac{1}{8}$

$\frac{1}{10}$	$\frac{1}{10}$	$\frac{1}{10}$	$\frac{1}{10}$	$\frac{1}{10}$	$\frac{1}{10}$	$\frac{1}{10}$	$\frac{1}{10}$	$\frac{1}{10}$	$\frac{1}{10}$

1 How many:

a halves in one whole? ______ b quarters in one whole? ______ c tenths in 1 whole? ______

d thirds in one whole? ______ e sixths in 1 whole? ______ f eighths in 1 whole? ______

2 Complete.

a $\frac{\square}{2} = 1$ b $\frac{\square}{10} = 1$ c $\frac{4}{\square} = 1$ d $\frac{3}{3} = \square$ e $\frac{\square}{6} = 1$

3 a $\frac{1}{2} = \frac{\square}{4}$ b $\frac{1}{3} = \frac{\square}{6}$ c $\frac{1}{5} = \frac{\square}{10}$ d $\frac{1}{4} = \frac{\square}{8}$ e $\frac{1}{2} = \frac{\square}{8}$

4 Use the diagram.

a $1 - \frac{1}{3} =$ ______ b $1 - \frac{1}{6} =$ ______ c $1 - \frac{3}{4} =$ ______ d $1 - \frac{2}{5} =$ ______ e $1 - \frac{2}{3} =$ ______

f $1 - \frac{4}{8} =$ ______ g $1 - \frac{9}{10} =$ ______ h $1 - \frac{5}{6} =$ ______ i $1 - \frac{6}{8} =$ ______ j $1 - \frac{9}{10} =$ ______

5 Find a fraction which is equal to:

a $\frac{1}{2} =$ ____ b $\frac{1}{3} =$ ____ c $\frac{1}{6} =$ ____ d $\frac{3}{4} =$ ____ e $\frac{4}{5} =$ ____ f $\frac{2}{3} =$ ____

Unit 5 Fractions on a number line

Order fractions $\frac{1}{2}$

1 Draw diagrams to show:

a $\frac{1}{3}$

b $\frac{3}{8}$

c $\frac{4}{6}$

2 Write these on the number lines.

a $\frac{1}{3}$, $\frac{2}{3}$ 0 1

b $\frac{1}{6}$, $\frac{3}{6}$, $\frac{4}{6}$ 0 1

c $\frac{1}{10}$, $\frac{3}{10}$, $\frac{7}{10}$, $\frac{9}{10}$ 0 1

d $\frac{1}{8}$, $\frac{1}{4}$, $\frac{3}{8}$, $\frac{3}{4}$ 0 1

These fractions are all smaller than 1.

3 a John had 6 cherries and gave $\frac{1}{3}$ to Nala.

How many did Nala get?

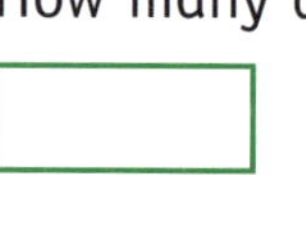

b Cherie ate $\frac{1}{4}$ of her 12 biscuits.

How many did she eat?

c Maisie sold $\frac{1}{6}$ of her 42 sheep.

How many did she sell?

d Class 5X has $\frac{1}{8}$ of its 32 students away ill.

How many are at school?

4 Write your own fraction problem which has an answer of 5 pencils.

 AC9M5N03 • AC9M5N07 Number MA3-RQF-01 • MA3-RQF-02 Representing quantity fractions A • Compare and order common unit fractions • Representing quantity fractions B • Find fractional quantities of whole numbers (halves, quarters, fifths and tenths)

Unit 5 Tenths

Tenths can be written as decimals.
$\frac{1}{10} = 0{\cdot}1 \quad \frac{6}{10} = 0{\cdot}6$

1 Write the fraction and decimal for the coloured part.

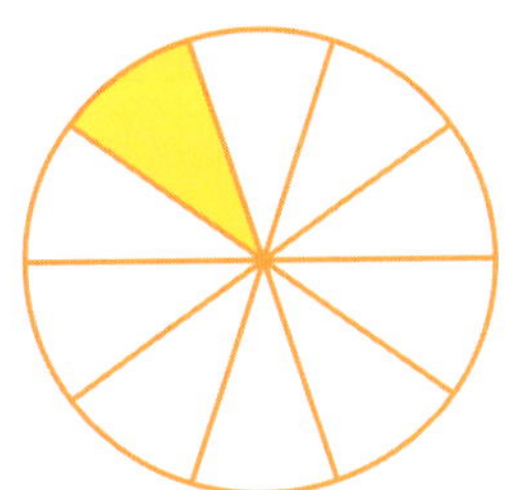  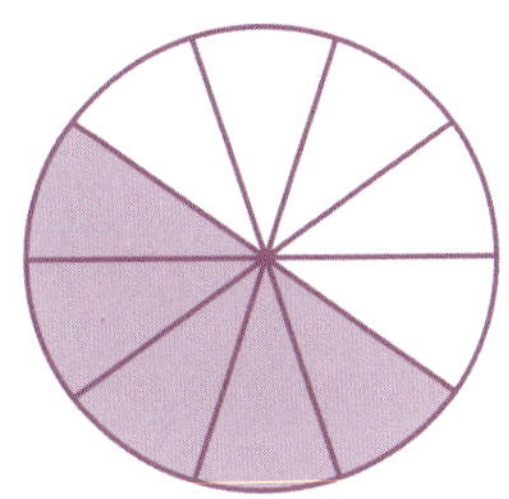 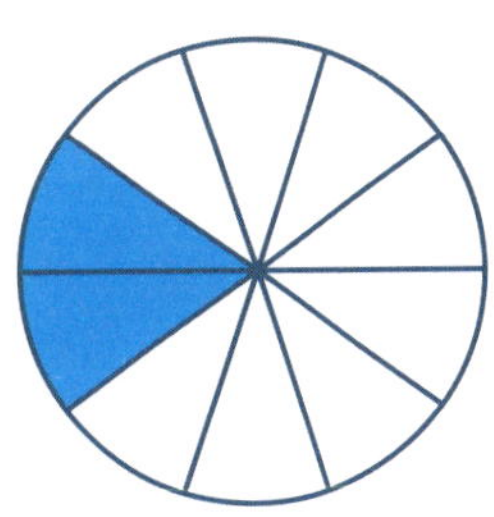 

a $\frac{\_\_}{10}$ = 0·__ b $\frac{\_\_}{10}$ = 0·__ c $\frac{\_\_}{10}$ = 0·__ d $\frac{\_\_}{10}$ = 0·__ e $\frac{\_\_}{10}$ = 0·__

2 Colour the fraction given and write the decimal.

 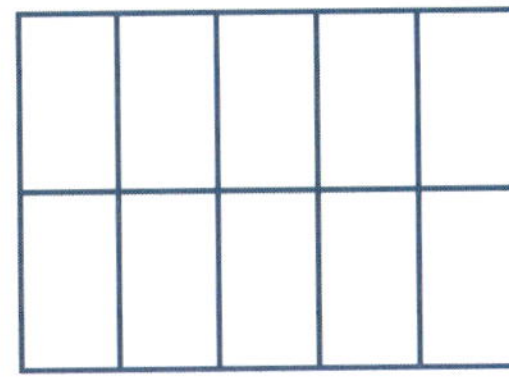 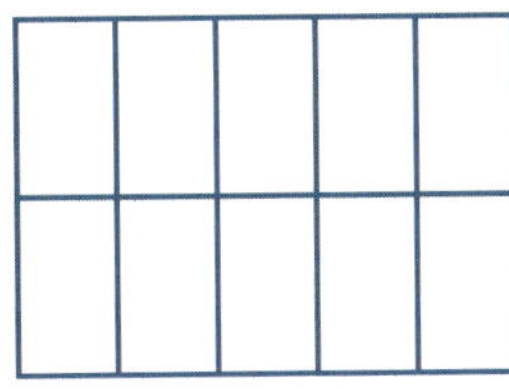 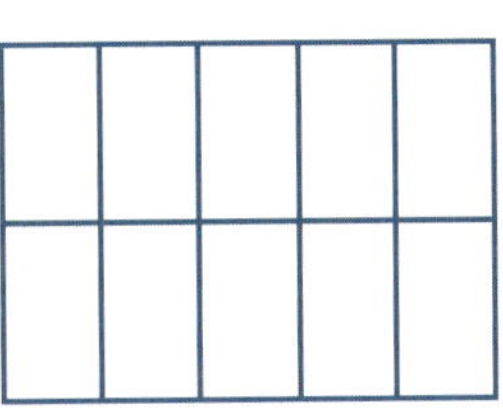 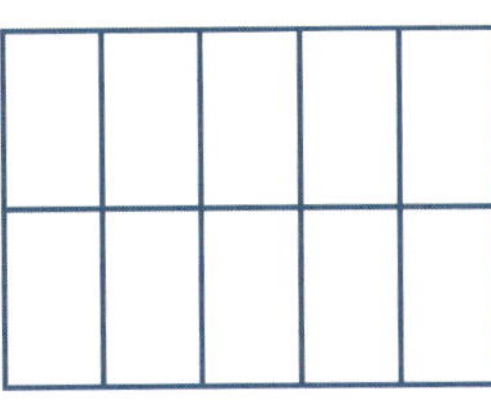

a $\frac{7}{10}$ = 0· __ b $\frac{4}{10}$ = 0· __ c $\frac{9}{10}$ = 0· __ d $\frac{6}{10}$ = 0· __ e $\frac{1}{2}$ = 0· __

3 Write the decimal and the fraction.

a nought point three ____ ___ b nought point nine ____ ___

c nought point six ____ ___ d nought point one ____ ___

4 Write the fraction.

a two thirds ___ b one eighth ___ c one sixth ___ d three fifths ___

e one half ___ f four sixths ___ g eight tenths ___ h three quarters ___

i one fifth ___ j seven eighths ___ k five sixths ___ l four eighths ___

5 Use $<$, $>$ or $=$ to make these true. You can look at page 19 if you need help.

a $\frac{1}{2}$ ___ $\frac{3}{6}$ b $\frac{1}{2}$ ___ $\frac{4}{5}$ c $\frac{1}{4}$ ___ $\frac{1}{6}$ d $\frac{1}{5}$ ___ $\frac{1}{3}$ e $\frac{2}{4}$ ___ $\frac{5}{10}$

f $\frac{1}{10}$ ___ 0·1 g 0·1 ___ $\frac{4}{10}$ h $\frac{7}{10}$ ___ 0·7 i $\frac{1}{3}$ ___ $\frac{3}{6}$ j $\frac{5}{10}$ ___ 0·9

Draw a diagram

A diagram will help you answer this. $\frac{2}{3} + \frac{5}{6} =$ ☐

Unit 5 Fractions of amounts

To calculate a fraction of an amount, divide by the denominator, eg $\frac{1}{4}$ means divide by 4. $\frac{1}{4}$ of 20 is 20 ÷ 4 = 5

To calculate a decimal part of an amount, change the decimal to a fraction first. eg 0·5 = $\frac{1}{2}$, 0·2 = $\frac{2}{10}$.

1 Mark the parts of a metre and write how many centimetres in:

a 0·5 m? ________ b 0·25 m? ________ c 0·1 m? ________

d 0·3 m? ________ e 0·2 m? ________ f 0·8 m? ________

2 Mark the fractions of a kilometre and write how many metres in:

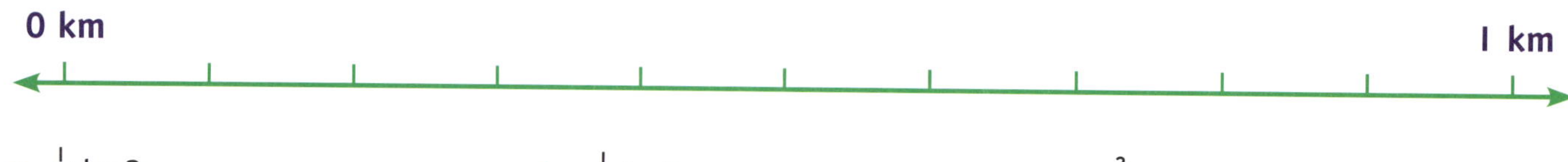

a $\frac{1}{2}$ km? ________ b $\frac{1}{5}$ km? ________ c $\frac{3}{5}$ km? ________

d $\frac{1}{10}$ km? ________ e $\frac{1}{4}$ km? ________ f $\frac{3}{4}$ km? ________

3 Mark the fractions of a group of 20 people and write how many people in:

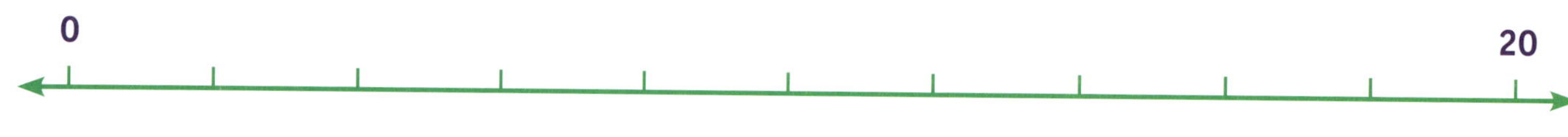

a $\frac{1}{4}$ of 20? ________ b $\frac{3}{4}$ of 20? ________ c $\frac{1}{10}$ of 20? ________

d $\frac{7}{10}$ of 20? ________ e $\frac{1}{5}$ of 20? ________ f $\frac{3}{5}$ of 20? ________

4 Calculate the following by dividing then multiplying.

a $\frac{1}{3}$ of 15 ________ b $\frac{2}{5}$ of 15 ________ c $\frac{2}{5}$ of 30 ________

d $\frac{1}{10}$ of 30 ________ e $\frac{1}{4}$ of 48 ________ f $\frac{3}{8}$ of 48 ________

g $\frac{5}{8}$ of 48 ________ h $\frac{3}{4}$ of 48 ________ i $\frac{9}{10}$ of 70 ________

5 $\frac{1}{3}$ of 60 children are late. $\frac{1}{10}$ of 60 children are early. How many were on time?

________ late ________ early ________ on time

 AC9M5N01 • AC9M5N07 Number MA3-RQF-02 Representing quantity fractions B • Find fractional quantities of whole numbers (halves, quarters, fifths and tenths)

Unit 5 Finding quantities

Find $\frac{1}{3}$ of 21 tomatoes = 7 tomatoes

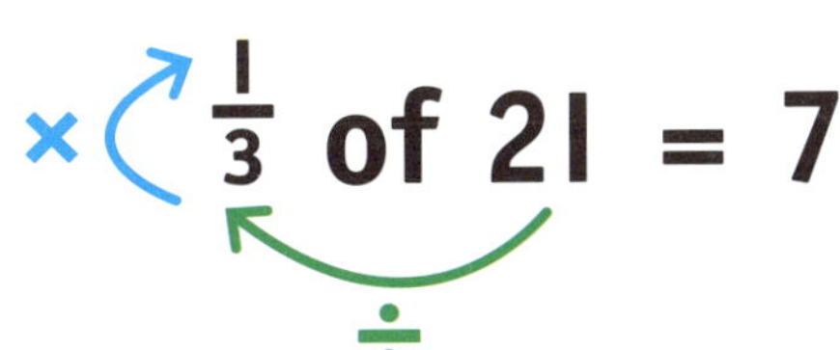

1 Work out the quantities.

a $\frac{1}{5}$ of 20 onions = _____ onions

b $\frac{1}{2}$ of 30 capsicums = _____ capsicums

c $\frac{1}{4}$ of 28 oranges = _____ oranges

d $\frac{1}{10}$ of 50 apples = _____ apples

e $\frac{1}{2}$ of 120 plums = _____ plums

f $\frac{1}{4}$ of 100 grapes = _____ grapes

g $\frac{1}{5}$ of 60 apricots = _____ apricots

h $\frac{1}{2}$ of 80 carrots = _____ carrots

i $\frac{1}{10}$ of 70 cucumbers = _____ cucumbers

j $\frac{1}{5}$ of 25 mangoes = _____ mangoes

k $\frac{1}{2}$ of 70 zucchinis = _____ zucchinis

l $\frac{1}{10}$ of 40 rockmelons = _____ rockmelons

m $\frac{1}{4}$ of 24 watermelons = _____ watermelons

n $\frac{1}{4}$ of 32 apples = _____ apples

2 Work out the fractions.

a 12 of 18 kiwi fruit = _____

b 16 of 24 dragonfruit = _____

c 30 of 40 strawberries = _____

d 14 of 42 radishes = _____

e 20 of 50 avocados = _____

f 12 of 48 pumpkins = _____

3 Work out the quantities.

a $\frac{3}{5}$ of _____ sausages = 15 sausages

b $\frac{4}{10}$ of _____ bread rolls = 20 bread rolls

c $\frac{2}{5}$ of _____ onions = 8 onions

d $\frac{7}{10}$ of _____ zucchinis = 70 zucchinis

e $\frac{4}{5}$ of _____ capsicums = 8 capsicums

f $\frac{3}{10}$ of _____ olives = 18 olives

g $\frac{8}{10}$ of _____ salamis = 64 salamis

h $\frac{6}{10}$ of _____ pumpkins = 24 pumpkins

i $\frac{2}{10}$ of _____ grapefruit = 6 grapefruit

Mastery Checklist

I can:
- ☐ identify equivalent fractions
- ☐ subtract a fraction from 1
- ☐ show fractions on a number line
- ☐ solve fraction problems
- ☐ connect fractions and decimals
- ☐ find a fraction of an amount or group.

Problem solving

Logos

1 The Stareye Company marketing department designed a new logo for their business. The art department was told to make it half blue, a quarter red and a quarter yellow. Design their logo using these rules.

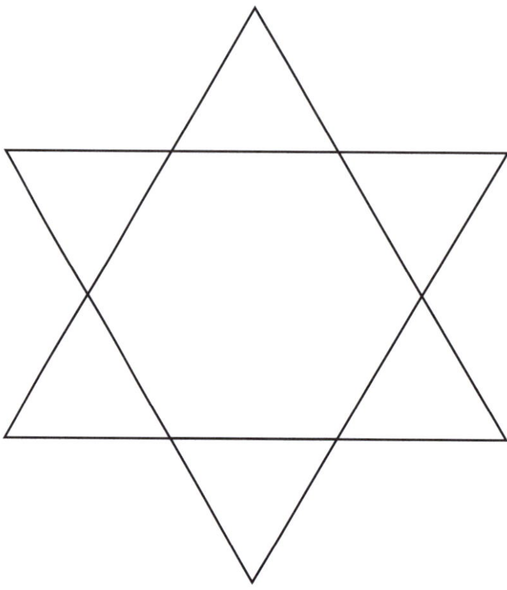

2 The Smiddley Company designed this logo for their games department. They want it to be half purple, one-eighth green and three-eighths silver. What would be your suggestion for their logo?

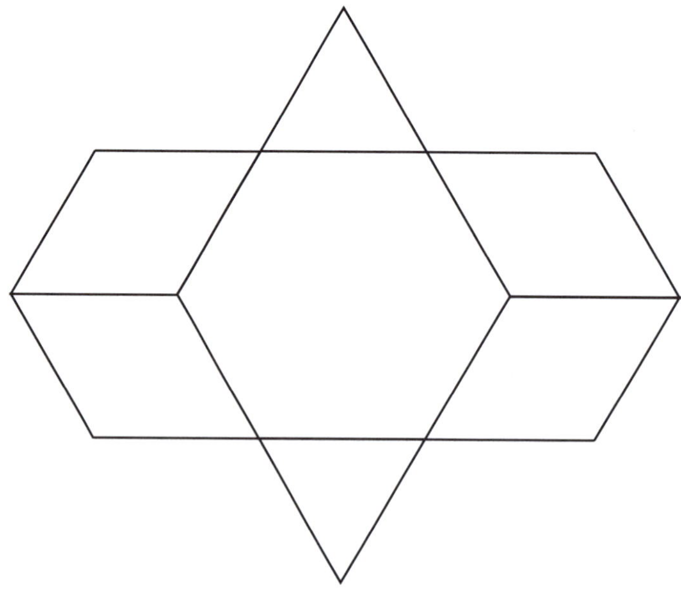

I can solve problems by:

☐ understanding fractions ☐ adding fractions with the same denominator.

Unit 6 Chance

The Smiths are holding a garage sale.

GARAGE SALE

A Some customers will arrive by hot-air balloon.

B Someone will buy Basil our family pet.

C All the toys will be sold.

D It will rain.

E The chair will be sold for $40.

SOLD OUT!

G Everything will be sold.

F Some people will need bags to carry their goods.

1 Put these chance words in their correct place on the line.

GOOD CHANCE | IMPOSSIBLE | FIFTY-FIFTY | CERTAIN | POOR CHANCE

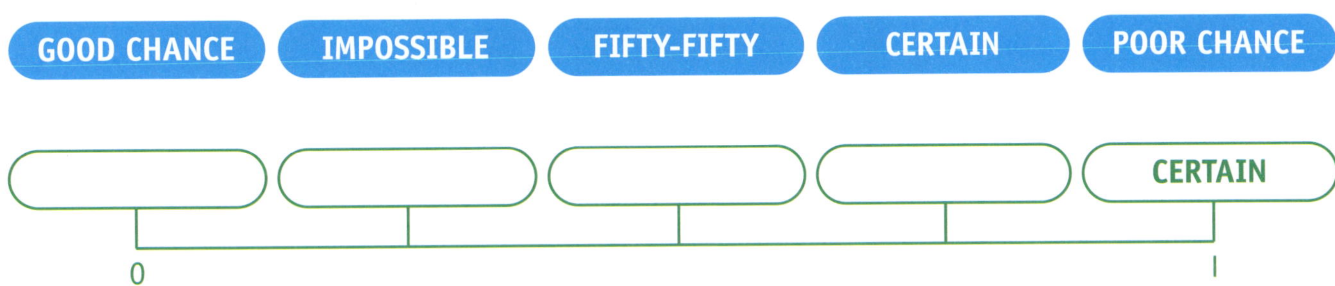

2 Write the letter for each of the above events under their most likely heading.

Unit 6 Chance experiment

Work in a group of 4.

In a box, place:

3 $1 coins.

4 10c coins.

2 20c coins.

1 5c coin.

1 If you were to close your eyes and pick out one coin, what are the chances it will be:

a $1? ______ b 10c? ______ c 20c? ______ d 5c? ______

2 Carry out the experiment. Take turns to close your eyes and choose a coin.

Record the results here.

3 Did the results match your predictions? ______

4 Write some observations. ______

______

5 Can you think of anything that influenced the result? ______

______

6 If you have all 4 types of coin in a box in different combinations, is there a way you can:

a be certain to pick $1? ______

b almost sure to pick $1? ______

c be certain not to pick $1? ______

d have a fifty-fifty chance of picking $1? ______

Unit 6 What is the chance?

A The person to next enter the room will be male.	**B** I will listen to music today.
C I will have a party on my next birthday.	**D** My pen will sing a song.
E I will be at school all week.	**F** We will play sport next week.
G My dog will run away.	**H** It will rain tomorrow.
I If I drop my toast, it will land butter side down.	**J** My family will go on holiday this year.

1 Give each card a value. 0 is impossible and 1 is certain.

If something has a 1 in 2 chance of it happening, it is $\frac{1}{2}$.

A ____ **B** ____ **C** ____ **D** ____ **E** ____ **F** ____ **G** ____ **H** ____ **I** ____ **J** ____

2 Draw a letter card, eg **A**, on the probability line for each.

0 ———————————————————————————— 1

Mastery Checklist I can:
- ☐ identify the probability of events happening
- ☐ conduct repeated chance experiments
- ☐ observe and record results
- ☐ describe probability using a scale of 0 to 1.

Games Day Carnival

Investigation 1

You are helping to organise a Games Day Carnival. There are 96 students with 6 available teachers. What activities with even groups could you suggest to your Sports teacher? eg 4 teams of 24 students playing capture the flag

1 What size teams can you divide 96 students into evenly?
eg 4 teams of 24 students

CHECK:
Number of kids in a team?
Number of teams?
Number of games?
Teachers per game?
Points?
Time allowed?

2 Make a list of games that could be played and the size of the teams, eg capture the flag – 2 or more in a team.

3 Choose the games and team numbers. List them here.

4 How will you decide the winning team for the day?

 AC9M5N02 • AC9M5N07 Number **MAO-WM-01** Working mathematically • choosing and applying mathematical techniques to solve problems • communicating thinking and reasoning coherently and clearly • **MA3-MR-01** Multiplicative relations A • Determine products and factors • Multiplicative relations B • Select and apply strategies to solve problems involving multiplication and division with whole numbers

5 Write a roster for the teams to play each other in the games.

6 Write a timetable for the day, including lunch and morning tea, as well as time to gather everyone to get organised at the beginning and end of the day.

To carry out these tasks, I need to:

- [ ] work with factors of 96 to make equal teams for games
- [ ] make a roster for the teams to play each other
- [ ] use logical reasoning to make a points score
- [ ] make a timetable for the day's activities
- [ ] work well in a group.

I enjoyed this task!

Revision

1 How many thousandths in this number?

523·619

5 ◯ 9 ◯ 3 ◯ 1 ◯

2 Which is the same as:

69 + 54

60 + 50 + 9 + 4 ◯ 60 + 90 + 5 + 4 ◯ 69 + 50 + 40 ◯ 6 + 9 + 5 + 4 ◯

3 Stan bought 1 cake. He paid with a $5 note and received $3.25 change. Which cake did he buy?

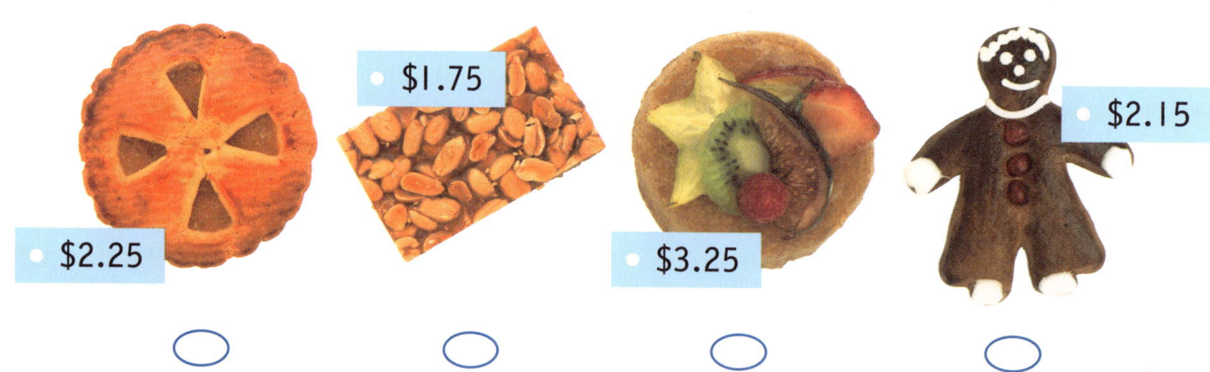

4 What is a common factor for each of these numbers?

2 ◯ 3 ◯ 7 ◯ 9 ◯

Revision

5 What is the Highest Common Factor (HCF) of 21 and 30?

Shade one bubble.

○ 3 ○ 5 ○ 6 ○ 10

6 What is the Lowest Common Multiple (LCM) of 4 and 12?

○ 4 ○ 8 ○ 12 ○ 24

7

$$\begin{array}{r} 608 \\ \times \quad 9 \\ \hline \\ \hline \end{array}$$

○ 5427 ○ 6102 ○ 5472 ○ 5427

8 $\frac{8}{10}$ of this circle is coloured.

Write this fraction as a decimal.

Write your answer in the box.

[ ]

9 What is $\frac{4}{6}$ of 36?

Shade one bubble.

○ 6 ○ 12 ○ 20 ○ 24

10 Which event is impossible?

○ It will rain today.
○ I will roll a 6 on a die.
○ The day after Tuesday will be Monday.
○ I will eat chicken for dinner.

Unit 7 Number patterns

1 Work out the rule and then complete the pattern.

a

Rule ____________________

b

Rule ____________________

c

Rule ____________________

d

Rule ____________________

e

Rule ____________________

f

Rule ____________________

2 Make up two patterns. Swap with a friend to write the rules and complete the patterns.

a Rule ____________________

b Rule ____________________

Unit 7 Inverse operations

Inverse operations

An inverse operation reverses the effect of another operation, eg addition is the inverse of subtraction.

17 + ? = 20

Solve using the inverse operation.

20 − 17 = 3

so 17 + 3 = 20

1 a The inverse of addition is ______

b The inverse of multiplication is ______

c The inverse of division is ______

d The inverse of subtraction is ______

2 15 + ? = 22

Use the inverse operation: 22 − 15 = 7

Test your solution: 15 + 7 = 22 ✓

3 In the problem 19 + ? = 27, how does the number sentence 27 − 19 = 8 help to solve it?

______

______

______

4 Write the inverse operation (number sentence) to solve:

a ? − 7 = 6 ______ b 19 + ? = 26 ______ c ? − 17 = 7 ______

d ? + 15 = 24 ______ e 25 + ? = 32 ______ f ? − 8 = 28 ______

5 a ? × 9 = 54 ______ b ? ÷ 9 = 4 ______ c ? ÷ 7 = 8 ______

d ? ÷ 6 = 8 ______ e ? ÷ 9 = 7 ______ f 8 × ? = 72 ______

6 Write a number sentence equivalent to the one given, eg 31 + 4 = 27 + 8.

a 17 + 12 = ______ b 2 × 16 = ______ c 60 ÷ 5 = ______

d 27 − 13 = ______ e 6 × 15 = ______ f 16 × 4 = ______

7 Show inverse operations above and below the number line.

a 34 + 26 = 60

34

b 7 × 6 = 42

Unit 7 Find the value

1 Check the answer for each one using inverse operations.

a ☐ + 7 = 11
☐ = ______
Check ______

b 9 × ☐ = 72
☐ = ______
Check ______

c 49 ÷ ☐ = 7
☐ = ______
Check ______

d ☐ − 9 = 8
☐ = ______
Check ______

e 36 − ☐ = 15
☐ = ______
Check ______

f 43 + ☐ = 62
☐ = ______
Check ______

g ☐ ÷ 9 = 11
☐ = ______
Check ______

h 53 × ☐ = 159
☐ = ______
Check ______

i 19 × ☐ = 76
☐ = ______
Check ______

j 164 ÷ ☐ = 41
☐ = ______
Check ______

k ☐ + 62 = 91
☐ = ______
Check ______

l ☐ − 24 = 51
☐ = ______
Check ______

m ☐ × 9 = 108
☐ = ______
Check ______

n 43 + ☐ = 106
☐ = ______
Check ______

o 155 − ☐ = 82
☐ = ______
Check ______

p ☐ ÷ 3 = 62
☐ = ______
Check ______

q 91 ÷ ☐ = 13
☐ = ______
Check ______

r ☐ × 20 = 360
☐ = ______
Check ______

s ☐ − 115 = 171
☐ = ______
Check ______

t 112 ÷ ☐ = 7
☐ = ______
Check ______

2 Write a number sentence to solve each problem.

a Bella ate 43 sweets. She had 19 left. How many did she have to start with? ______

☐ − 43 = 19
☐ = ______

b Dylan has Dalmatian dogs. Each dog had 7 pups. If there were 56 pups, how many adult dogs does Dylan have? ______

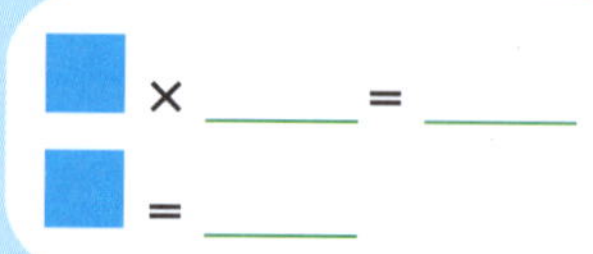

☐ × ______ = ______
☐ = ______

Mastery Checklist I can:
- ☐ find the rules for number patterns
- ☐ create my own number patterns
- ☐ use inverse operations to find a missing number
- ☐ use inverse operations to check answers.

AC9M5A01 • AC9M5A02 Number **MA3-AR-01** Additive relations A • Apply efficient mental and written strategies to solve addition and subtraction problems • **MA3-MR-01** Multiplicative relations B • Select and apply strategies to solve problems involving multiplication and division with whole numbers

Unit 8 Length

1 Estimate the distance travelled by each vehicle or person.

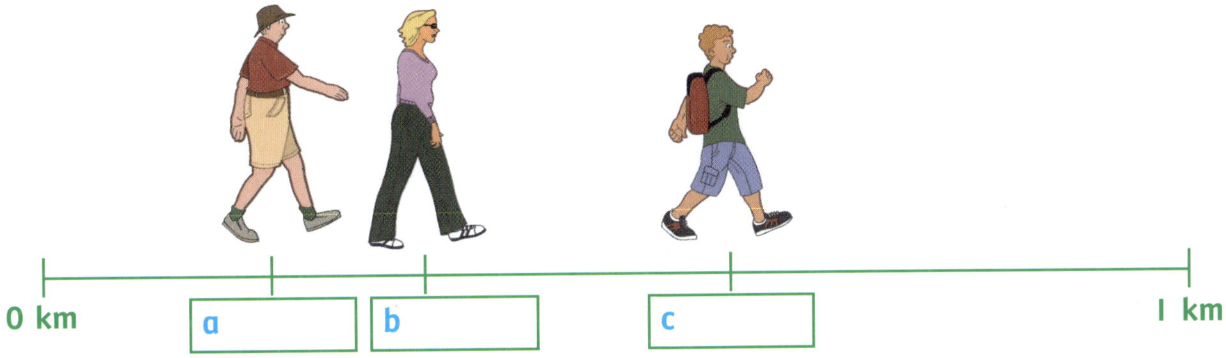

0 km
a
b
c
1 km

0 km
d
e
f
100 km

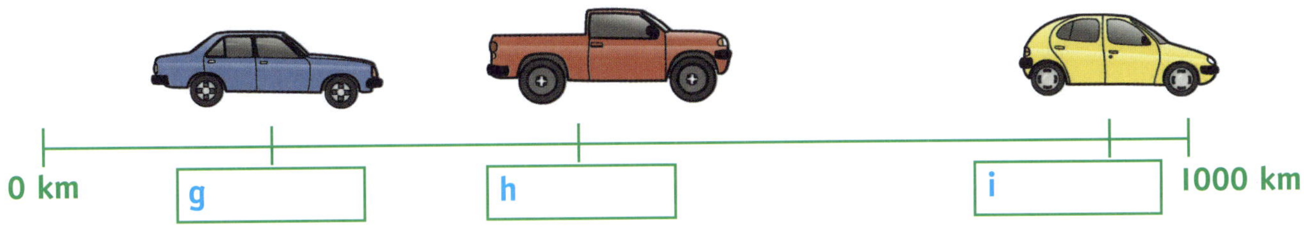

0 km
g
h
i
1000 km

2 Mark the distance travelled.

a Sam the snail crawled 50 cm.

0 m — 1 m

b Jay rode 400 m.

0 km — 1 km

c Dan rode 70 000 m.

0 km — 100 km

d Leo ran 150 km.

0 km — 1000 km

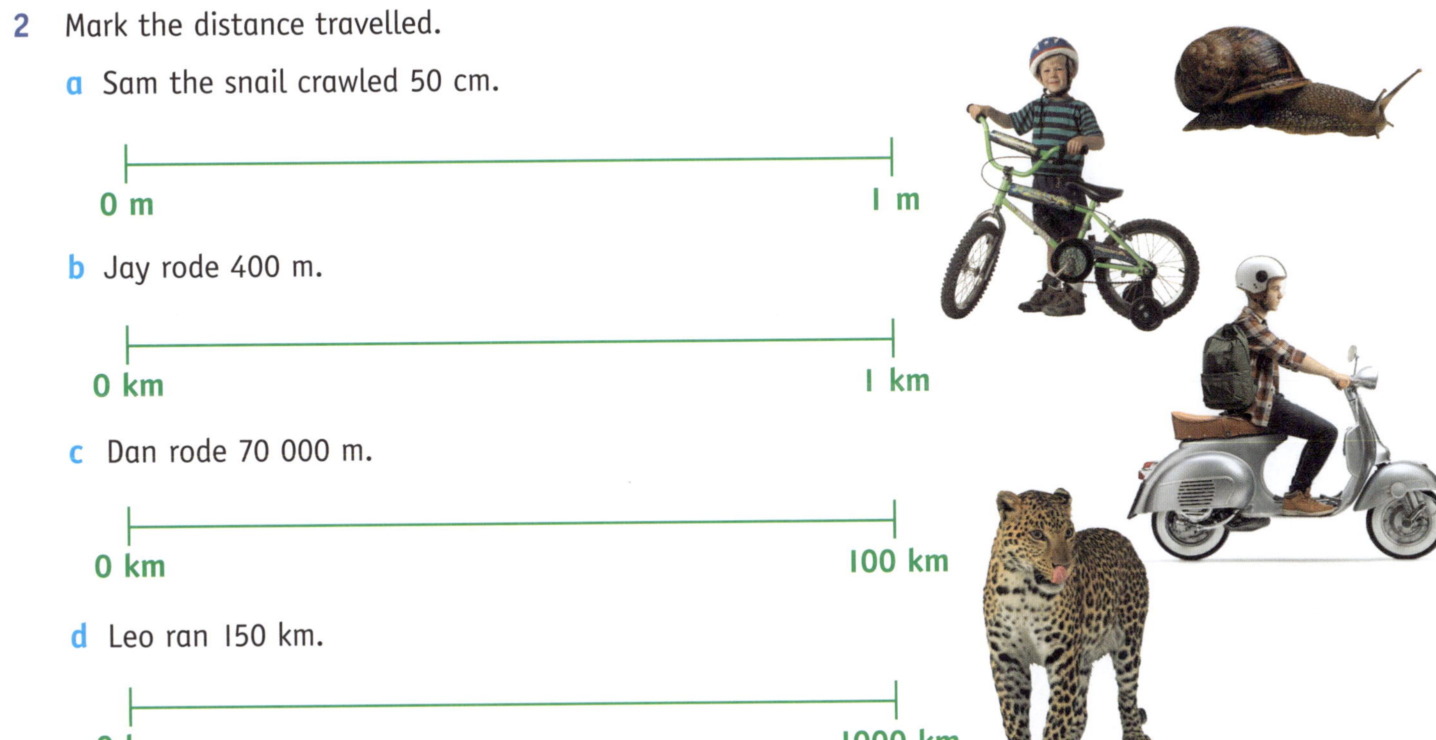

Unit 8 Estimating length

estimate and measure to check

1 What measurement tool would you use to measure the length of:

a a book? ____________ b your garden? ____________

c the perimeter of your school? ____________ d a hair ribbon? ____________

e some curtain fabric? ____________ f your fingernail? ____________

g the road between two towns? ____________ h a ship's anchor chain? ____________

i a skipping rope? ____________ j a football field? ____________

2 What unit of measurement would you use for each of the items in question 1?

a ________ b ________ c ________ d ________ e ________

f ________ g ________ h ________ i ________ j ________

3 Estimate the length of:

a your finger. ________ b the blackboard. ________ c the teacher's desk. ________

d a pen. ________ e this book. ________ f your classroom. ________

g the window. ________ h the door. ________ i your big toe. ________

j Explain how you estimated these lengths. ____________________________________

____

4 Measure accurately each item in question 3.

a ________ b ________ c ________ d ________ e ________

f ________ g ________ h ________ i ________

j Circle the answers that are close to your estimates.

5 These friends had a competition to see who could estimate closest to their average height.

Person	Height	Estimated Average Height
George	1 m 15 cm	1 m 11 cm
David	97 cm	1 m 2 cm
Cassie	1 m 9 cm	1 m 5 cm

a Write each height in cm.

George ________ David ________

Cassie ________

b Write each height in m.

George ________ David ________

Cassie ________

c What is their average height? ________

d Who was closest? ________

Work backwards

The Taylor family drove 274 km 318 m to their holiday house. They drove 98 km 517 m before they had a flat tyre and then 79 km 740 m before they stopped for lunch.

How far did they drive on the last leg of their trip? ________

Unit 8 Kilometres

kilometre (km)
1 km = 1000 m
Long distances are measured in kilometres.

1 Name four lengths that are measured in metres.

a ______ b ______

c ______ d ______

2 Name four lengths that are measured in kilometres.

a ______ b ______

c ______ d ______

3 Colour the distances you would measure in kilometres.

a the length of a bus

b the distance to New Zealand

c the width of the playground

d your height

e the length of a river

f the distance to Melbourne

g the width of a road

4 Change to kilometres.

a 5000 m ______ b 1000 m ______ c 9000 m ______ d 21 000 m ______ e 15 000 m ______

5 Change to kilometres and metres.

a 3200 m = ___ km ______ m b 8746 m = ___ km ______ m c 2460 m = ___ km ______ m

d 11 803 m = ___ km ______ m e 4055 m = ___ km ______ m f 36 203 m = ___ km ______ m

6 Change to metres.

a 6 km = ______ b 10 km = ______ c 4 km = ______

d 17 km = ______ e 43 km = ______ f 1 km 615 m = ______

g 3 km 750 m = ______ h 9 km 208 m = ______ i 28 km 85 m = ______

7 Write the shortest distance between:

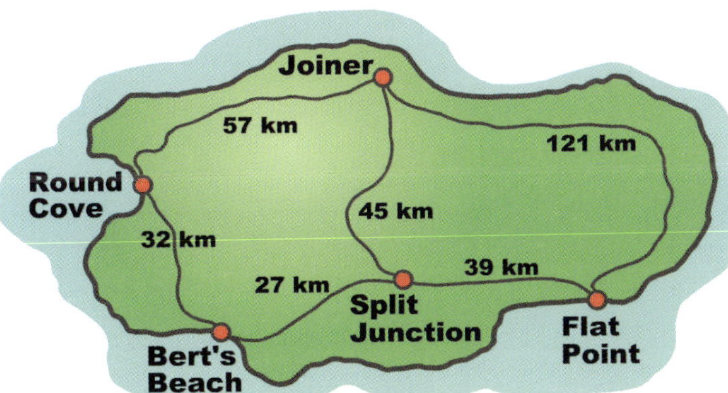

a Round Cove and Split Junction. ______

b Flat Point and Joiner. ______

c Joiner and Bert's Beach. ______

d Flat Point and Round Cove. ______

e How far is it to drive around the island?

______

f Estimate the length of the island and its width.

______

Challenge! Use the library or Internet to find the distance in kilometres from your school to every capital city in Australia.

Unit 8 Millimetres, centimetres, metres

millimetre mm
centimetre cm
metre m
kilometre km
10 mm = 1 cm
100 cm = 1 m
1000 mm = 1 m
1000 m = 1 km

1 Colour **red** the things measured in **millimetres**, **yellow** the things measured in **centimetres** and **blue** the things measured in **metres**.

a width of a pencil
b length of classroom
c width of a river
d width of a Maths book
e length of a hair ribbon
f height of a pole vault
g length of a flea's leg
h length of a train

2 Change to millimetres.

a 3 cm ______ b 12 cm ______
c 5.5 cm ______ d 6·8 cm ______

13 mm = 1·3 cm
215 cm = 2·15 m

3 Change to centimetres.

a 50 mm ______ b 72 mm ______ c 98 mm ______ d 160 mm ______
e 385 mm ______ f 2 m ______ g 5·91 m ______ h 12·04 m ______

4 Change to metres.

a 700 cm ______ b 1200 cm ______ c 815 cm ______ d 372 cm ______
e 5813 cm ______ f 2 m 61 cm ______ g 11 m 15 cm ______ h 17 km ______

5 Measure the length and width of each shape in millimetres.
Write its perimeter in millimetres and then in centimetres.

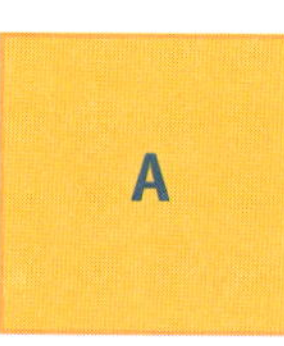

B

C

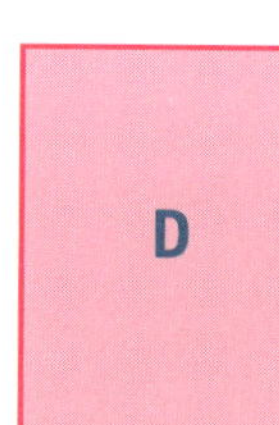

A =	mm =	cm
B =	mm =	cm
C =	mm =	cm
D =	mm =	cm

6 Write each perimeter in metres and then in centimetres.

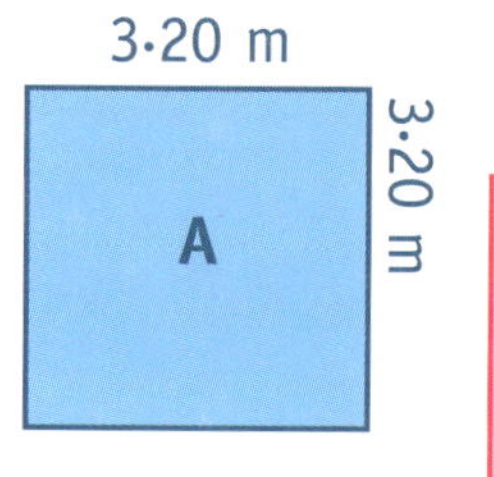

1·85 m
B
3·74 m

10·25 m
C
1·40 m

8·36 m
D
2·21 m

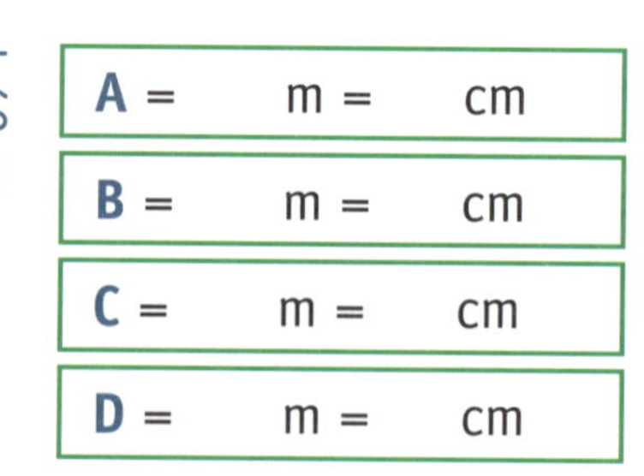

A =	m =	cm
B =	m =	cm
C =	m =	cm
D =	m =	cm

Mastery Checklist

I can:
- ☐ estimate lengths in cm, m and km
- ☐ estimate lengths and measure to check
- ☐ convert cm, m and km
- ☐ find the perimeter of a rectangle.

Problem solving

Mini orienteering

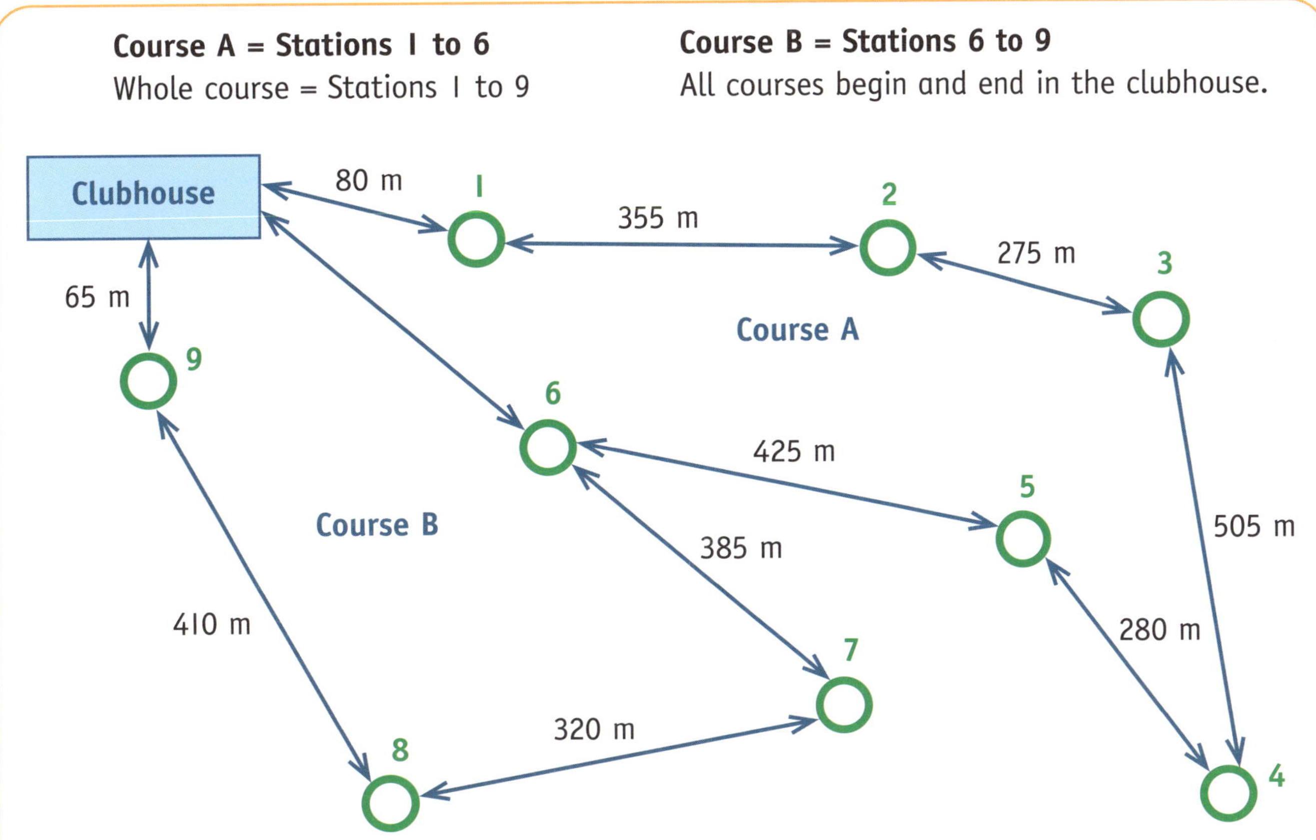

1 Total each course in exact measurements and in rounded terms, eg 2·85 km is a little less than 3 kilometres.

a The whole course of 9 stations starting and ending in the clubhouse.

____

b The **A** course, starting and ending in the clubhouse.

____

c The **B** course, starting and ending in the clubhouse.

____

2 Col has an injured ankle and can't go on to finish his course. He phones for help and explains that he doesn't know the number of the last station he passed, but he says his pedometer is showing 1·5 km from his start. He says he is walking one of the courses in reverse order. Between which two stations might he be?

____

I can solve problems by:

☐ adding numbers understanding length ☐ writing algorithms.

Unit 9 Measuring angles

Describe and measure the angles in the following pictures.

Highlight the angle with a coloured pencil and ruler.

Remember, an acute angle is less than 90°, a right angle is exactly 90° and an obtuse angle is between 90° and 180°.

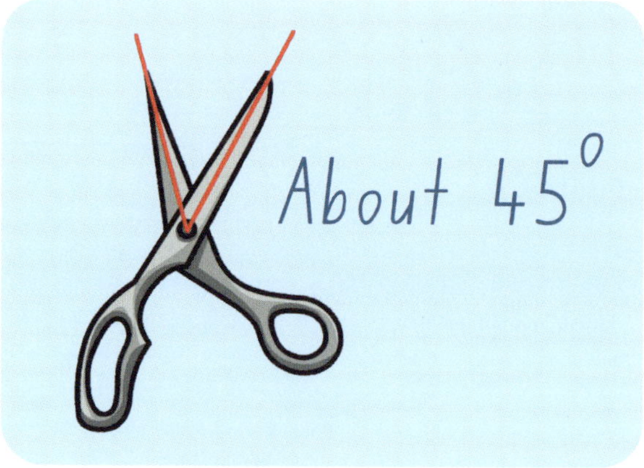

About 45°

a

b

c

d

e

f

g

Unit 9 Angles

A protractor is used to measure angles.

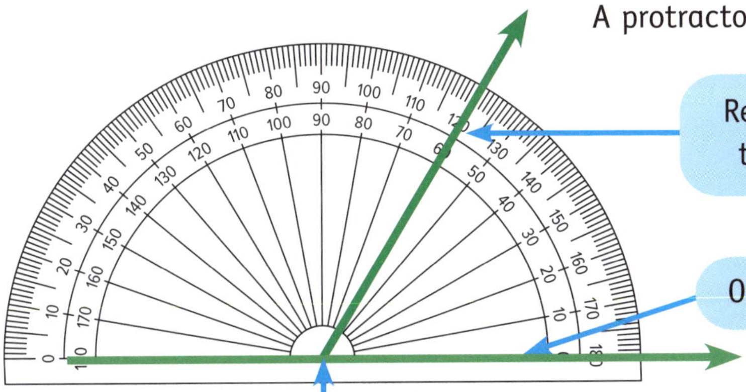

Read the number for this arm to tell the angle size. (60°)

One arm is along the base line. (0°)

The vertex is at the centre point.

An angle is measured in degrees. 50 degrees is written as 50°.

1 Write the size of each angle.

a

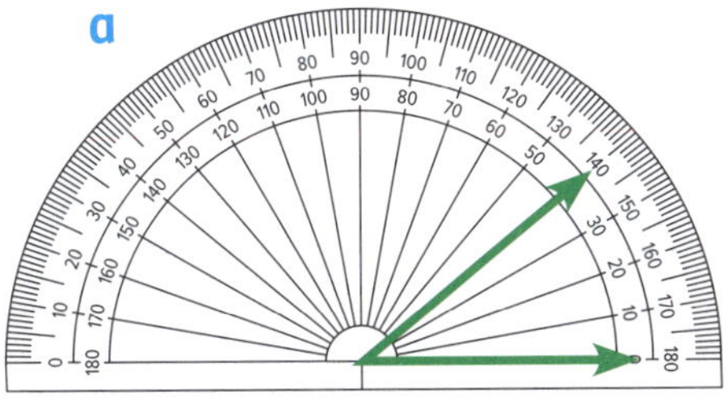

b

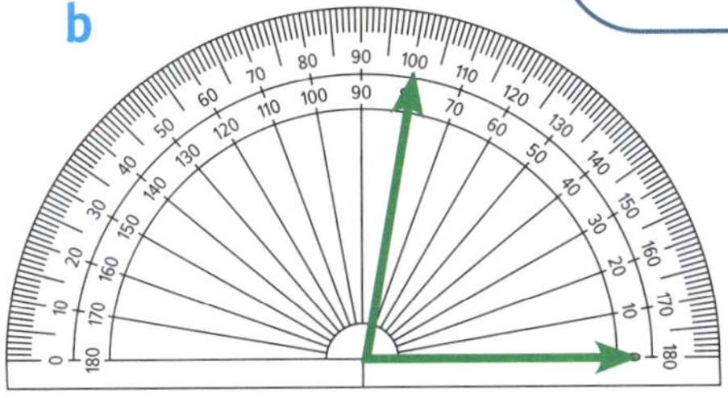

c

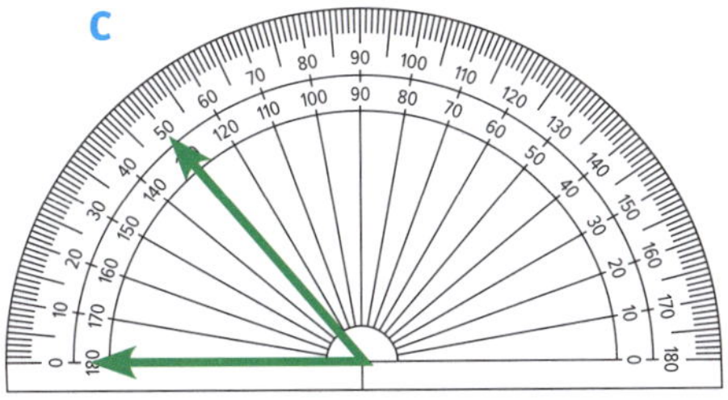

d

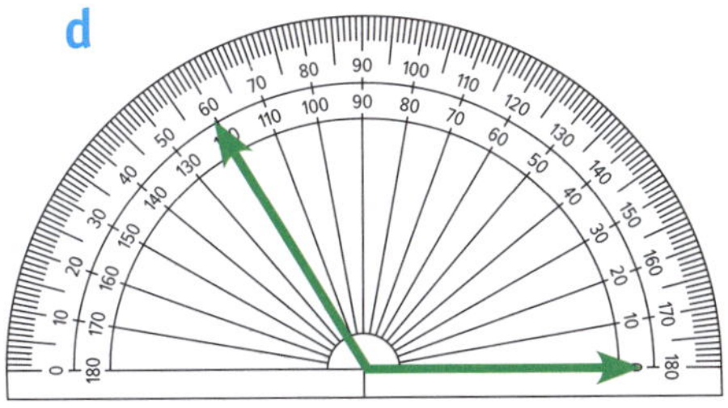

e

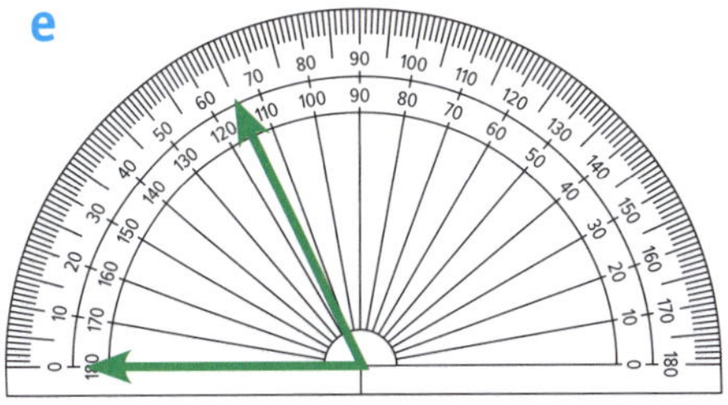

f

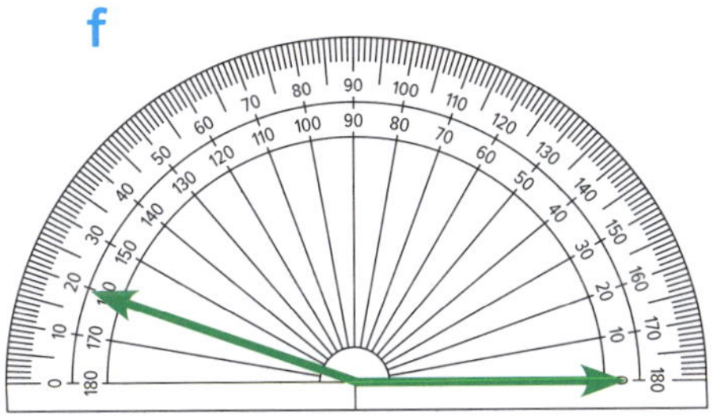

g

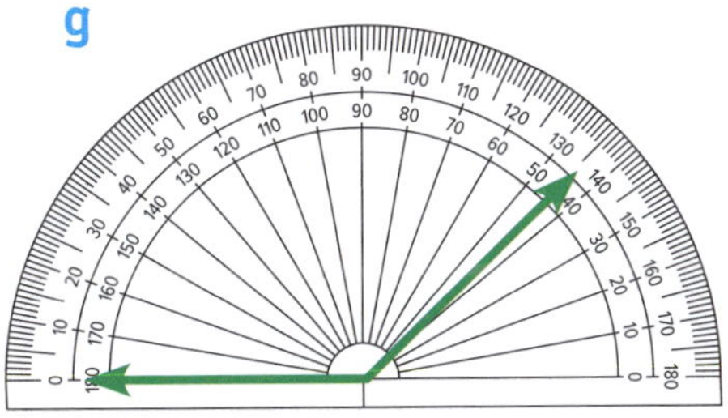

h

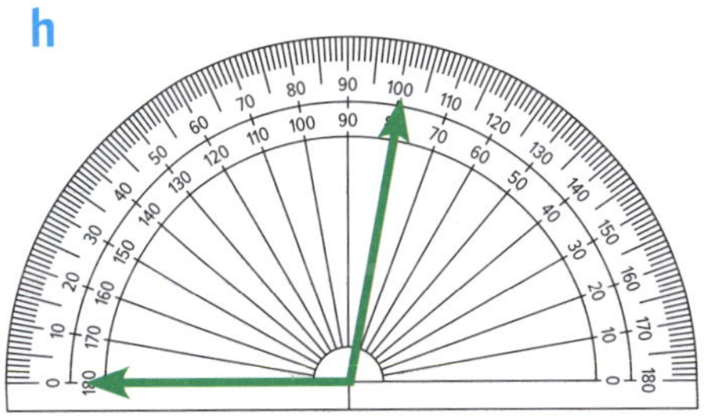

Challenge! Work with a friend. Look around and use your protractor to find:

a 3 angles less than 40°.

b 3 angles between 40° and 90°.

c 3 angles of 90°.

d 3 angles more than 90°.

Unit 9 Measuring and drawing angles

estimate and measure to check

1 Estimate the size of each angle. Then measure it accurately.

a

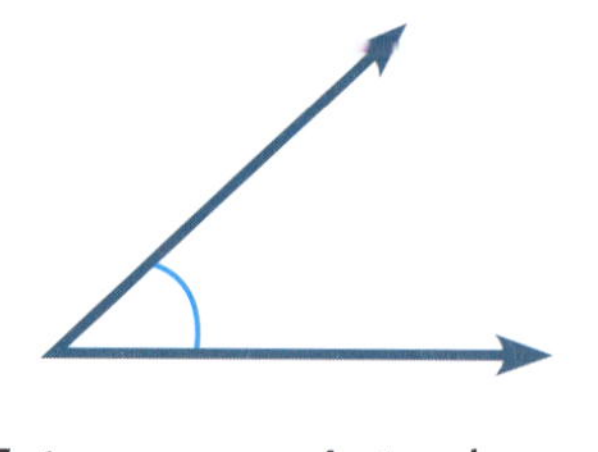

Est. ______ Actual ______

b

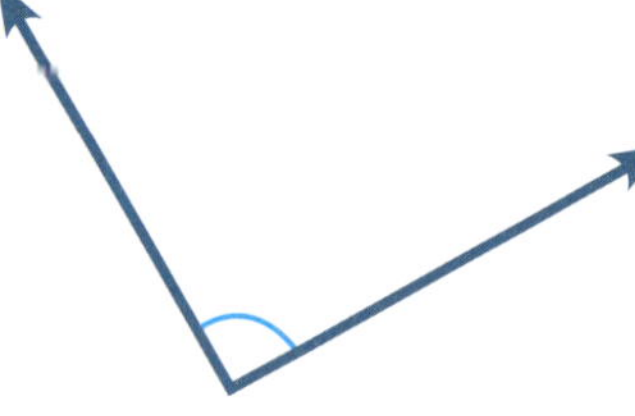

Est. ______ Actual ______

c

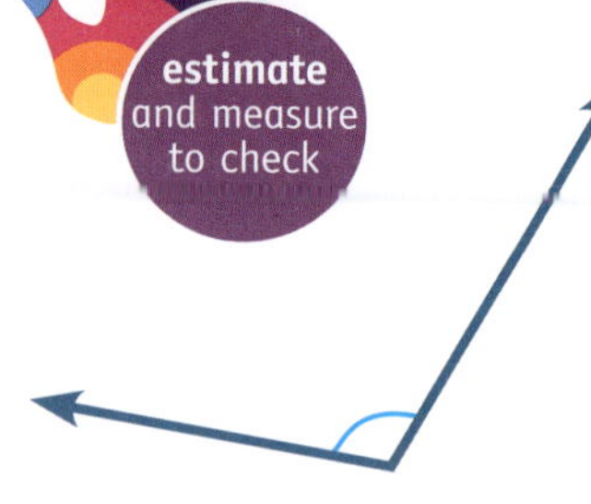

Est. ______ Actual ______

d

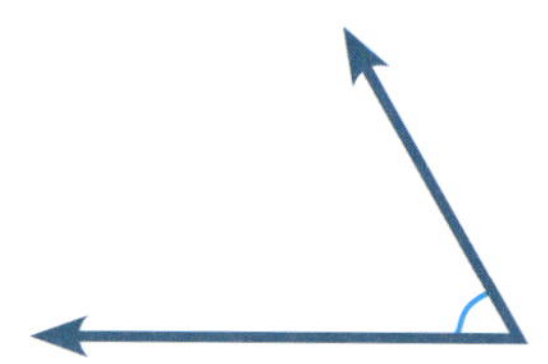

Est. ______ Actual ______

e

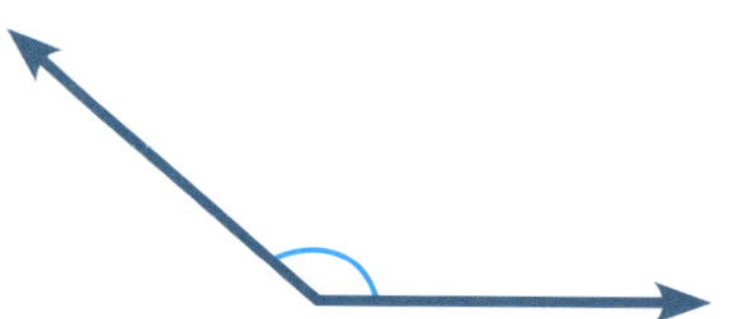

Est. ______ Actual ______

f

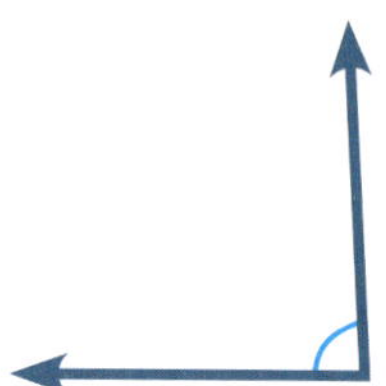

Est. ______ Actual ______

g

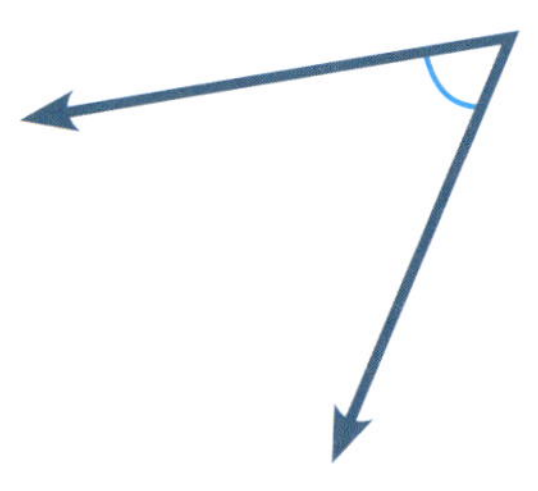

Est. ______ Actual ______

h

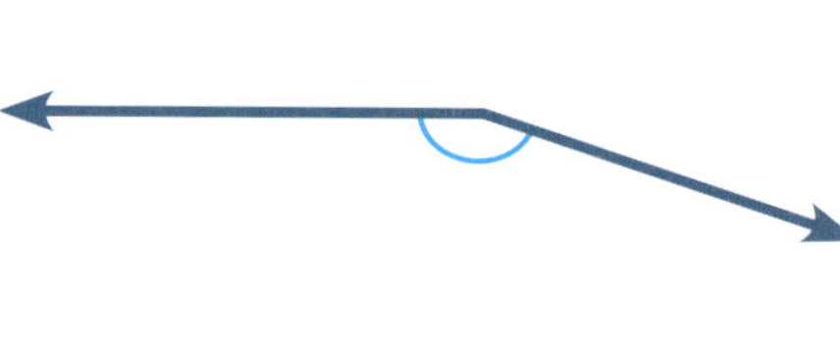

Est. ______ Actual ______

i

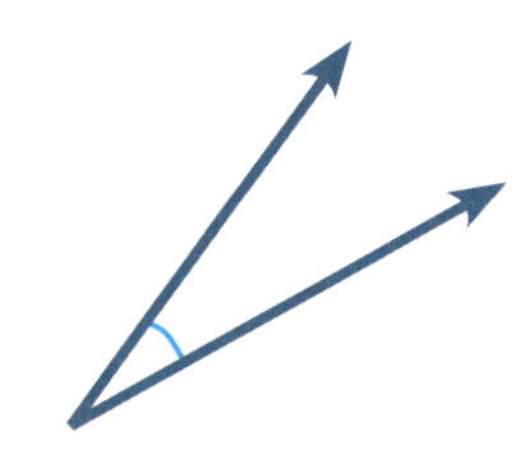

Est. ______ Actual ______

2 Use a protractor to draw these angles.

a 35°

b 130°

c 20°

d 116°

e 68°

f 109°

Unit 9 More angles

1 Label each angle as **acute, right, obtuse, straight, reflex** or **revolution.**

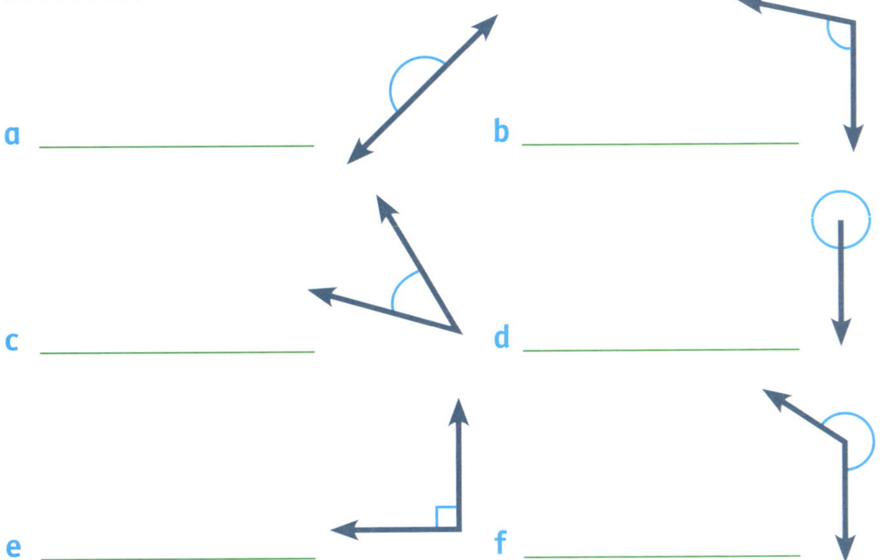

a ____________

b ____________

c ____________

d ____________

e ____________

f ____________

2 Classify these angles as **acute, right, obtuse, straight, reflex** or **revolution.**

a 36° ____________ b 300° ____________

c 90° ____________ d 360° ____________

3 Find the complementary angle for each of these angles.

a 43° ____________ b 82° ____________

c 30° ____________ d 10° ____________

4 Determine the supplementary angle for each of these angles.

a 116° ____________ b 60° ____________

c 175° ____________ d 90° ____________

e 62° ____________ f 178° ____________

5 What is the size of the missing angle in each revolution?

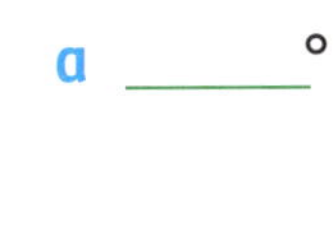

a ______°

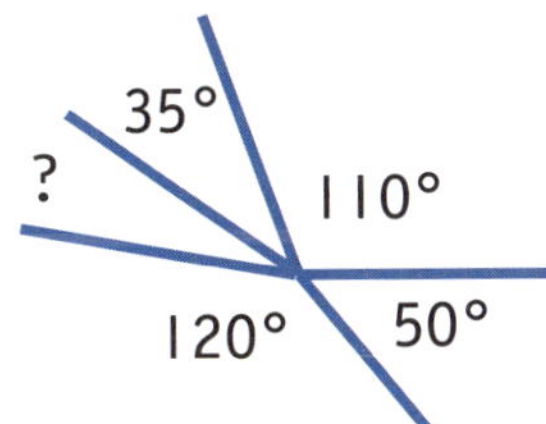

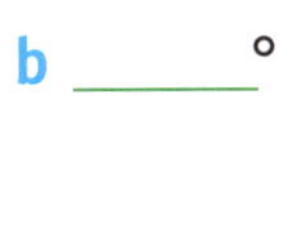

b ______°

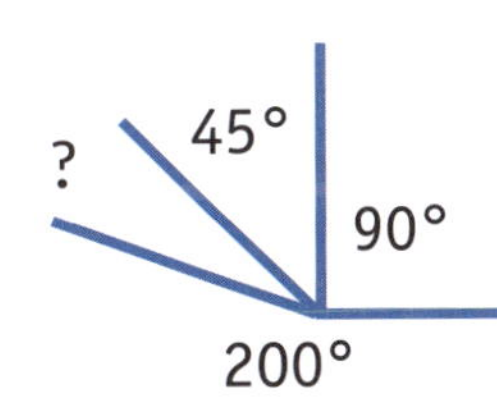

arm

vertex

Acute angles less than 90°

Right angles always 90°

Obtuse angles more than 90° less than 180°

Straight angles always 180°

Reflex angles more than 180° less than 360°

Revolutions are always 360°

Vertically opposite angles are equal

110° 70° **Supplementary angles add up to 180°**

70° 20° **Complementary angles add up to 90°**

Mastery Checklist

I can:
- ☐ use a protractor to measure angles
- ☐ describe angles as acute, right, obtuse, straight, reflex or revolution
- ☐ estimate the size of angles and measure to check
- ☐ draw angles.

Unit 10 Dot plots

Year 5 birthdays

○ = 2 people

Month	
January	○ ○
February	○ ○ ○
March	○ ○ ○ ○ ○
April	○ ○ ○ ○
May	○ ○
June	○ ○ ○
July	○
August	○ ○
September	○ ○ ○
October	○ ○ ○ ○
November	○ ○ ○
December	○ ○

1 How could you collect this information about your class?

____

____

2 How many birthdays were in:

a January? ________ b March? ________ c May? ________

d July? ________ e October? ________ f December? ________

3 Which season has the most birthdays? ________________

4 a Who would use a graph like this? ________________

b Why? ____

5 a Would every class's graph of birthdays look like this? ________

b Why? ____

6 Why does a dot plot suit this information?

____

____

____

Unit 10 Draw a dot plot

Graphs 2 

This shows the numbers of brothers and sisters of children in Year 6.

0 siblings	1 sibling	2 siblings	3 siblings	4 siblings	over 4 siblings
14	16	15	13	12	14

1 Draw a dot plot to show this information. **Key** ☐ **= 2 students**

2 Give the graph a title.

3 How would you collect this information from your class?

____

____

4 Who would use the information in this graph? ____________________

5 How would they use it? ____________________

6 Why is a dot plot the best kind of graph for this information? ____________________

____

7 What questions are answered by this graph?

____

Unit 10 Tally marks

Data 1

1 Use tally marks to show these counts. Books sold in a week: Adventure 21, Young Adult 29, Thriller 11, Mystery 37, Comedy 15.

Tally marks are used to count large numbers. They are in groups of 5. The 5th mark makes a bundle.

𝍸 = 5

Book	Tally	Total
Adventure		
Young Adult		
Thriller		
Mystery		
Comedy		

2 Farmer Blake kept a tally of the number of boxes of mangos that were picked each day for a week.

Day	Tally	Total
Sunday	𝍸 |	
Monday	𝍸 𝍸 𝍸	
Tuesday	𝍸 𝍸 ||	
Wednesday	𝍸 𝍸 𝍸 𝍸	
Thursday	𝍸 𝍸 ||||	
Friday	𝍸 𝍸 𝍸 |||	
Saturday	𝍸	

Complete the total column.

Sunday	☆
Monday	
Tuesday	
Wednesday	
Thursday	
Friday	
Saturday	

Key ☆ = 5 boxes

3 Why did she choose a 5-pointed star for the graph?

____

4 **a** Use the key to complete the graph. **b** Give the graph a title.

5 How many boxes were picked:

a on Thursday? ________ **b** on Wednesday? ________ **c** on the weekend? ________

d altogether? ________

6 **a** On which day did she pick four times as many boxes as on Saturday? ________

b Why do you think she picked so few boxes on Saturday? ________

____

7 On one day she had help for a few hours. Which day do you think it was? ________

Why? ______________________________

Unit 10 Column graph

The next week Farmer Blake decided to draw a column graph.

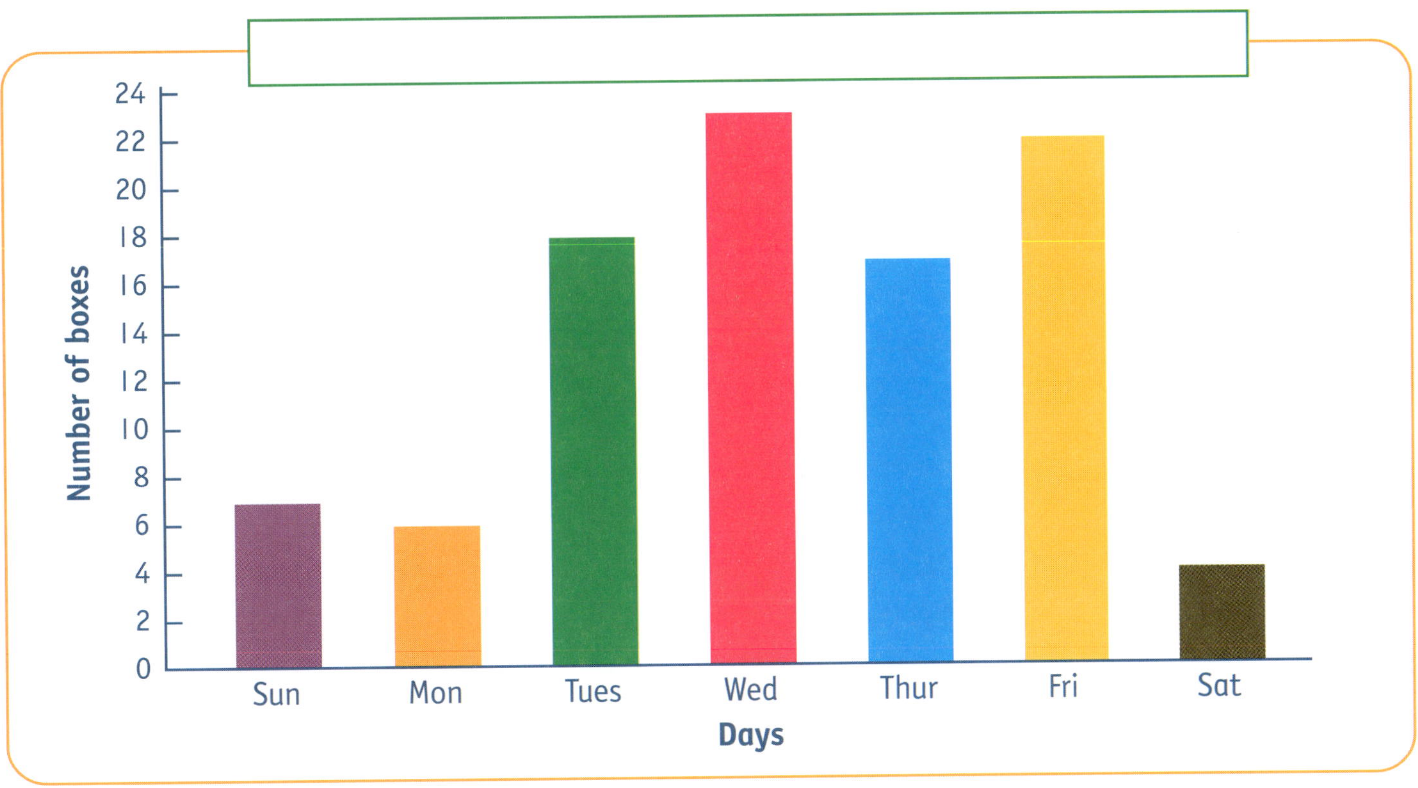

1 Write a title for the graph.

2 a Complete her tally chart.

b How many boxes did she pick altogether that week? ________

c How does this compare with the previous week?

____

Day	Tally	Total

3 On which day did she:

a pick the most? ________

b pick the least? ________

4 Write one possible reason:

a why so few boxes were picked on Monday. ________

b why so many boxes were picked on Wednesday. ________

5 What do you think happens on weekends? ________

6 a Is it easier for you to read the tally chart or the column graph? ________

b Why? ________

Mastery Checklist I can:

- ☐ interpret a dot plot
- ☐ draw a dot plot
- ☐ use tally marks
- ☐ complete a pictograph
- ☐ interpret a column graph.

Revision Term 1

1 p 2

6 0 7 5 2 9

Use the cards to make:

a the largest number. ______

b the smallest number. ______

2 Write in words. p 2

a 850 002 ______

______

b 200 174 ______

______

3 How many times smaller is the 5 in 520 than the 5 in 650 000? p 3

______

4 Round to the nearest thousand. p 3

a 856 900 ______

b 13 886 ______

5 Expand these numbers. p 4

a 459 008 ______

______

b 801 600 ______

______

6 p 7

a $\begin{array}{r} 403 \\ +\ 294 \\ \hline \end{array}$ ______

b $\begin{array}{r} 574 \\ +\ 228 \\ \hline \end{array}$ ______

c $\begin{array}{r} 358 \\ +\ 429 \\ \hline \end{array}$ ______

7 p 10

$9.80/kg

$6.50/kg

$7.45/kg

$5.20/kg

Pete had $10.

What change does he get if he buys 1 kg of:

a bananas? ______ b grapes? ______

c apples? ______ d strawberries? ______

8 p 11

a 39 − 28 = ______

b 61 − 32 = ______

c 86 − 42 = ______

d 58 − 29 = ______

9 Use the number lines. p 12

a 411 − 128 = ______

b 723 − 386 = ______

10 p 13

$\begin{array}{r} 527 \\ -\ 263 \\ \hline \end{array}$ ______

check $\begin{array}{r} 263 \\ +\ \\ \hline \end{array}$ ______

11 Colour the factors of 28. p 14

14 8 4 7 6

28 1 3 2

12 Write the first 4 multiples. p 15

a 9 ______ ______ ______ ______

b 7 ______ ______ ______ ______

13 Use doubles. p 17

a 16 × 4 = ______ b 15 × 8 = ______

14 Use factors. p 18

a 15 × 9 = ______ b 47 × 6 = ______

15 Kai picks 374 cherries from each of 6 trees. How many altogether? p 18

Revision Term 1

16 Complete. p 19

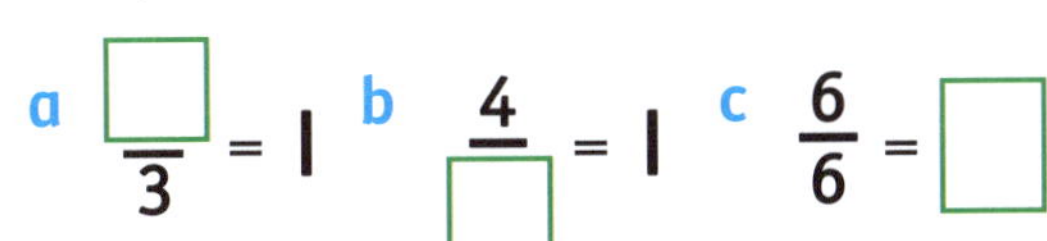

a $\frac{\square}{3} = 1$ b $\frac{4}{\square} = 1$ c $\frac{6}{6} = \square$

17 a $1 - \frac{1}{3} =$ _____ b $1 - \frac{7}{12} =$ _____ p 19

18 Order these fractions smallest to largest. p 20

$\frac{1}{2}$, $\frac{4}{10}$, $\frac{7}{8}$ ______________________

19 Colour the fraction. p 21

a

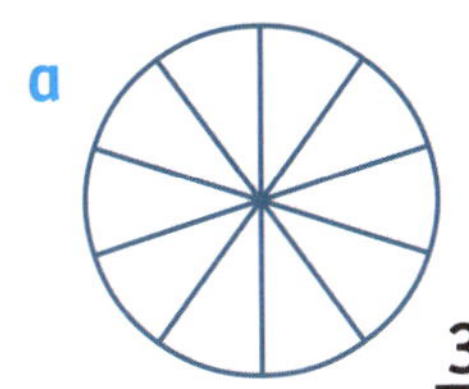

$\frac{3}{10}$

b

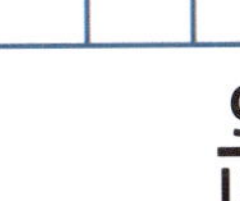

$\frac{9}{10}$

20 Write the fraction and the decimal for the coloured part. p 21

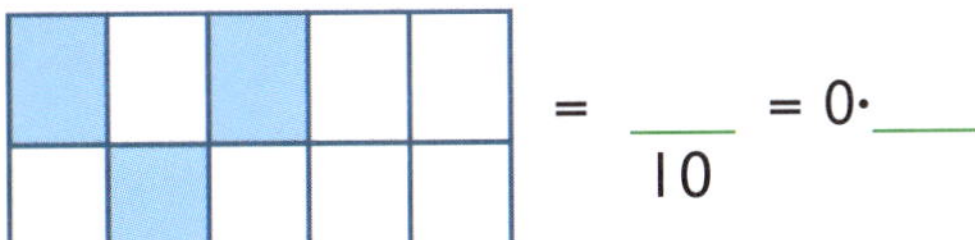

= $\frac{\_\_\_}{10}$ = 0·___

21 What is: p 22

a $\frac{1}{10}$ of 1 metre? _______

b $\frac{1}{4}$ of 1 kilometre? _______

22 Write something for next week that: p 25

a is certain to happen.

____

b is impossible to happen.

____

c will probably happen.

____

23 What is the inverse operation of multiplication? p 33

____

24 What is the inverse operation of subtraction? p 33

____

25 Would you use cm, m or km to measure the length of: p 36

a a pencil? _____ b a room? _____

c a person? _____ d a town? _____

26 a 3 km = _______ m p 37

b 6 m = _______ cm

c 4 cm = _______ mm

d 3·91 m = _____ cm

e 74 mm = _____ cm f 27 km = _______ m

27 p 38

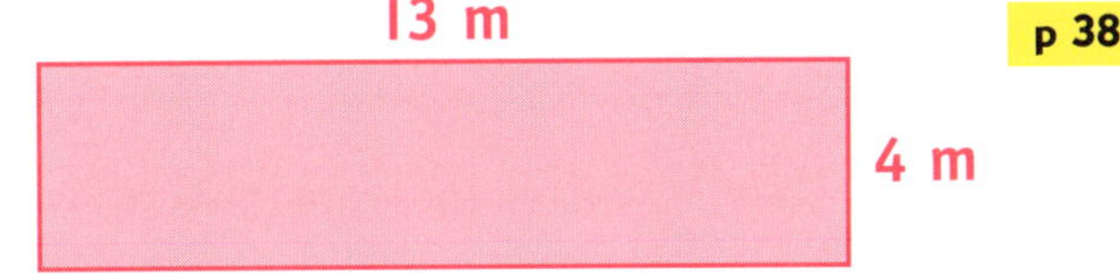

Perimeter = _________

28 Use a protractor to draw a right angle. p 42

29 A revolution measures 360°. p 43

What is the size of the missing angle?

_______°

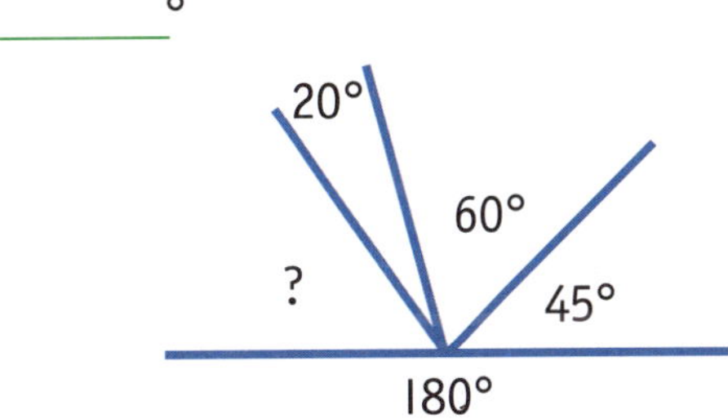

30 Count the tally marks. Write the total. p 46

a  _______

b 𝍸 𝍸 𝍸 𝍸 𝍸 𝍸 𝍸 | _______

c 𝍸 𝍸 𝍸 𝍸 || _______

NAPLAN* practice

This is a test to see how well you understand what you have learnt.

Instructions

Read each question carefully. There are three different ways to show your answer:

- Shade the bubble next to the correct answer.
- Write a word in a box.
- Write a number in a box.

Use a pencil. DO NOT use a pen. If you make a mistake, rub it out and try again.

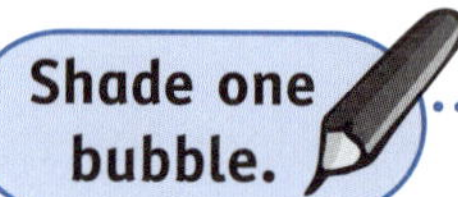

1 Which one of these is the same as 43 600?

40 + 300 + 6000 ◯ 600 + 4300 ◯ 43 000 + 60 ◯ 40 000 + 600 + 3000 ◯

2 This pattern is made by translating a regular shape.

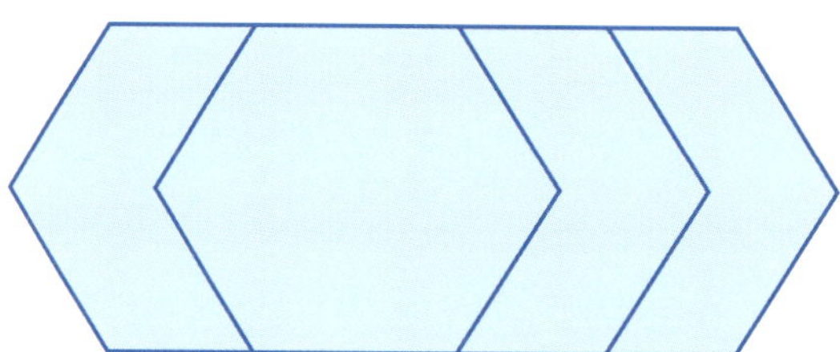

What shape is it?

triangle ◯ trapezium ◯ hexagon ◯ quadrilateral ◯

3 Which one of these has the same value as the sum of 46 and 38?

40 + 36 + 8 ◯ 38 + 50 − 6 ◯ 30 + 40 + 16 ◯ 50 + 36 ◯

4 Tad bought lunch and used a $10 note. He received change of $1.15.
What did he buy for lunch?

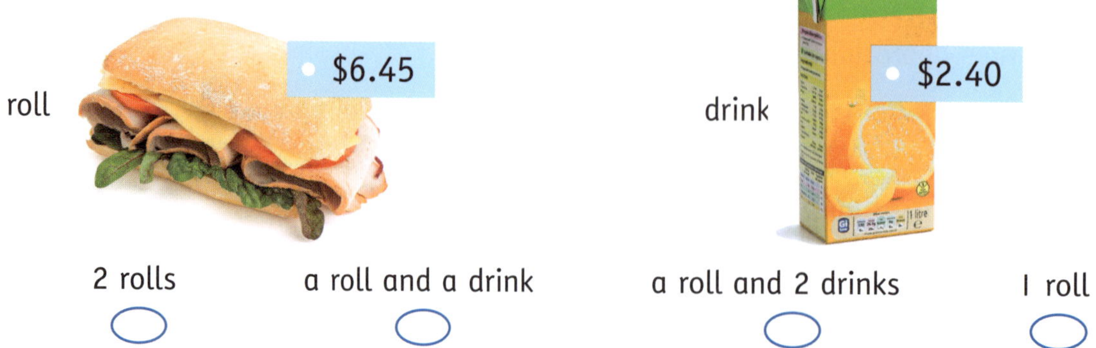

2 rolls ◯ a roll and a drink ◯ a roll and 2 drinks ◯ 1 roll ◯

* This is not an officially endorsed publication of the NAPLAN program and is produced independently of Australian governments.

Test practice

5 Jody wrote some factors of 30.

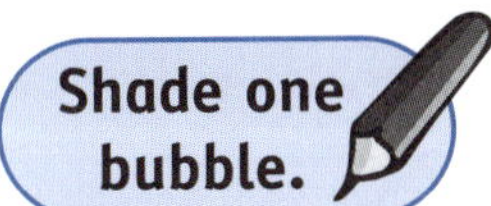

1, 2, 5, 6, 10, 15, 30

She missed one. Which factor did she miss?

4 ◯ | 12 ◯ | 3 ◯ | 8 ◯

6 260 children have to travel by bus.

Write your answer in the box.

A bus holds 40 children.

How many buses will they need? 

7 There are 30 books. Mr Jones can take one fifth of the books in one load.

How many books can he take in one load? 

8 Jem has two $1 coins and three 50c pieces in a purse. With her eyes closed, what is her chance of taking out a $1 coin?

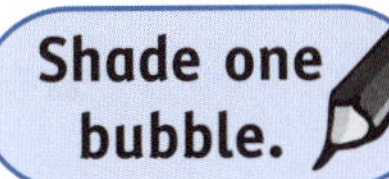

1 in 5 ◯ | 1 in 3 ◯ | 2 in 3 ◯ | 2 in 5 ◯

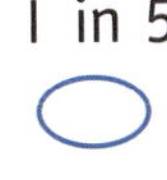

9 You make 5 stacks of blocks with different odd numbers of blocks in each stack. What is the least number of blocks you could use?

27  | 25  | 23  | 21 ◯

Test practice

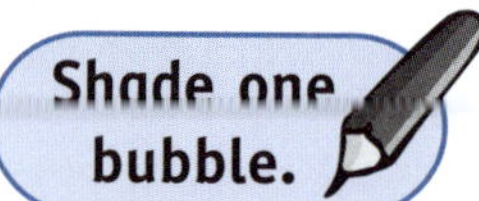

10 This graph shows test scores for a class.

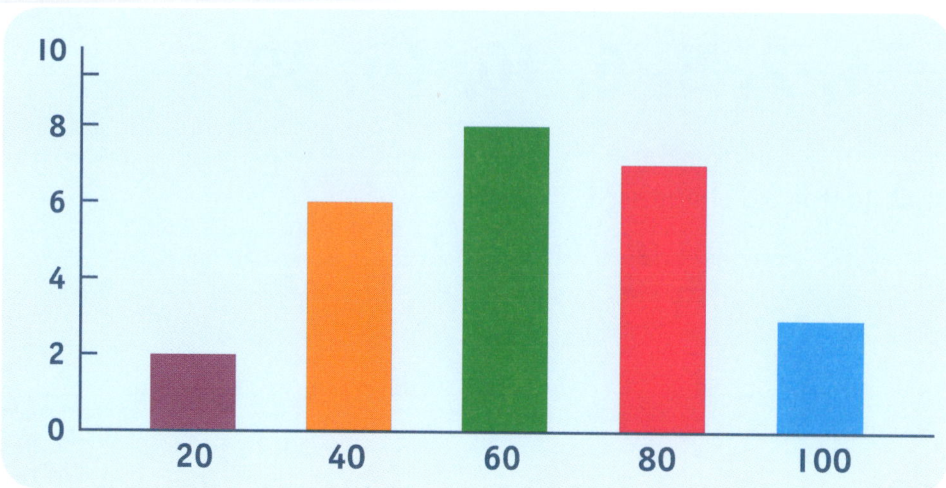

50% is a pass. How many children passed the test?

8 ○ 20 ○ 17 ○ 18 ○

11 This line shows a 20 km road. How far has the car driven?

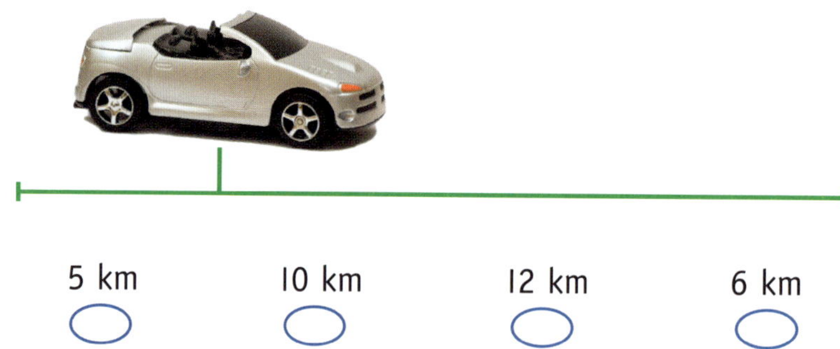

5 km ○ 10 km ○ 12 km ○ 6 km ○

12 I made a pentagonal prism out of cardboard shapes. How many rectangles did I use?

2 ○ 10 ○ 5 ○ 7 ○

13 What is the smallest 4-digit number Ale can make with the digits on the cards?

0354 ○ 0345 ○ 3045 ○ 3054 ○

Test practice

14 Study these scales.

How many apples weigh the same as a mango?

1	2	3	4

15 Four children worked out the cost of 20 flags at 85c each.

Which method did not give the correct result?

\$8.50 + \$8.50	850c × 2	10 + \$8.50 + 85c	2 × 85c × 10
◯	◯	◯	

16 When you add ten thousand to this number, which digit will change?

74 690

6	7	4	9
	◯	◯	◯

17 Ash has 22 jelly babies, Vinn has 17, but Liam only has 12. Ash can give Liam some jelly babies and they will all have the same number. How many jelly babies should Ash give Liam?

3	4	5	6
		◯	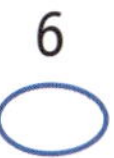

Test practice

Shade one bubble.

18

	Chocolate left to eat
Jill	$\frac{2}{5}$
Freda	25%
Tom	$\frac{3}{10}$
Tilly	0·35

Who has the most chocolate left?

Tilly ◯ Jill ◯ Freda ◯ Tom ◯

19 24 people are at my party. One quarter is my family. One half are my school friends. The rest are neighbours.

How many neighbours are at my party?

8 ◯ 6 ◯ 4 ◯ 10 ◯

20 If Cam turns right from Delli Road into Peters Road, what angle will his car's turn make?

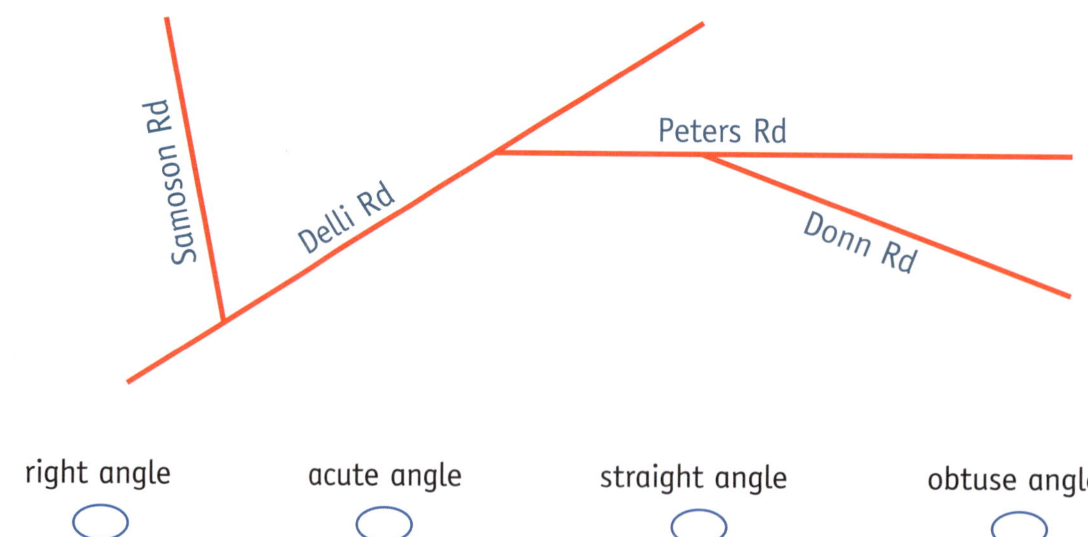

right angle ◯ acute angle ◯ straight angle ◯ obtuse angle ◯

Test practice

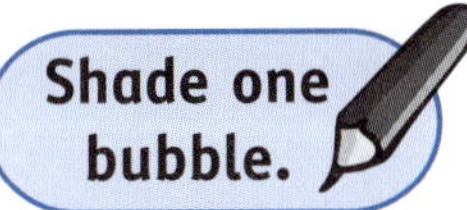

21 Which container is holding 1·5 L of water?

22 Which piece is missing from this symmetrical design?

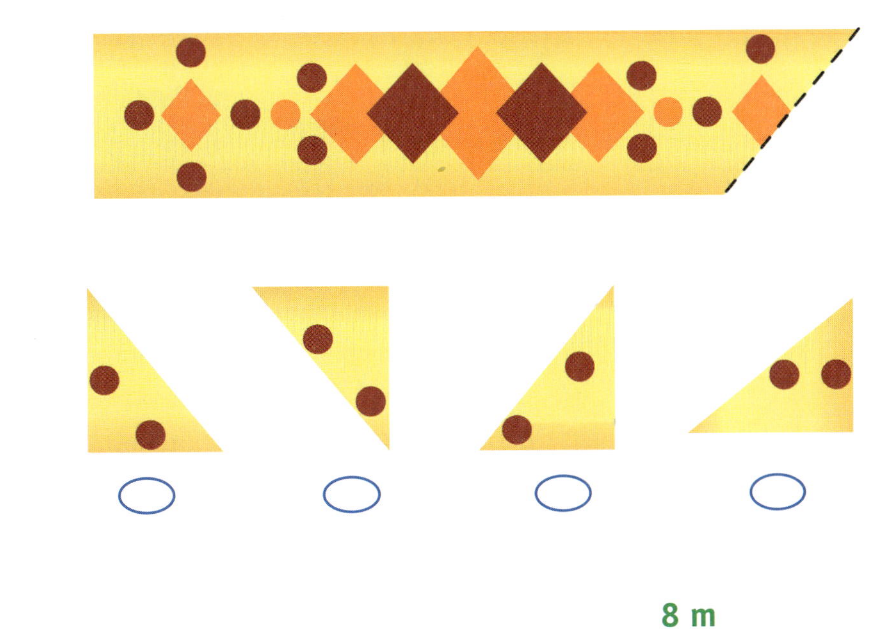

23 Which garden is half the area of Dan's?

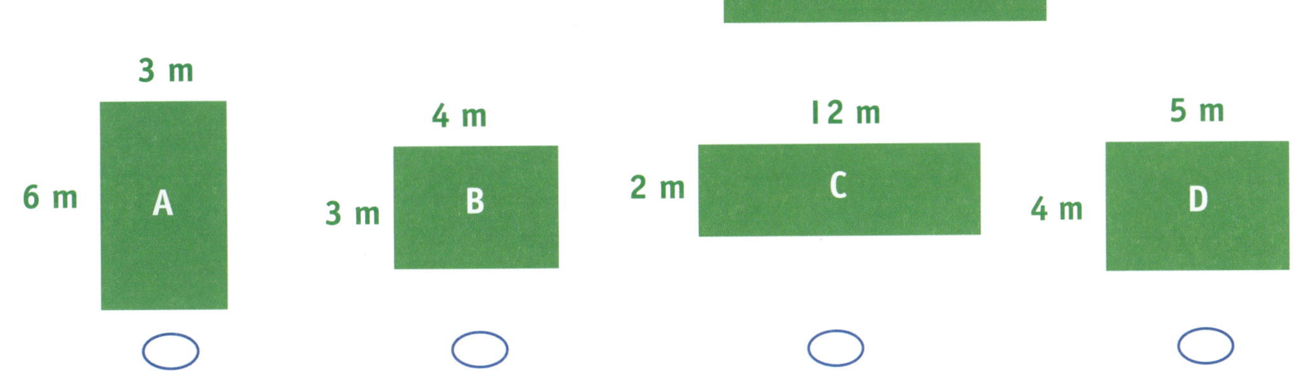

Test practice

Write your answer in the box.

24 It's 27th November. How many days does Terry have to wait until his birthday on 4th January?

☐

25 One is a square number and also a triangular number. What is another number <50 which is a square number and a triangular number?

☐

26 This is my bus departure timetable.

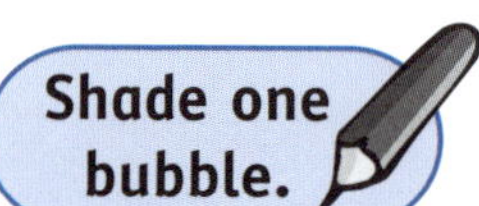

Ringa	7:00	7:15	7:30
Valle	7:08	7:23	7:38
Patters	7:20	7:35	7:40
Tempty	7:26	7:41	7:46

The 7:15 from Ringa leaves 4 minutes late. If the bus continues without further delays, at what time will it leave Patters?

7:39 ◯ 7:35 ◯ 7:27 ◯ 7:31 ◯

27

```
  3 4 0 0
-   5 6 4
---------
  2 ? 3 ?
```

The missing digits are:

1 and 4 ◯ 8 and 6 ◯ 1 and 6 ◯ 9 and 4 ◯

Test practice

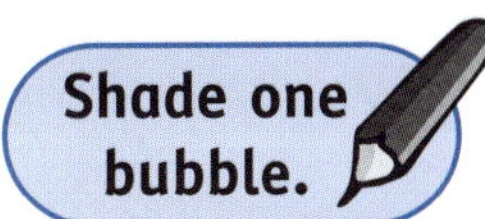

28 Chris built this tower. If he built another tower with the same number of cubes but made it 4 cubes wide and 2 cubes deep, how many cubes high would it be?

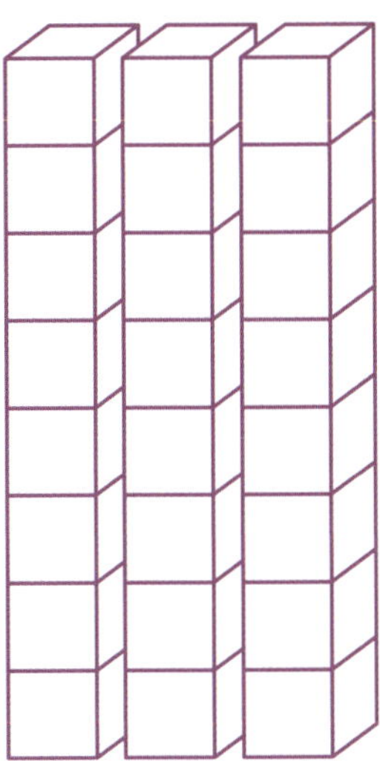

3 ◯

4 ◯

5 ◯

6 ◯

29 In a relay totalling 1200 metres, 8 children have to run an equal distance. How far will each run?

100 metres ◯ 15 metre ◯ 150 metres ◯ 20 metres ◯

30 I am looking at a 3D object which has three triangular sides and a triangular base.

Write your answer in the box.

What is it?  

31 Jamie put a sticker on every face of this object. How many stickers did he use? 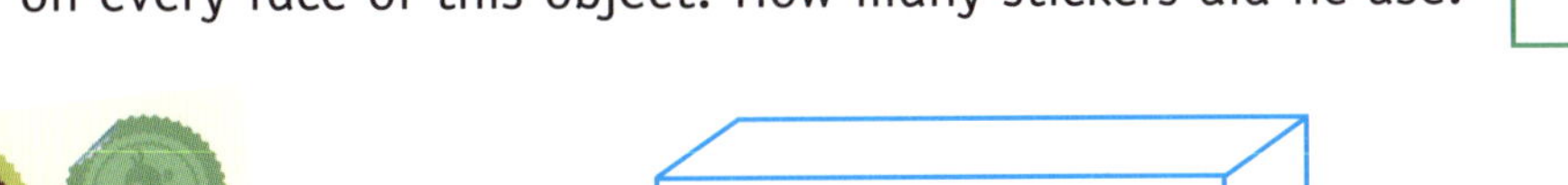

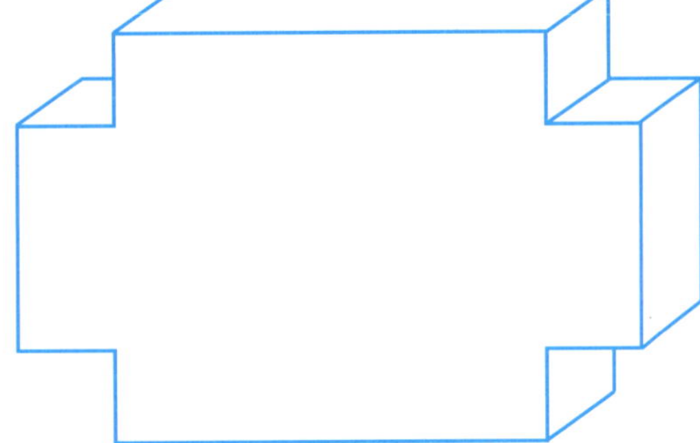

Unit 11 Large numbers

A

Population	
Cairns	169 300
Canberra	472 000
Geelong	271 000
Gold Coast	711 000
Hobart	253 000
Newcastle	461 900
Sunshine Coast	359 000
Wollongong	312 600

B

Population	
Adelaide	1 345 000
Brisbane	2 439 800
Melbourne	5 061 200
Perth	2 067 600
Sydney	5 200 000

Samira and Riley are reading the latest population boards.

1 What is the difference between the two boards? ______________________

____

____

2 a Which place has the largest population? ______________________

b Which place has the smallest population? ______________________

3 Which place has a population closest to:

a one million people? ______________________

b one hundred thousand people? ______________________

c half a million people? ______________________

d a quarter of a million? ______________________

4 Place the cities on board B on this number line.

1 000 000 ———————————————————————— 6 000 000

Unit 11 Working with large numbers

1 Write these populations in words.

a Canberra ______________________________

____

b Sunshine Coast ______________________________

____

c Melbourne ______________________________

____

2 Write the cities on board A in descending order of population.

____

____

3 Give the value of the 5 in:

a Hobart ____________ b Melbourne ____________ c Adelaide ____________

4 Which city has:

a the second largest population? ____________

b the second smallest population? ____________

5 Round each city on Board B to the nearest thousand.

a Adelaide ____________ b Brisbane ____________ c Melbourne ____________

d Perth ____________ e Sydney ____________

6 Round each city on Board A to the nearest hundred thousand.

a Cairns ____________ b Canberra ____________ c Geelong ____________

d Gold Coast ____________ e Hobart ____________ f Newcastle ____________

g Sunshine Coast ____________ h Wollongong ____________

7 Match.

a 50 000 + 9000 + 300 000

b 50 000 + 6000

c 400 000 + 2000 + 70 000

d 300 000 + 5000 + 1 000 000 + 40 000

A Adelaide

B Hobart

C Canberra

D Sunshine Coast

Challenge! Find:

a 5 cities with populations more than ten million.

b 5 countries with populations more than fifty million.

Unit 11 Place value

1 Complete the labels.

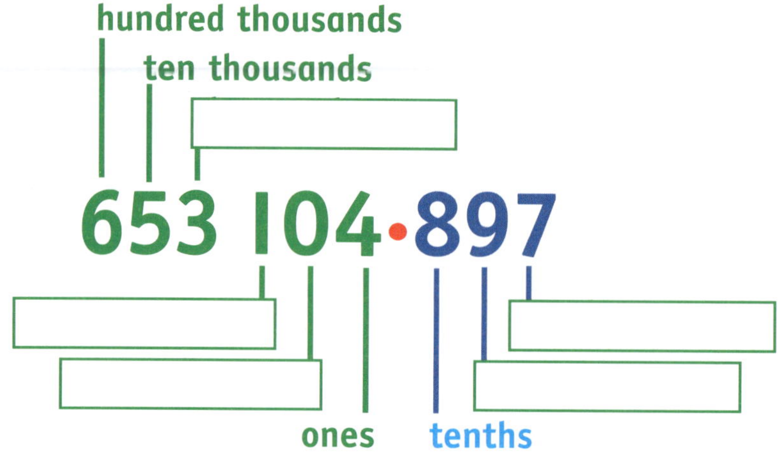

2 Complete.

a 72 894·356 = 72 894 + $\frac{3}{10}$ + $\frac{5}{100}$ + $\frac{6}{1000}$

b 83 245·62 = ______ + $\frac{\square}{10}$ + $\frac{\square}{100}$ + $\frac{\square}{1000}$

c 1305·805 = ______ + $\frac{\square}{10}$ + $\frac{\square}{100}$ + $\frac{\square}{1000}$

d 901·340 = ______ + $\frac{\square}{10}$ + $\frac{\square}{100}$ + $\frac{\square}{1000}$

e 6·098 = ______ + $\frac{\square}{10}$ + $\frac{\square}{100}$ + $\frac{\square}{1000}$

f 16·92 = ______ + $\frac{\square}{10}$ + $\frac{\square}{100}$ + $\frac{\square}{1000}$

g 5 950 205·763 = ______ + $\frac{\square}{10}$ + $\frac{\square}{100}$ + $\frac{\square}{1000}$

h 7 643 296·004 = ______ + $\frac{\square}{10}$ + $\frac{\square}{100}$ + $\frac{\square}{1000}$

i 5984·203 = ______ + $\frac{\square}{10}$ + $\frac{\square}{100}$ + $\frac{\square}{1000}$

j 6 732 001·592 = ______ + $\frac{\square}{10}$ + $\frac{\square}{100}$ + $\frac{\square}{1000}$

k 3·010 = ______ + $\frac{\square}{10}$ + $\frac{\square}{100}$ + $\frac{\square}{1000}$

l 839·6 = ______ + $\frac{\square}{10}$ + $\frac{\square}{100}$ + $\frac{\square}{1000}$

m 34 952·80 = ______ + $\frac{\square}{10}$ + $\frac{\square}{100}$ + $\frac{\square}{1000}$

n 5 930 546·003 = ______ + $\frac{\square}{10}$ + $\frac{\square}{100}$ + $\frac{\square}{1000}$

Unit 11 Working with large numbers

1 Use red to circle the whole number and use blue to circle the decimal.

a 342 683·594 b 895·23 c 7435·682

d 7·003 e 436·829 f 14 596·25

g 897·329 h 6·49 i 1·2

j 124 987·2 k 38·481 l 9·123

2 Answer yes or no.

a 8·093 has 9 hundredths. ____________

b 643 284·210 has 1 thousandth. ____________

c 29·3 has 3 tenths. ____________

d 749·083 has 4 tens. ____________

e 1529·210 has 2 tenths. ____________

f 68 491·35 has 3 hundredths. ____________

g 265 429·384 has 6 ten thousands. ____________

h 17·563 has 6 tens. ____________

i 8495·030 has 4 hundreds. ____________

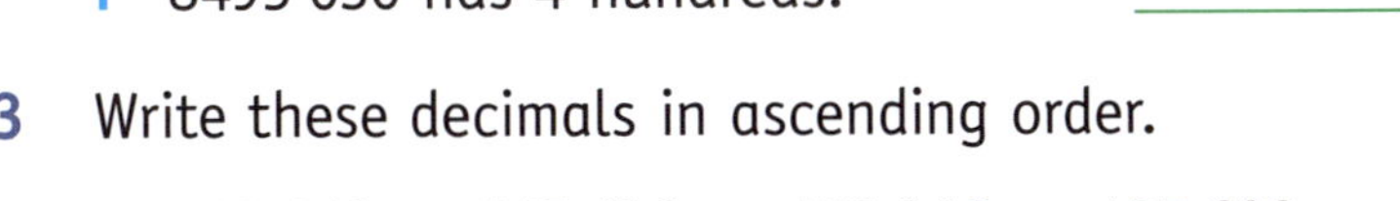

3 Write these decimals in ascending order.

a 542·649 245·496 452·946 425·609 524·708

____________ ____________ ____________ ____________ ____________

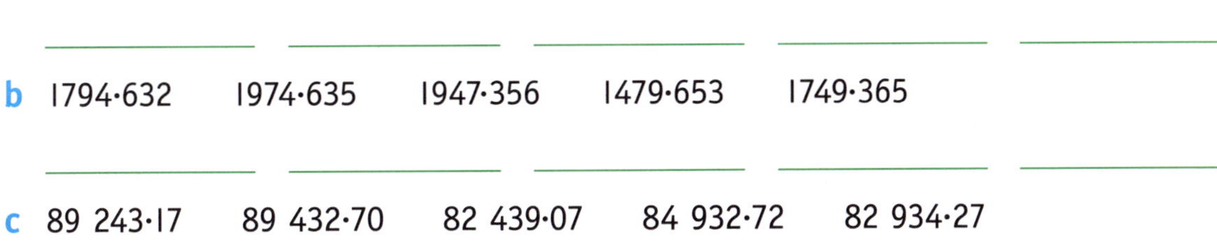

b 1794·632 1974·635 1947·356 1479·653 1749·365

____________ ____________ ____________ ____________ ____________

c 89 243·17 89 432·70 82 439·07 84 932·72 82 934·27

____________ ____________ ____________ ____________ ____________

4 Write these decimals in descending order.

a 638·429 683·942 638·249 643·829 643·982

____________ ____________ ____________ ____________ ____________

b 9386·280 9863·820 9683·082 9368·280 9836·208

____________ ____________ ____________ ____________ ____________

c 38 420·983 38 024·389 38 240·398 38 283·409 38 823·904

____________ ____________ ____________ ____________ ____________

Unit 11 Value of numbers

Word problems

1 What is the value of the underlined number?

a 5 439 673 9000 b 1 629 542 ______ c 8 314 279 ______

d 6 732 405 ______ e 7 523 086 ______ f 9 867 453 ______

g 4 682 309 ______ h 5 096 037 ______ i 3 459 802 ______

2 What is the value of the 5?

a 2 493 056 50 b 4 095 321 ______ c 6 593 324 ______

d 5 432 096 ______ e 8 369 035 ______ f 9 352 639 ______

g 7 325 399 ______ h 3 498 528 ______ i 1 234 756 ______

3 Write a number in the millions that has a 7 in the listed place. Make sure each number is different!

a ones place ______ b hundreds place ______

c millions place ______ d thousands place ______

e ten thousands place ______ f hundred thousands place ______

4 Write in words each number you wrote for question 3.

a ______

b ______

c ______

d ______

e ______

f ______

Mastery Checklist I can:

- [ ] use place value from millions to thousandths
- [ ] partition numbers
- [ ] compare and order numbers.

Unit 12 Addition of money

LUKE'S LAVISH LUNCHES

Sashimi $7.55

Indian Tray $9.50

Taco $8.65

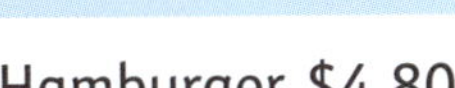

Hamburger $4.80

Grilled sandwich $5.35

Pizza slice $6.25

Every work day three friends go to Luke's Lavish Lunches for lunch.
Each day they choose a different combination of dishes.

1 Write down the dishes they might choose and the total cost for each day.

- a Monday Sashimi + Sandwich + Taco = $ ______
- b Tuesday ______
- c Wednesday ______
- d Thursday ______
- e Friday ______

2
- a Estimate the cost of ordering all six dishes. ______
- b Use a calculator to find the actual cost. ______
- c Was the calculator useful? ______ Why? ______

______

Unit 12 Addition practice

Word problems

1 a

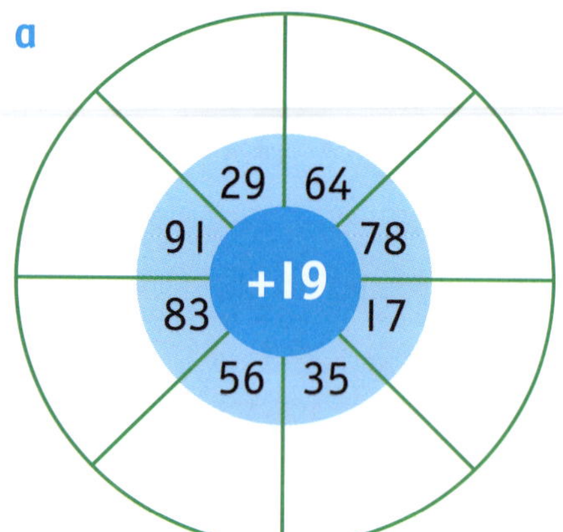

b

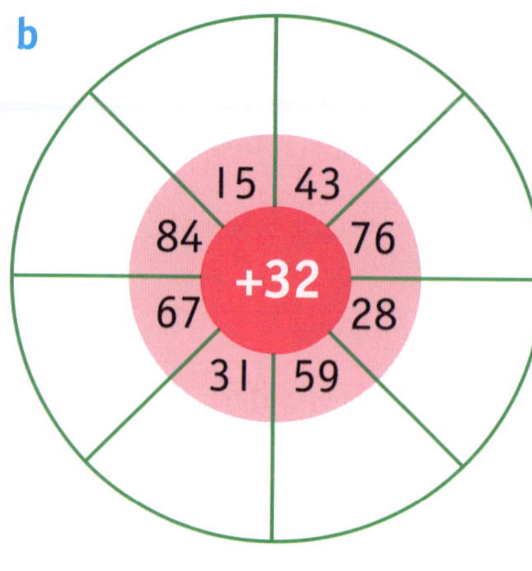

c

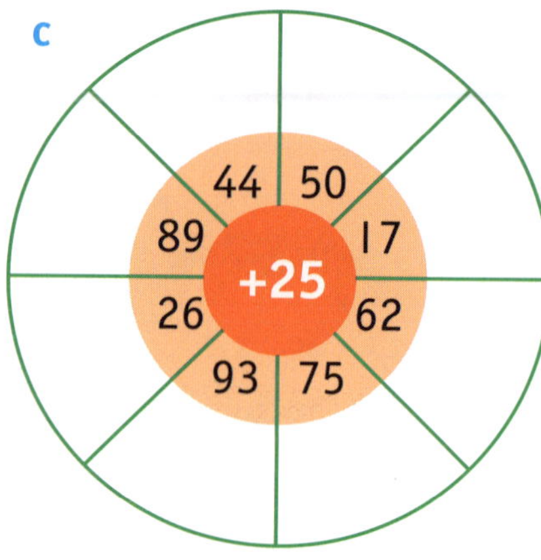

2 a
```
  384
   17
+ 291
-----

-----
```
b
```
   63
  594
+  27
-----

-----
```
c
```
  305
   28
+   9
-----

-----
```
d
```
  764
  458
+  95
-----

-----
```
e
```
    8
  815
+  39
-----

-----
```

3 Estimate answers first.

a John sold 318 oranges, 257 apples and 98 pineapples. How many pieces of fruit did he sell?

Est. ______

Answer ______

b Jo sold 536 roses, 94 lilies and 425 carnations. How many flowers did she sell?

Est. ______

Answer ______

c Sui sold 304 biscuits, 58 pizzas, 27 bread rolls and 481 loaves of bread.

How many items did she sell?

Est. ______

Answer ______

d Ali sold 94 mice, 67 puppies, 483 goldfish and 159 birds. How many pets did he sell?

Est. ______

Answer ______

Trial and error

Amanda, Lynda and Nat had 684 hair ribbons altogether. Nat had more than Amanda but less than Lynda. How many ribbons might each girl have?

Amanda ______ Lynda  Nat ______

AC9M5N08 • AC9M5N09 Number MA3-AR-01 Additive relations A • Apply efficient mental and written strategies to solve addition and subtraction problems • Use estimation and place value understanding to determine the reasonableness of solutions

Unit 12 Four-digit addition

1 a 5 + 3 = ______
50 + 30 = ______
500 + 300 = ______
5000 + 3000 = ______

b 4 + 5 = ______
40 + 50 = ______
______ + ______ = ______
______ + ______ = ______

c 3 + 4 = ______
______ + ______ = ______
______ + ______ = ______
______ + ______ = ______

2
a $\begin{array}{r} 1694 \\ +\ 5282 \\ \hline \end{array}$
b $\begin{array}{r} 4715 \\ +\ 4563 \\ \hline \end{array}$
c $\begin{array}{r} 2068 \\ +\ 7912 \\ \hline \end{array}$
d $\begin{array}{r} 3706 \\ +\ 5265 \\ \hline \end{array}$
e $\begin{array}{r} 3907 \\ +\ 3764 \\ \hline \end{array}$
f $\begin{array}{r} 6270 \\ +\ 1895 \\ \hline \end{array}$
g $\begin{array}{r} 7695 \\ +\ 2178 \\ \hline \end{array}$
h $\begin{array}{r} 9238 \\ +\ 4758 \\ \hline \end{array}$

3 Write three examples where an exact 4-digit or 5-digit answer would be needed.
a ______
b ______
c ______

4 Write three examples where an approximate answer using more than 3 digits is acceptable.
a ______
b ______
c ______

5
a $\begin{array}{r} 3750 \\ 216 \\ 1907 \\ \hline \end{array}$
b $\begin{array}{r} 85 \\ 347 \\ 5291 \\ \hline \end{array}$
c $\begin{array}{r} 512 \\ 7090 \\ 68 \\ \hline \end{array}$
d $\begin{array}{r} 8759 \\ 7 \\ 618 \\ \hline \end{array}$
e $\begin{array}{r} 28 \\ 63 \\ 4045 \\ \hline \end{array}$
f $\begin{array}{r} 8290 \\ 6548 \\ 7 \\ \hline \end{array}$

Looking for patterns

Use the constant addition function on your calculator to find two different addition patterns.

Show your patterns to the class and explain them.

Mastery Checklist

I can:
- ☐ add money amounts
- ☐ estimate and use a calculator to check
- ☐ complete addition algorithms
- ☐ add 4-digit numbers
- ☐ complete addition patterns.

Unit 13 Division facts

YEAR K
Boys 23
Girls 25

YEAR 1
Boys 19
Girls 17

YEAR 2
Boys 15
Girls 20

YEAR 3
Boys 31
Girls 23

YEAR 4
Boys 29
Girls 35

YEAR 5
Boys 31
Girls 32

YEAR 6
Boys 36
Girls 36

These are the enrolments for Dividy school.

Teachers like to form groups for various activities.

1 Which years can form exact groups of:

a 2? ____________________

b 3? ____________________

c 4? ____________________

d 5? ____________________

e 6? ____________________

f 7? ____________________

g 8? ____________________

2 Which year can make separate boys and girls groups of:

a 5? __________ b 4? __________ c 3? __________

3 What exact groups can you make in your class? ____________________

Unit 13 Divide mentally

Work mentally.

1 Divide these by 10.

a 70 ______ b 90 ______ c 100 ______
d 130 ______ e 47 ______ f 69 ______
g 84 ______ h 91 ______ i 52 ______
j 131 ______ k 128 ______ l 375 ______
m 480 ______ n 619 ______ o 927 ______

Some tricks

To ÷ by 10
cross off the last number (it is the remainder).
eg $73 \div 10 = 7\frac{3}{10}$

To ÷ by 5
divide by 10 and double.
eg $72 \div 5 = 7\frac{2}{10} \times 2$
$= 14\frac{4}{10}$

2 Divide these by 5.

a 80 ______ b 90 ______ c 110 ______ d 240 ______ e 160 ______
f 61 ______ g 54 ______ h 102 ______ i 311 ______ j 423 ______
k 480 ______ l 263 ______ m 370 ______ n 127 ______ o 235 ______

3 Divide these by 2.

a 36 ______ b 90 ______ c 68 ______
d 76 ______ e 144 ______ f 268 ______
g 183 ______ h 371 ______ i 692 ______

4 Divide these by 4.

a 64 ______ b 76 ______ c 92 ______
d 108 ______ e 216 ______ f 252 ______
g 340 ______ h 165 ______ i 286 ______

5 Divide these by 8.

a 112 ______ b 120 ______ c 136 ______
d 176 ______ e 168 ______ f 272 ______
g 360 ______ h 409 ______ i 724 ______

More tricks (with even numbers)

To ÷ by 2
halve the number.
$84 \div 2 = 42$

To ÷ by 4
halve then halve again.
$124 \div 4 = 62 \div 2$
$= 31$

To ÷ by 8
halve, halve and halve.
$96 \div 8 = 48 \div 4$
$= 24 \div 2 = 12$

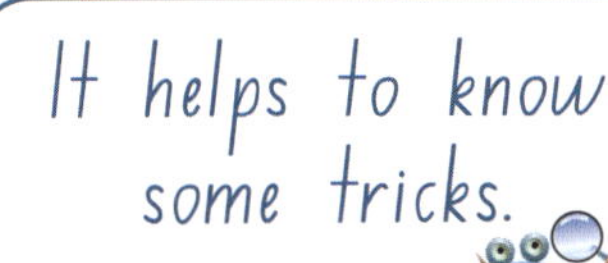

6 Jo and Terry were sorting the school supplies. They shared:

a 390 exercise books between 10 classes. How many each? ______

b 165 pencils between 4 classes. How many each? ______

How many were left over? ______

c 104 rulers between 8 classes. How many each? ______

d 97 tennis balls between 5 classes. How many each? ______

How many left over? ______

7 Write a division story for your class to solve. ____________________

____

Unit 13 Division algorithms

1 Colour the numbers that are exactly:

a divisible by 2.

84 29 76 138 221 610 905

b divisible by 10.

90 110 245 103 680 301 500

c divisible by 5.

95 83 170 502 151 315 132

d divisible by 3.

63 81 35 72 133 213 105

e divisible by 4.

116 220 114 208 318 340 132

Divisibility

A number is divisible by:

2 if it is even.

3 if the sum of its digits is divisible by 3.

eg 174 → 1 + 7 + 4 = 12

12 is divisible by 3 so 174 is divisible by 3.

4 if the last 2 digits are divisible by 4.

eg 516 → 16 is divisible by 4 so 516 is divisible by 4.

5 if it ends in 0 or 5.

10 if it ends in 0.

2

a $4\overline{)76}$ b $5\overline{)95}$ c $7\overline{)94}$ d $6\overline{)87}$

e $3\overline{)84}$ f $8\overline{)89}$ g $4\overline{)83}$ h $5\overline{)58}$

Division reminder

$$\begin{array}{r} 16 \\ 6\overline{)96} \end{array}$$

6 into 9 goes 1 with 3 over.

6 into 36 goes 6.

∴ 96 ÷ 6 = 16

$$\begin{array}{r} 21\text{ r }1 \\ 4\overline{)85} \end{array}$$

85 ÷ 4 = 21 r 1

3

a $3\overline{)693}$ b $5\overline{)560}$ c $6\overline{)678}$ d $7\overline{)896}$

e $2\overline{)748}$ f $4\overline{)564}$ g $5\overline{)705}$ h $6\overline{)696}$

4 These all have remainders.

a $5\overline{)609}$ b $3\overline{)734}$ c $4\overline{)857}$ d $9\overline{)996}$ e $6\overline{)689}$

f $7\overline{)792}$ g $4\overline{)877}$ h $3\overline{)955}$ i $2\overline{)737}$ j $6\overline{)883}$

Challenge!

Find the highest number that will divide into every number in the cloud. Use a calculator.

Mastery Checklist

I can:
- ☐ make equal groups
- ☐ use different strategies for mental division
- ☐ solve division with remainders
- ☐ complete division algorithms.

AC9M5N02 Number MA3-MR-01 Multiplicative relations A • Select and apply strategies to divide a number with 3 or more digits by a one-digit divisor • Multiplicative relations B • Select and apply strategies to solve problems involving multiplication and division with whole numbers

Problem solving

Testing division

1 These numbers must cross the river. They can only move down or across onto numbers they divide into exactly. Colour their paths.

4 7 8 9

2 At the Frolic Fair, customers can buy lucky tickets for $5.
They win prizes if their numbers are divisible by two, three or four numbers.

divisible by two factors – money back	divisible by three factors – $10	divisible by four factors – $50

Which three ticket numbers over one hundred would you want to buy?

Why?

I can solve problems by:
☐ using division ☐ writing algorithms.

Unit 14 Hundredths

1 How many small squares in each shape? ______

2 Write the number coloured in each shape as a fraction and a decimal.

a $\frac{10}{100}$ = 0·10

b $\frac{\_\_}{100}$ = ______

c $\frac{\_\_}{100}$ = ______

d $\frac{\_\_}{100}$ = ______

e $\frac{\_\_}{100}$ = ______

f $\frac{\_\_}{100}$ = ______

g $\frac{\_\_}{100}$ = ______

h $\frac{\_\_}{100}$ = ______

i $\frac{\_\_}{100}$ = ______

j $\frac{\_\_}{100}$ = ______

k $\frac{\_\_}{100}$ = ______

l $\frac{\_\_}{100}$ = ______

m $\frac{\_\_}{100}$ = ______

n $\frac{\_\_}{100}$ = ______

o $\frac{\_\_}{100}$ = ______

3 Write the decimals in ascending order.

______

______

4 Write: a the largest fraction. ______ b the smallest fraction. ______

Unit 14 Percentages

Percent means out of 100.
5% is $\frac{5}{100}$
60% is $\frac{60}{100}$

1 Express each of the diagrams on page 70 as a fraction and a percentage.

a $\frac{10}{100}$ = 10% b $\frac{\_\_}{100}$ = ____ c $\frac{\_\_}{100}$ = ____ d $\frac{\_\_}{100}$ = ____ e $\frac{\_\_}{100}$ = ____

f $\frac{\_\_}{100}$ = ____ g $\frac{\_\_}{100}$ = ____ h $\frac{\_\_}{100}$ = ____ i $\frac{\_\_}{100}$ = ____ j $\frac{\_\_}{100}$ = ____

k $\frac{\_\_}{100}$ = ____ l $\frac{\_\_}{100}$ = ____ m $\frac{\_\_}{100}$ = ____ n $\frac{\_\_}{100}$ = ____ o $\frac{\_\_}{100}$ = ____

2 Write the percentages in descending order.

____ ____ ____ ____ ____ ____ ____ ____ ____ ____ ____ ____ ____ ____ ____

3 Colour to show:

a 20%
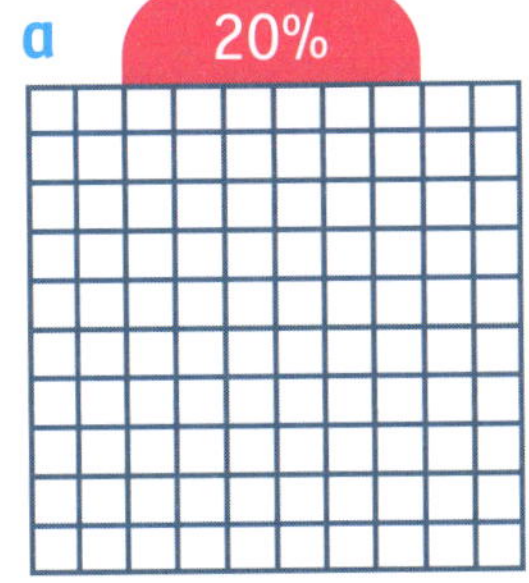
b 50%

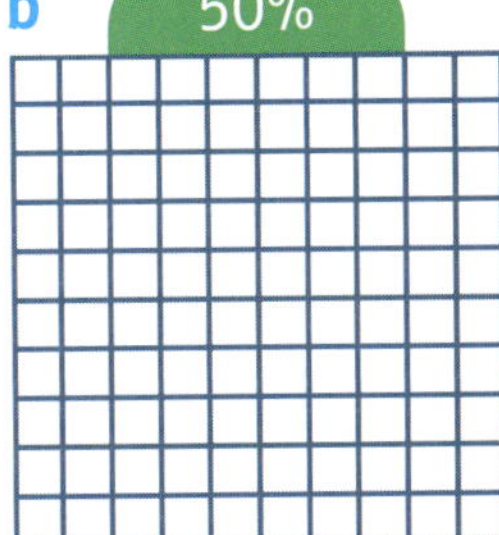
c 75%
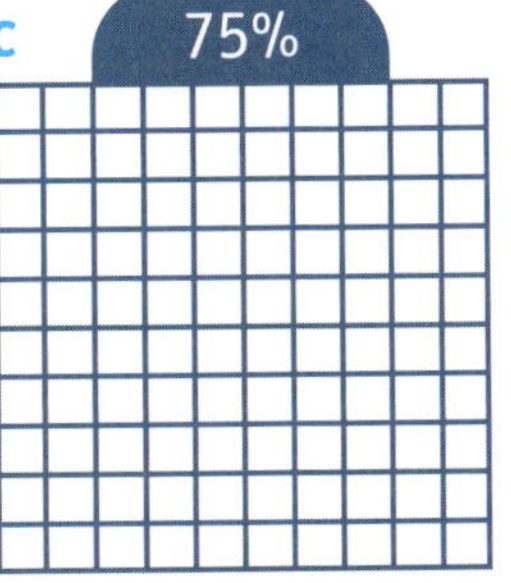
d 10%
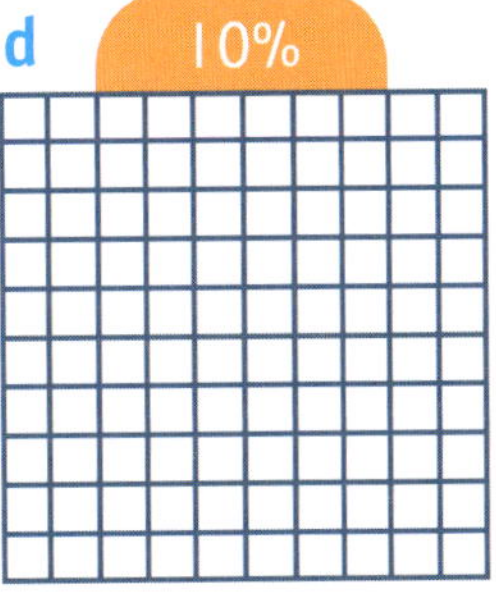
e 80%

4 Draw lines to match a fraction to its decimal and percentage.

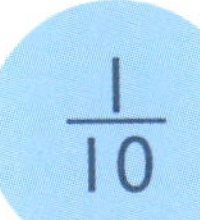

$\frac{1}{2}$ $\frac{1}{10}$ $\frac{4}{10}$ $\frac{9}{10}$ $\frac{25}{100}$ $\frac{30}{100}$

0·10 0·9 0·5 0·4 0·3 0·25

40% 50% 90% 10% 25% 30%

Draw a diagram

Draw diagrams to help you complete these.

$\frac{1}{5} = \frac{?}{100}$ $\frac{1}{4} = \frac{?}{100}$ $\frac{1}{20} = \frac{?}{100}$ $\frac{7}{10} = \frac{?}{100}$ $\frac{3}{4} = \frac{?}{100}$

Unit 14 Everyday percentages

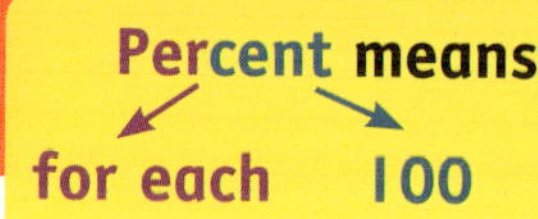

1 Fill in the table.

	Percent	Fraction	Fraction in lowest terms	Decimal
a	50%	$\frac{50}{100}$	$\frac{1}{2}$	0.50
b	25%			
c	75%			
d	10%			
e	20%			

2 Draw to show:

a 50% of an apple.

b 75% of a pizza.

c 10% of a chocolate bar.

3

Colour:

a 10% blue. b 25% red. c 50% green. d 10% yellow.

e How many are not coloured? ________

f What % is this? ________

4 Find:

a 75% of 1 hour = ________ minutes

b 50% of 1 minute = ________ seconds

c 20% of $30 = ________

d 10% of 1 decade = ________ years

e 25% of 1 dozen = ________

f 75% of 1 year = ________ months

Challenge!

Item	Price	New price with 50% increase	New price with 25% increase	New price with 10% increase
a Shoes	$35			
b Shirt	$28			

Unit 14 Percentages all around us

Collect some advertising brochures and look for percentage amounts of 10%, 25% and 50%. Make a collage of six advertisements on this page.

Write a brief explanation for each one.
eg 10% – this is discount on new scooters.

Unit 14 Discounts

SPORTSWORLD SALE

Here are the original prices. Work out the sale price.

1 Hats

a $20 ________% off. Sale price = ________

b $30 ________% off. Sale price = ________

2 Shorts

a $100 ________% off. Sale price = ________

b $55 ________% off. Sale price = ________

3 Shoes

a $150 ________% off. Sale price = ________

b $200 ________% off. Sale price = ________

4 Bags

a $120 ________% off. Sale price = ________

b $150 ________% off. Sale price = ________

5 Shirts

a $50 ________% off. Sale price = ________

b $70 ________% off. Sale price = ________

Working Space

Mastery Checklist I can:

- ☐ connect fractions, decimals and percentages
- ☐ calculate percentages
- ☐ calculate % price increases and discounts
- ☐ understand real world percentages.

Unit 15 Decimals

1 Write the decimals on the number line below.

1·25 0·09 1·3 3·5 0·75 1·0 0·35 0·53

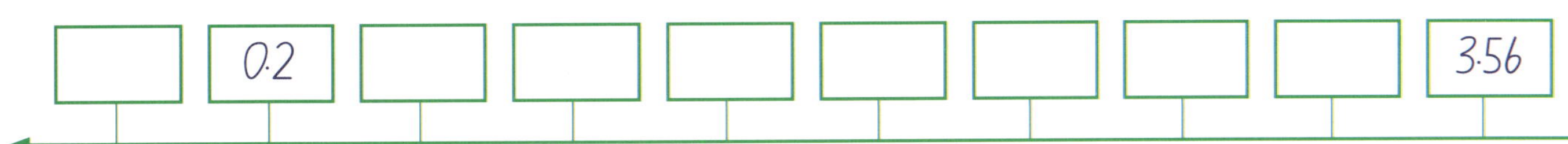

2 Write **is more than** or **is less than** to make the sentences true.

a 0·35 ____________________ 0·4

b 1·62 ____________________ 1·7

c 5·84 ____________________ 5·95

d 2·93 ____________________ 2·39

e 6·77 ____________________ 6·84

f 3·58 ____________________ 3·8

g 0·41 ____________________ 0·5

h 4·029 ____________________ 4·29

i 9·06 ____________________ 9·6

j 8·32 ____________________ 8·39

k 0·64 ____________________ 0·06

l 7·99 ____________________ 7·89

3 Write **>**, **<** or **=** to complete the statements.

6·35 + 1·2 [<] 7·89 + 0·9
7.55 ______ 8.79

- Work out each side and write the answers on the lines.
- Then work out which symbol to write in the box: **>**, **<** or **=**.

a 3·09 + 2·32 [ ] 6·43 + 1·23
______ ______

b 7·14 − 0·9 [ ] 6·27 + 1·32
______ ______

c 8·36 − 4·2 [ ] 7·62 − 1·32
______ ______

d 5·85 + 2·75 [ ] 10·35 − 3·79
______ ______

e 7·23 + 4·83 [ ] 15·2 − 5·63
______ ______

f 0·93 + 0·6 [ ] 1·25 − 0·2
______ ______

g 6·20 + 1·03 [ ] 3·03 + 4·5
______ ______

h 9·09 + 3·9 [ ] 7·36 + 3·95
______ ______

AC9M5N01 Number **MA3-RN-02** Represents numbers A • Decimals and percentages: Compare, order and represent decimals • **MA3-AR-01** Additive relations B • Apply known strategies to add and subtract decimals

Unit 15 Rounding decimals

1 Round each decimal to the nearest tenth.

a	6 459 623·73	6 459 623.7	b	35·09	________
c	5·29	________	d	5 243 781·36	________
e	7498·98	________	f	147·32	________
g	688·77	________	h	53·86	________
i	6·31	________	j	763 249·91	________
k	493 261·09	________	l	70 324·62	________
m	68 012·18	________	n	3210·88	________
o	485·28	________	p	7 841 872·22	________
q	58·679	________	r	98·248	________

2 Round each decimal to the nearest hundredth.

a	5 963 240·667	5 963 240.67	b	871·425	________
c	219·286	________	d	6·895	________
e	0·496	________	f	6 495 826·724	________
g	973 141·844	________	h	14·372	________
i	48·246	________	j	952 437·810	________
k	95 926·124	________	l	76 242·996	________
m	6821·158	________	n	7495·637	________
o	58 741·298	________	p	687 805·189	________
q	8 746·271	________	r	8 968·984	________

3 Round each decimal to the nearest whole number.

a	5 249 824·376	5 249 824	b	362 498·38	________
c	75 349·127	________	d	6824·36	________
e	137·92	________	f	52·879	________
g	0·82	________	h	5 324 802·194	________
i	436 821·493	________	j	89 499·99	________
k	7762·582	________	l	749·378	________
m	41·158	________	n	1·387	________
o	87·547	________	p	99.489	________
q	87 247·005	________	r	8 958 248·574	________

Unit 15 Decimal addition and subtraction

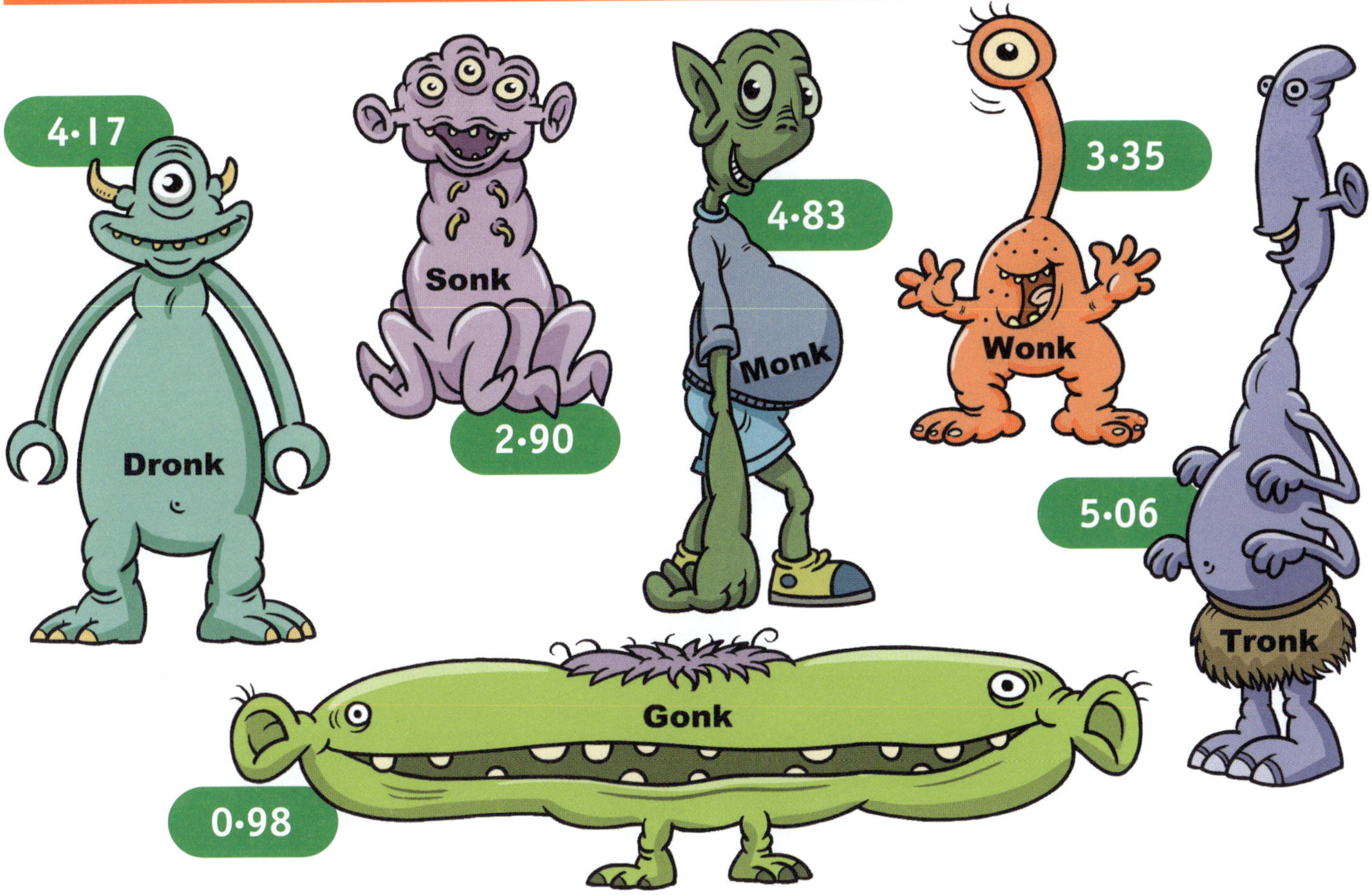

These aliens are from ONKUTO where everyone is a different height.

Dronk is 4·17 m, Sonk is 2·90 m, Monk is 4·83 m, Wonk is 3·35 m, Tronk is 5·06 m, Gonk is 0·98 m.

1 Order them from tallest to shortest.

____

2 What measurement is the decimal part of their height? __________

3 What is the difference in height between?

a Dronk and Wonk?	b Tronk and Gonk?	c Monk and Sonk?	d Tronk and Monk?
4·17 − 3·35 ______ ______ m			

4 What is the total height of:

a Monk, Dronk and Sonk?	b Gonk, Wonk and Tronk?	c all of them?

Unit 15 Decimals

1 First estimate in whole numbers and then work out the answers.

a
```
   7·6
   3·8
 + 1·4
 _____
 _____
```
Est. ______

b
```
   9·4
   4·8
 + 0·6
 _____
 _____
```
Est. ______

c
```
   11·2
    0·8
 + 24·5
 ______
 ______
```
Est. ______

d
```
   3·85
   2·07
 + 1·92
 ______
 ______
```
Est. ______

e
```
   5·63
   8·71
 + 4·58
 ______
 ______
```
Est. ______

f
```
   7·09
   0·38
 + 9·17
 ______
 ______
```
Est. ______

+, − decimals

- **Keep decimal points under each other.**
- **Put a decimal point in the answer.**

```
   7 · 3 4      Est. 7 + 2 = 9
 + 1 · 6 9      3/10 + 9/100
 _________
   9 · 0 3
```

Hint Put the decimal point in the answer first so you don't forget.

2 a
```
   3·9
 − 1·7
 _____
 _____
```
Est. ______

b
```
   8·6
 − 5·1
 _____
 _____
```
Est. ______

c
```
   9·7
 − 5·2
 _____
 _____
```
Est. ______

d
```
   6·1
 − 2·6
 _____
 _____
```
Est. ______

e
```
   5·4
 − 3·5
 _____
 _____
```
Est. ______

f
```
   4·93
 − 1·61
 ______
 ______
```
Est. ______

g
```
   7·75
 − 3·44
 ______
 ______
```
Est. ______

h
```
   8·07
 − 2·36
 ______
 ______
```
Est. ______

i
```
   6·52
 − 3·78
 ______
 ______
```
Est. ______

j
```
   9·40
 − 5·76
 ______
 ______
```
Est. ______

3

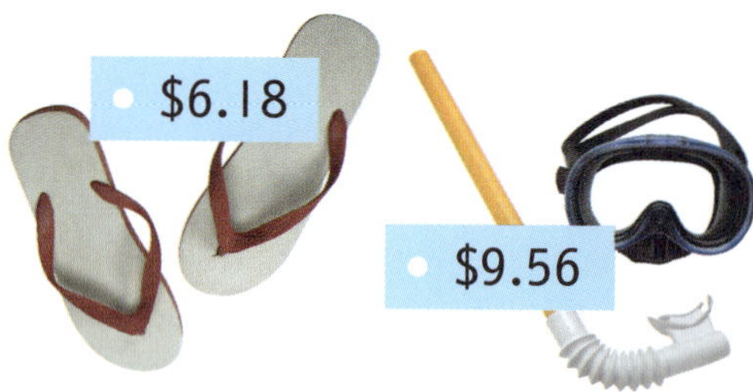

How much did they spend?

a Zuri bought thongs, a ball and a snorkel set. ______

b Kirra bought a hat, sunscreen and a ball. ______

c Bob bought a snorkel set, sunscreen and thongs. ______

d Tracy bought a hat, a snorkel set and a ball. ______

How much change?

e Issa had $7.40 and bought sunscreen. ______

f Jason had $9.05 and bought thongs. ______

g Ruby had $5 and bought a ball. ______

Working

AC9M5N01 Number MA3-AR-01 Additive relations A • Apply efficient mental and written strategies to solve addition and subtraction problems • Additive relations B • Apply known strategies to add and subtract decimals

Unit 15 Multiplication of decimals

1 On page 77 the heights are in metres.

a Why are there two numerals after the decimal point?

____

Tens	Ones		Tenths	Hundredths
7	2	·	3	9

$70 + 2 + \frac{3}{10} + \frac{9}{100}$

b Write their height in centimetres.

Dronk ________ Sonk ________ Monk ________ Wonk ________ Tronk ________ Gonk ________

2 A  7·8 kg

B  27·6 kg

C  35·4 kg

D  11·7 kg

E  18·9 kg

What is the mass of:

a 4 of **A**?	b 6 of **B**?	c 9 of **C**?	d 7 of **D**?	e 5 of **E**?
7·8 × 4 ____ ____				

f Order the dogs' masses from lightest to heighest.

☐ ☐ ☐ ☐ ☐

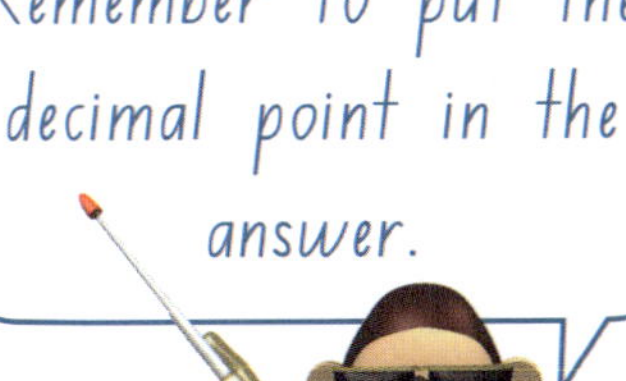

3 a 7·23 × 3 = ____ b 4·95 × 5 = ____ c 7·64 × 8 = ____ d 6·71 × 9 = ____

e 7·38 × 9 = ____ f 3·47 × 7 = ____ g 8·02 × 6 = ____ h 5·29 × 3 = ____

4 a $7.55 × 6 = ____ b $5.91 × 3 = ____ c $9.04 × 4 = ____ d $8.60 × 9 = ____ e $6.07 × 8 = ____

Mastery Checklist

I can:
- ☐ order decimals on a number line
- ☐ use >, < and = to compare decimals
- ☐ round decimals
- ☐ add and subtract decimals
- ☐ multiply decimals.

NewTime

Investigation 2

The Outtatime Committee is tired of remembering all the time equivalents (60 secs = 1 min, etc) and is going to petition the government to change the way time is measured. A day will still be the same length, but they have a chance to change the way it is measured. They will call the new measurements NewTime.

What changes could they make so that time is still accurate but there are not so many different time equivalents to learn and remember?

1 Work with a partner. Rename the times of the day and change the equivalents, eg 20 clicks = 1 sunny. Do not change the year measurements.

Times of a day:

2 Make up a new timetable for the day using your NewTime equivalents. Plan a school day, or a camp day, or a staying home day or another personal choice day.

3 How will you write your NewTime digitally? Write some examples and explain them.

4 Convert your NewTime into 24-hour time. Use a table to show how the times match up. Would the times match better with a number of hours other than 24?

5 a What would happen if NewTime were adopted by the Australian government?

b What would the government find difficult to put in place?

To carry out these tasks, I need to:

- ☐ understand the measurement of time
- ☐ make a timetable for a day
- ☐ convert times to 24-hour time
- ☐ use logical reasoning to predict outcomes of change
- ☐ work well with a partner.

I enjoyed this task! ☆☆☆☆☆

Revision

1

71 603·58

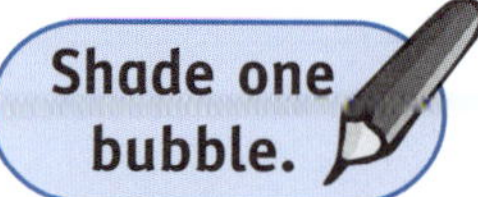

Round this number to the nearest whole number.

71 600	71 604	71 6036	70 000
◯	◯	◯	◯

2 What is a good estimation for:

3750 + 954 + 2105

7000	14 000	6000	10 000
◯	◯	◯	◯

3 Which division has a remainder of 1?

$3\overline{)251}$	$4\overline{)297}$	$5\overline{)870}$	$6\overline{)381}$
◯	◯	◯	◯

4 Drake went to bed at . Which clock shows this time?

◯	◯	◯	◯

5 Jaryd was asked to write the number that expands to 0·8 + 0·02 + 0·003.

What should he answer?

8·230	8·023	0·823	0·832
◯	◯	◯	◯

Revision

6

$$\begin{array}{r} 374 \\ 19 \\ +\ 208 \\ \hline \\ \hline \end{array}$$

600 ◯ 601 ◯ 611 ◯ 701 ◯

7

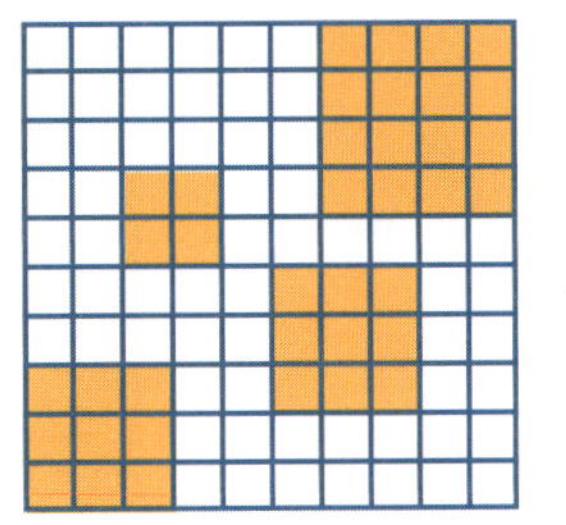

$\frac{38}{100}$ = ______

0·36 ◯ 0·30 ◯ 0·39 ◯ 0·38 ◯

8 Which decimal could go on the number line?

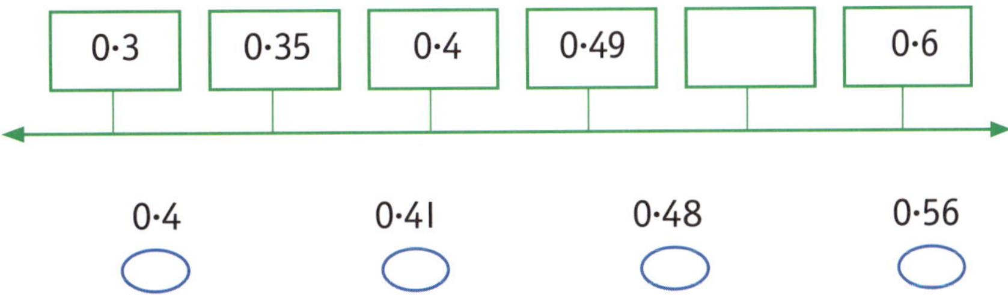

0·4 ◯ 0·41 ◯ 0·48 ◯ 0·56 ◯

9

$$\begin{array}{r} 8\cdot 29 \\ \times\ \ 6 \\ \hline \\ \hline \end{array}$$

49·75 ◯ 49·74 ◯ 50·74 ◯ 49·44 ◯

10 60% of 1 hour = ______ minutes

15 ◯ 30 ◯ 36 ◯ 38 ◯

Unit 16 Area and perimeter

a

b

c

d

e

f

1 Work out the area of each tile by using a square centimetre overlay. Write the area of each tile.

a ______ b ______ c ______

d ______ e ______ f ______

2 Measure accurately the length and width of each tile.

a L = ______ W = ______ b L = ______ W = ______ c L = ______ W = ______

d L = ______ W = ______ e L = ______ W = ______ f L = ______ W = ______

3 What is the perimeter of each tile?

a ______ b ______ c ______

d ______ e ______ f ______

To find the area of a rectangle, multiply its length by its width. A = L x W

4 Work out the area of each tile using the formula.

a A = ______ × ______ b A = ______ × ______ c A = ______ × ______

= ______ = ______ = ______

d A = ______ × ______ e A = ______ × ______ f A = ______ × ______

= ______ = ______ = ______

AC9M5M02 Measurement **MA3-GM-02** Geometric measure A • Length: Measure lengths to find perimeters • **MA3-2DS-02** Two-dimensional spatial structure A • Area: Calculate the areas of rectangles using familiar metric units

Unit 16 Area of a rectangle

1 Draw three rectangles.

a L = 8 cm W = 3 cm

b L = 12 cm W = 2 cm

c L = 6 cm W = 4 cm

Area is measured in squares.
1 square metre = 1 m^2
1 square centimetre = 1 cm^2

2 Work out the area for each using the formula A = L × W.

a A = ______ × ______
= ______

b A = ______ × ______
= ______

c A = ______ × ______
= ______

d What have you found? ____________________

3 Work out the perimeter of each.

a P = ____ + ____ + ____ + ____
= ______

b P = ____ + ____ + ____ + ____
= ______

c P = ____ + ____ + ____ + ____
= ______

d What have you found? ____________________

4 Write the length and width of 2 rectangles which have an area of 20 cm^2.

a L = ______ W = ______ b L = ______ W = ______

5 What are their perimeters? a P = ______ b P = ______

Challenge!

You have a new house. Use a sheet of centimetre grid paper to plan your new garden. You might want to include a pool, a shed, a barbecue area, etc. If each 1 cm^2 represents 1 m^2, work out the area occupied by each item in your garden.

AC9M5M02 Measurement **MA3-GM-02** Geometric measure A • Length: Measure lengths to find perimeters • **MA3-2DS-02** Two-dimensional spatial structure A • Area: Calculate the areas of rectangles using familiar metric units

Unit 16 Hectares

Hectare (ha)
Hectares are used to measure large areas, eg a paddock, a school.
1 ha = 10 000 m²

1 Square metres (m²) or hectares (ha)?

a playing field _____ b basketball court _____ c farm _____

d classroom _____ e National Park _____ f airport _____

g pool surface _____ h suburban block _____ i movie screen _____

2 Change to hectares.

a 30 000 m² _____ ha

b 70 000 m² _____

c 120 000 m² _____

d 360 000 m² _____

3 Change to square metres.

a 2 ha _____ m²

b 5 ha _____

c 17 ha _____

d $21\frac{1}{2}$ ha _____

4 a Cut three 10 cm squares from centimetre grid paper.

b Cut each square and rearrange it to make a rectangle.

c Paste the rectangles into your workbook.

d Write the dimensions of each rectangle.

A length _____ width _____ B length _____ width _____

C length _____ width _____

e Each centimetre represents 10 m. Work out the area for each rectangle. You can use a calculator.

A Area = _____ B Area = _____ C Area = _____

f Write about your answers. _____

_____

A hectare does not have to be a square.

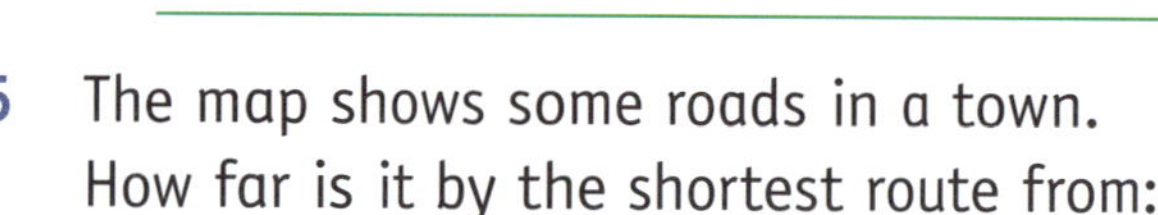

5 The map shows some roads in a town.
How far is it by the shortest route from:

a Post Office to Supermarket? _____

b School to Train Station? _____

c Bank to Cinema? _____

d Post Office to Petrol Station? _____

6 Work out in hectares the area of the block containing the:

a Cinema. _____

b Bank. _____

c Train Station. _____

d School. _____

e whole map. _____

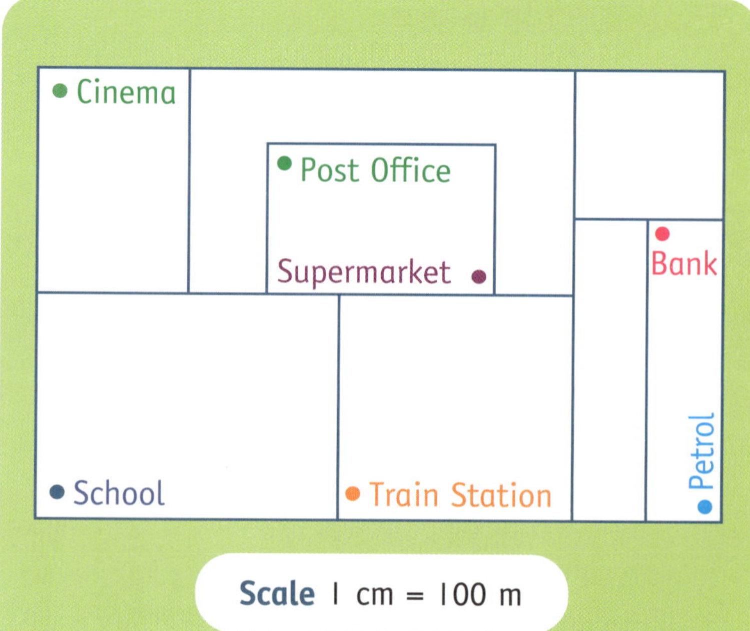

Unit 16 Large areas

1 These are all fields. Colour green the ones which are exactly one hectare. They are not drawn to scale.

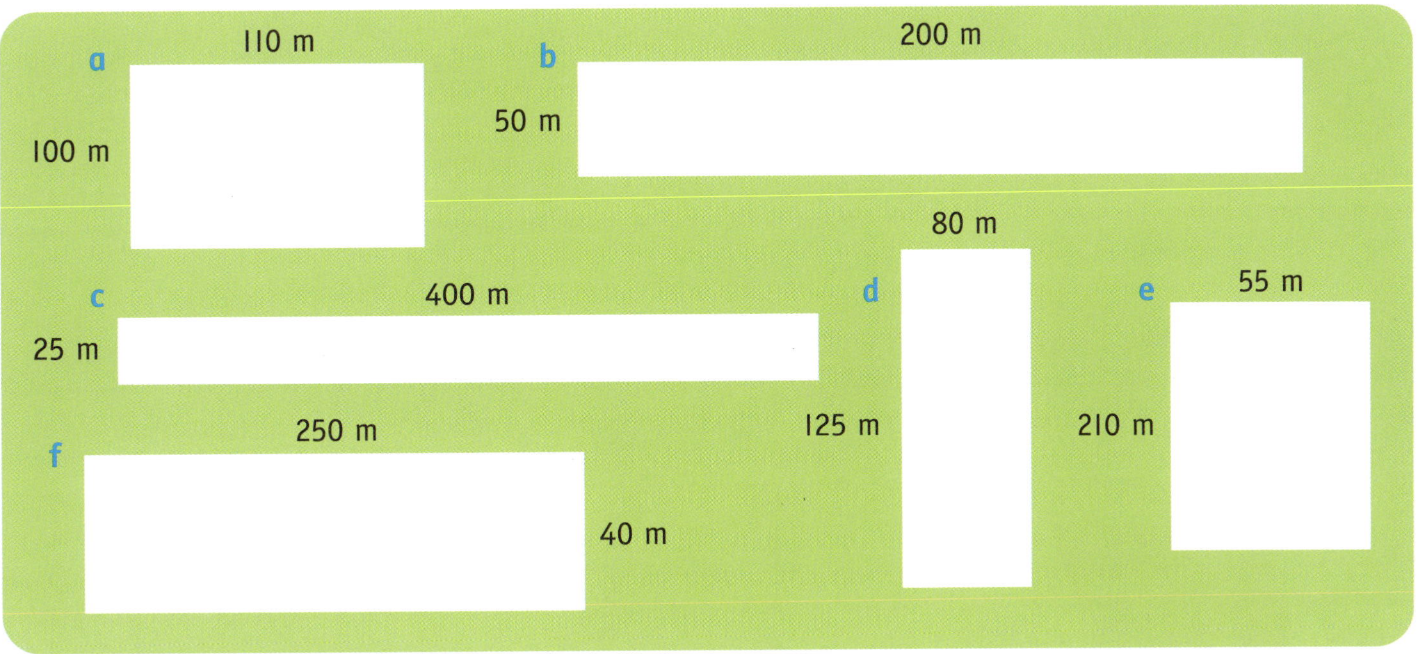

2 Jack bought a small farm. The two cattle paddocks are 150 m × 170 m and 120 m × 180 m. The sheep paddock is 205 m × 115 m. The wheat field is 250 m × 130 m and the house block is 80 m × 200 m.

What is the area of:

a cattle paddock 1? ______________

b cattle paddock 2? ______________

c the sheep paddock? ______________

d the wheat field? ______________

e the house block? ______________

f the whole farm to the nearest hectare? ______________

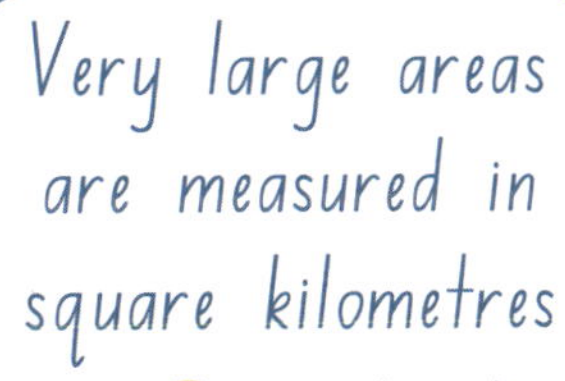

3 Very large areas are measured in square kilometres (km^2).

a Name 3 areas which could be measured in km^2.

______________ ______________ ______________

b Work with a friend to find the area of each state and territory.

NSW ______________ QLD ______________ VIC ______________

WA ______________ SA ______________ TAS ______________

NT ______________ ACT ______________

c Which state/territory has the largest area? ______________

smallest area? ______________

Unit 16 Parallelograms and triangles

A parallelogram is a 'pushed over' rectangle.

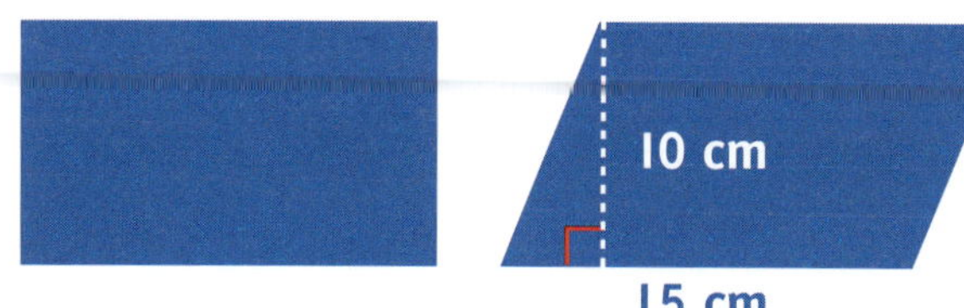

A parallelogram has the same area as a rectangle with the same length and width.

Area = length × width

= 15 cm × 10 cm

= 150 cm^2

A triangle is half a rectangle.

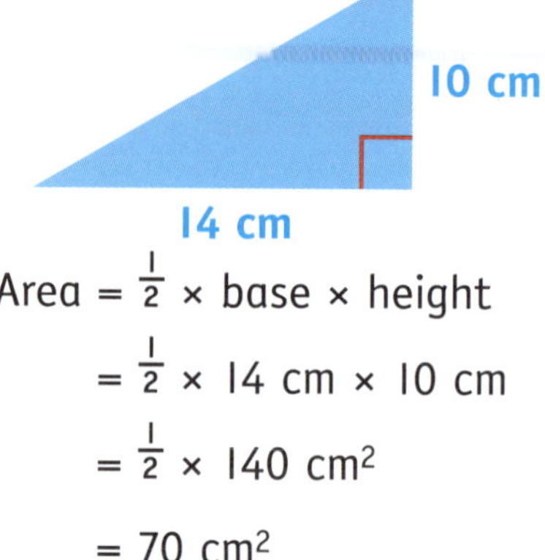

Area = $\frac{1}{2}$ × base × height

= $\frac{1}{2}$ × 14 cm × 10 cm

= $\frac{1}{2}$ × 140 cm^2

= 70 cm^2

1 Work out the area of the parallelograms.

Area = length × width

a

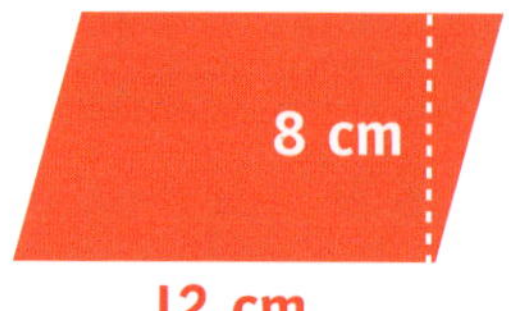

A = length × width

= ________ × ________

= ________ cm^2

b

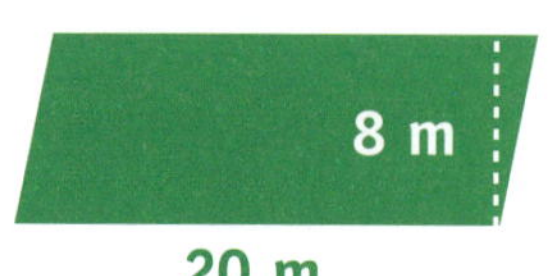

A = length × width

= ________ × ________

= ________ m^2

c

A = length × width

= ________ × ________

= ________ m^2

2 Work out the area of the triangles.

Area = $\frac{1}{2}$ × base × height

a

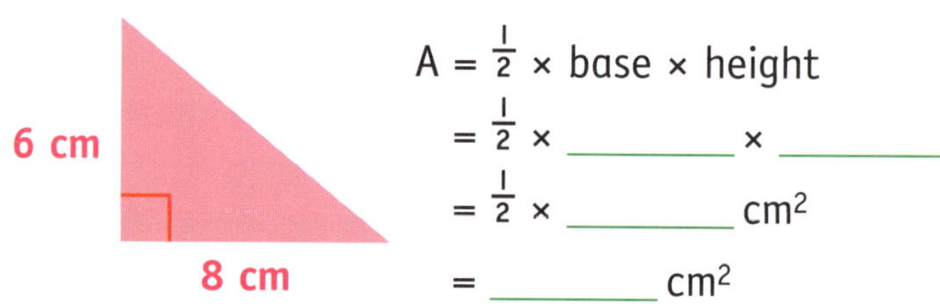

A = $\frac{1}{2}$ × base × height

= $\frac{1}{2}$ × ________ × ________

= $\frac{1}{2}$ × ________ cm^2

= ________ cm^2

b

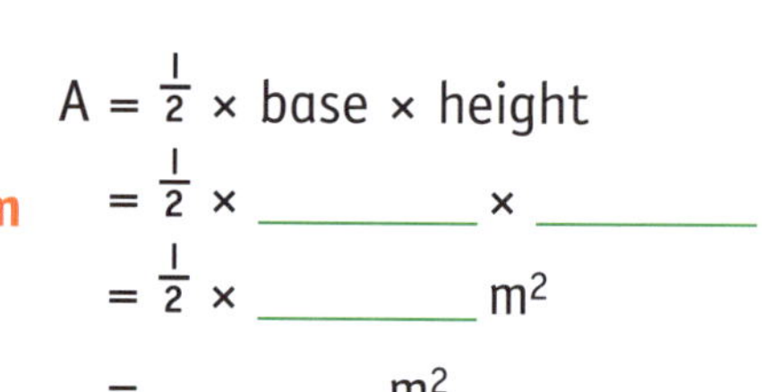

A = $\frac{1}{2}$ × base × height

= $\frac{1}{2}$ × ________ × ________

= $\frac{1}{2}$ × ________ m^2

= ________ m^2

c

10 cm

12 cm

A = $\frac{1}{2}$ × base × height

= $\frac{1}{2}$ × ________ × ________

= $\frac{1}{2}$ × ________ cm^2

= ________ cm^2

Mastery Checklist

I can:

- ☐ measure to find the area and the perimeter
- ☐ use the formula Area = length × width
- ☐ convert hectares to m^2
- ☐ measure areas in km^2
- ☐ find the area of parallelograms and triangles.

AC9M5M01 Measurement **MA3-2DS-03** Two-dimensional spatial structure B • Area: Calculate the area of a parallelogram using subdivision and rearrangement • Determine the area of a triangle

Unit 17 Volume and capacity

Volume
the amount of space something occupies.

Dimensions = 1 × 2 × 3
Volume = 6 cubic units

build objects with blocks

1 Build each model using cubic centimetre blocks.

A B C D E F

2 How many blocks did you use?

A ______ B ______ C ______ D ______ E ______ F ______

3 What is the volume of each model in cubic centimetres?

A ______ cm^3 B ______ C ______ D ______ E ______ F ______

Capacity is the amount of liquid a container can hold.

A 2 L

B 1 L

C 375 mL

D 500 mL

4 What is the capacity of each container?

A ______ B ______ C ______ D ______

5 Which container has:

a the largest capacity? ______

b the smallest capacity? ______

c a capacity of 375 mL? ______

d 500 mL capacity? ______

6 What is the difference in capacity between these containers?

a A and B ______ b B and C ______ c C and D ______ d A and D ______

Unit 17 Cubic centimetres

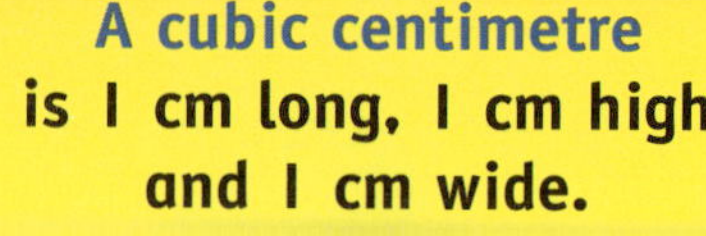

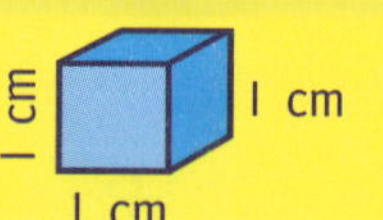

$1\text{ cm} \times 1\text{ cm} \times 1\text{ cm} = 1\text{ cm}^3$

Activity • Work with a friend

1 You need a small empty rectangular box and plenty of cubic centimetre blocks.

a Estimate how many blocks will be needed to fill the box. ______

b Fill the box with the blocks.

c How many blocks does it hold? ______

d What is the volume? ______

e Repeat with a different box.

2 Draw four objects whose volumes would be measured in cubic centimetres.

3 Estimate the volume of each of the objects you drew. Use a cube of 9 cm³ to help you estimate.

a ______ b ______ c ______ d ______

4 a Gather together 3 hardcover novels. Write their names here.

______

b Order the novels from least volume to greatest volume.

______

c Estimate each book's volume in cubic centimetres.

______ ______ ______

5 Estimate the volume of 12 of the biggest books. How could you pack these 12 books into a box?

______

______

Challenge!

Build 4 different models with a volume of 20 cm³.
Draw your models on isometric dot paper.

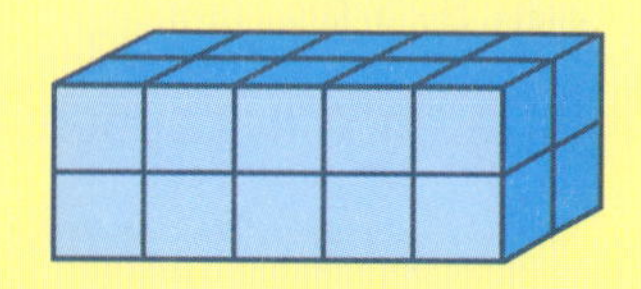

Unit 17 Cubic metres

1 Name four objects whose volumes would be measured in cubic metres.

a ____________________

b ____________________

c ____________________

d ____________________

A cubic metre
The volume of large objects can be measured in cubic metres (m^3).
$1\ m \times 1\ m \times 1\ m = 1\ m^3$

Activity • Cubic metres

2 • Using metre rods and fabric, construct a cubic metre as a class activity. Examine it carefully.

• Make a list of 3 objects which have a volume of:

a about $1\ m^3$. ____________________

b about $2\ m^3$. ____________________

c about $\frac{1}{2}\ m^3$. ____________________

• Estimate how many cubic metres would fit in the classroom. ____________

• Can you write an easy way to find the volume of a rectangular prism?

____

3 A space 6 metres long and 6 metres wide is covered in cubic metre blocks.
A crane builds a pyramid 1 metre shorter and 1 metre narrower in each layer.
How many cubic metre blocks are needed to complete the pyramid? ____________

How many blocks will be on the top layer? ____________

Hint: Build a model with Base 10 ones.

4 a A container is 3 m long, 2 m wide, 2·5 m high. Write the number sentence to work out its volume.

____

b Draw the container in this space and label its dimensions.

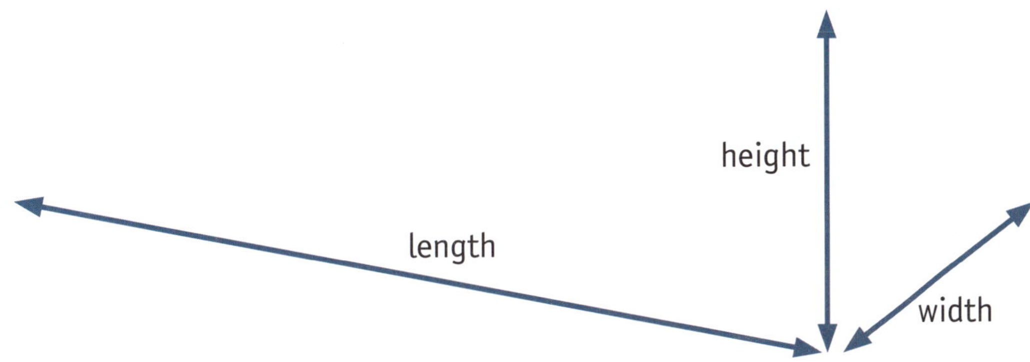

Unit 17 Volume of a rectangular prism

To find the volume of a rectangular prism, multiply the length by the width by the height. The answer will be in cubic units.

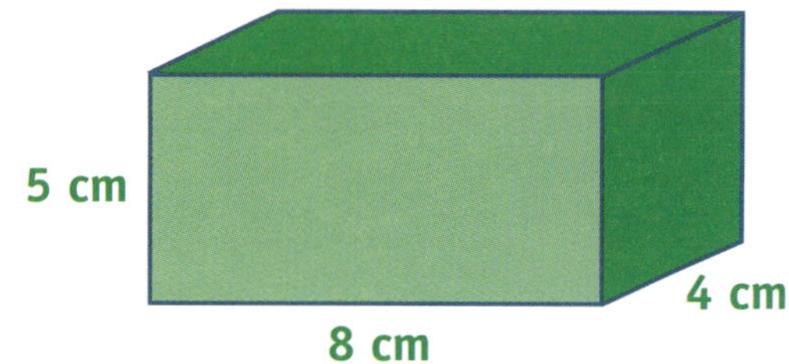

Volume = length (l) × width (w) × height (h)
= 8 cm × 5 cm × 4 cm
= 160 cm^3

1 Work out the volume.

a

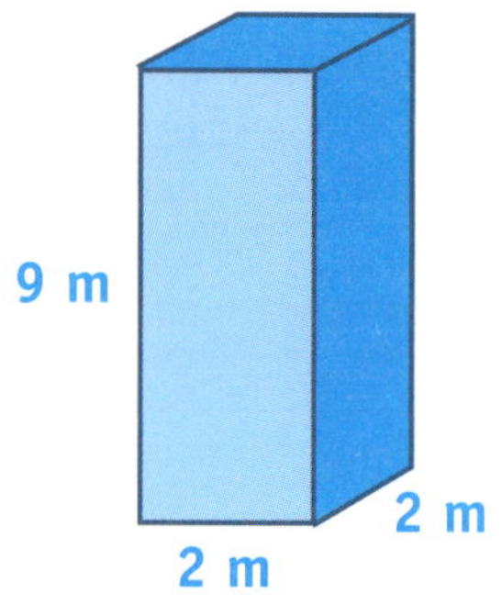

Volume = length (l) × width (w) × height (h)
= ________ × ________ × ________
= ________ m^3

b

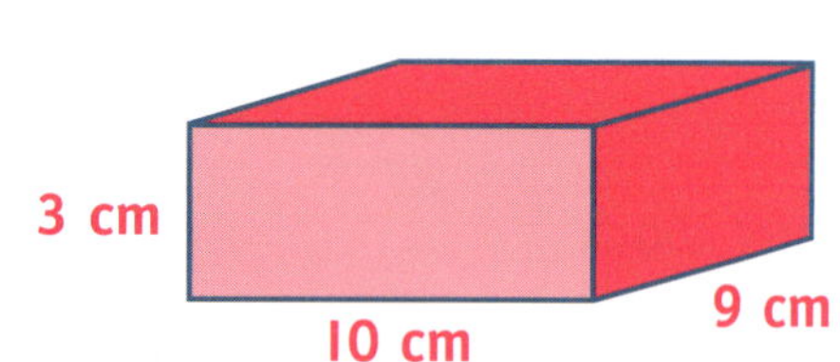

Volume = l × w × h
= ________ × ________ × ________
= ________ cm^3

c

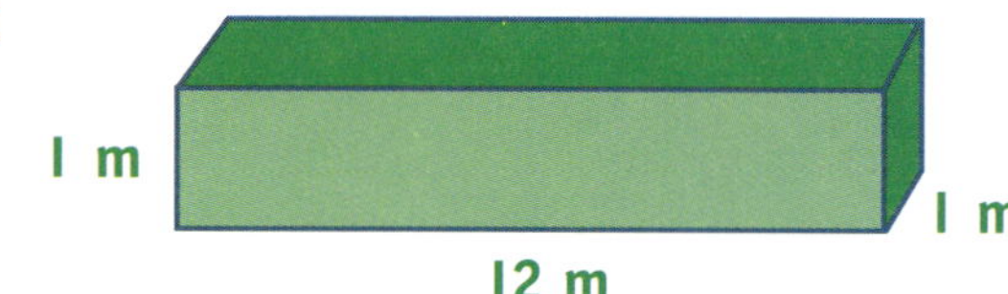

Volume = l × w × h
= ________ × ________ × ________
= ________ m^3

d

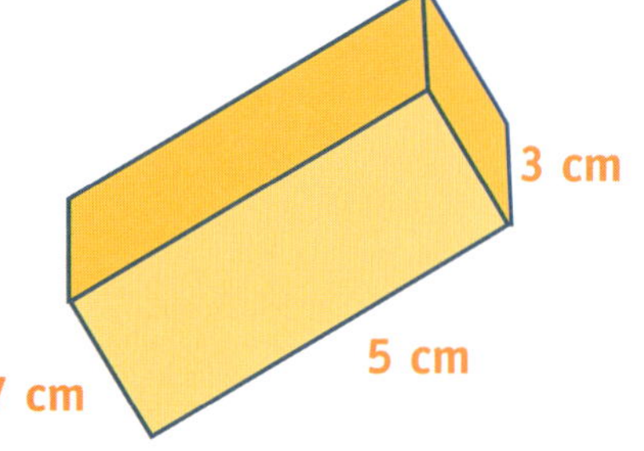

Volume = l × w × h
= ________ × ________ × ________
= ________ cm^3

Mastery Checklist I can:
- ☐ build models to find the volume
- ☐ compare capacities of containers
- ☐ use cubic centimetres and cubic metres to measure volume
- ☐ use a formula to work out the volume of a rectangular prism.

Unit 18 Twenty-four hour time

The local Council is running a LEARN HOW weekend with free classes.
Each poster tells the time that the class will start. Each class lasts two hours.

1 Write the classes in time order.

a ________ b ________ c ________ d ________

e ________ f ________ g ________ h ________

i ________ j ________

2 Which classes start in the morning? ________

____

3 Jim sleeps in and doesn't get up until 12:27.

Which is the first class he can attend? ________

4 a Jai wants to attend two classes after midday that are close together.

Which ones will she choose? ________

b Why? ________

Unit 18 Changing times

24-hour time

Look at page 93.

1 Write all the times in am or pm time from earliest to latest.

am stands for ante meridiem which means before midday.
pm stands for post meridiem which means after midday.

2 What time will these classes end? Use 24-hour time.

a Coin Collecting ______ b Face Painting ______ c Upholstery ______
d First Aid ______ e Banjo Playing ______ f Bread Making ______
g Pet Care ______ h Basket Weaving ______

3 If Mala attends Bread Making what is the next class she can attend? ______

4 Write these times using am or pm.

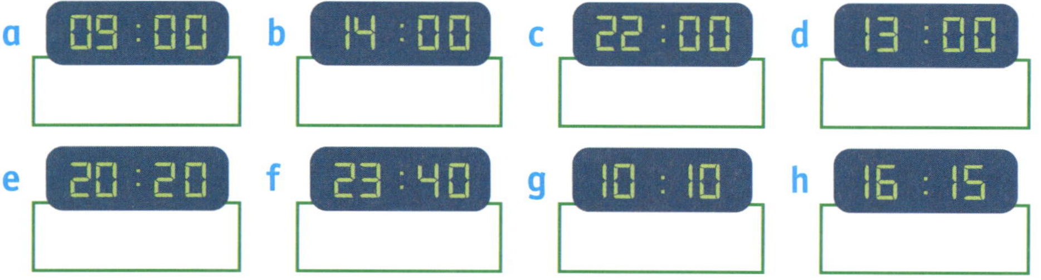

24-hour time always uses 4 digits.
1pm can be written as 13:00 or 1300.
1am can be written as 01:00 or 0100.

5 Write these times using 24-hour time.

These are am times.

These are pm times.

Unit 18 Duration

1 Are these 24-hour times am (morning) or pm (afternoon) times?

a 21:43 pm b 12:05 ______ c 09:48 ______

d 23:56 ______ e 06:14 ______ f 20:02 ______

g 01:26 ______ h 17:24 ______ i 07:50 ______

2 Write these 24-hour times in 12-hour format. Include am or pm.

a 16:34 4:34 pm b 07:43 ______

c 22:25 ______ d 14:36 ______

e 04:03 ______ f 13:15 ______

g 12:58 ______ h 10:49 ______

3 Calculate how much time has passed. Write your answer in hours and minutes.

a 08:36 to 14:41 6 hours 5 minutes

b 01:52 to 01:59 ______

c 17:58 to 19:32 ______

d 23:46 to 0:58 ______

e 06:38 to 10:57 ______

f 09:54 to 11:26 ______

g 18:44 to 19:12 ______

h 17:07 to 20:16 ______

4 What is the time $3\frac{1}{2}$ hours later? Answer in 24-hour time.

a 02:34 ______ b 14:44 ______ c 04:19 ______ d 16:51 ______

5 What is the time $4\frac{1}{4}$ hours later? Answer in 24-hour time.

a 21:09 ______ b 03:51 ______ c 19:27 ______ d 15:39 ______

6 Solve these time problems.

a A movie starts at 20:43 and runs for 2 hours and 12 minutes. What time will it end? Answer in 24-hour time.

______

b A store opened at 9:45 am and closed $8\frac{1}{2}$ hours later. What time was that? Answer in 24-hour time.

______

Mastery Checklist I can:

- ☐ understand and use 24-hour time
- ☐ solve time addition problems
- ☐ convert between 24-hour time and am or pm time
- ☐ calculate how much time has passed.

Problem solving

Right times

1 I live in NSW and have friends in every Australian capital city. I like to call them at midnight New Year's Eve and on their birthdays at 8 am their time. Complete my time schedule so I will know at what NSW time I have to ring them for each occasion. Don't forget Daylight Saving must be considered.

NSW time to call for:

Friend	Birthday	Location	New Year	Birthday
Kate	25th May	Hobart	00:00 1 Jan	08:00 25 May
Josie	13th August	Adelaide		
Helen	7th November	Brisbane		
Frank	15th March	Melbourne		
Kelly	10th January	Darwin		
Sam	4th September	Perth		
Barb	7th June	Canberra		

2 Make a timetable for Grandpa who was a pilot. He likes to follow 24-hour time. He likes to get up at 7 am, and he wants to finish breakfast, water the garden, buy his newspaper and have lunch before 2 pm. He likes to walk the dog and read his newspaper before dinner at 7 pm.

I can solve problems by:

☐ understanding 24-hour time ☐ making a timetable.

AC9M5M03 Measurement **MAO-WM-01** Working mathematically • choosing and applying mathematical techniques to solve problems • communicating thinking and reasoning coherently and clearly • **MA3-NSM-02** Non-spatial measure B • Time: Solve problems involving duration, using 12- and 24-hour time

Unit 19 Map reading

This is a map of Bliss Point and Reco Island.

1 What will you find at:

a B1? ______ b H3? ______ c I4? ______

d D3? ______ e J7? ______ f E7? ______

2 Give the coordinates for:

a the shipwreck. ______ b the castle. ______ c the motel. ______

d the bridge. ______ e the kiosk. ______ f the school. ______

3 Give two lots of coordinates for:

a the cliffs. ______ b Beauty Beach. ______ c the river. ______

4 Name one object that is:

a north of the lighthouse. ______ b south of the castle. ______

c east of Ferry Street Wharf. ______ d west of Beauty Beach. ______

e north of the library. ______ f east of the kiosk. ______

g north of the store. ______ h south of the motel. ______

Unit 19 Coordinates

Coordinates are two numbers which tell an exact point on a grid or map. The bottom (horizontal) number comes first and the side (vertical) number comes second.

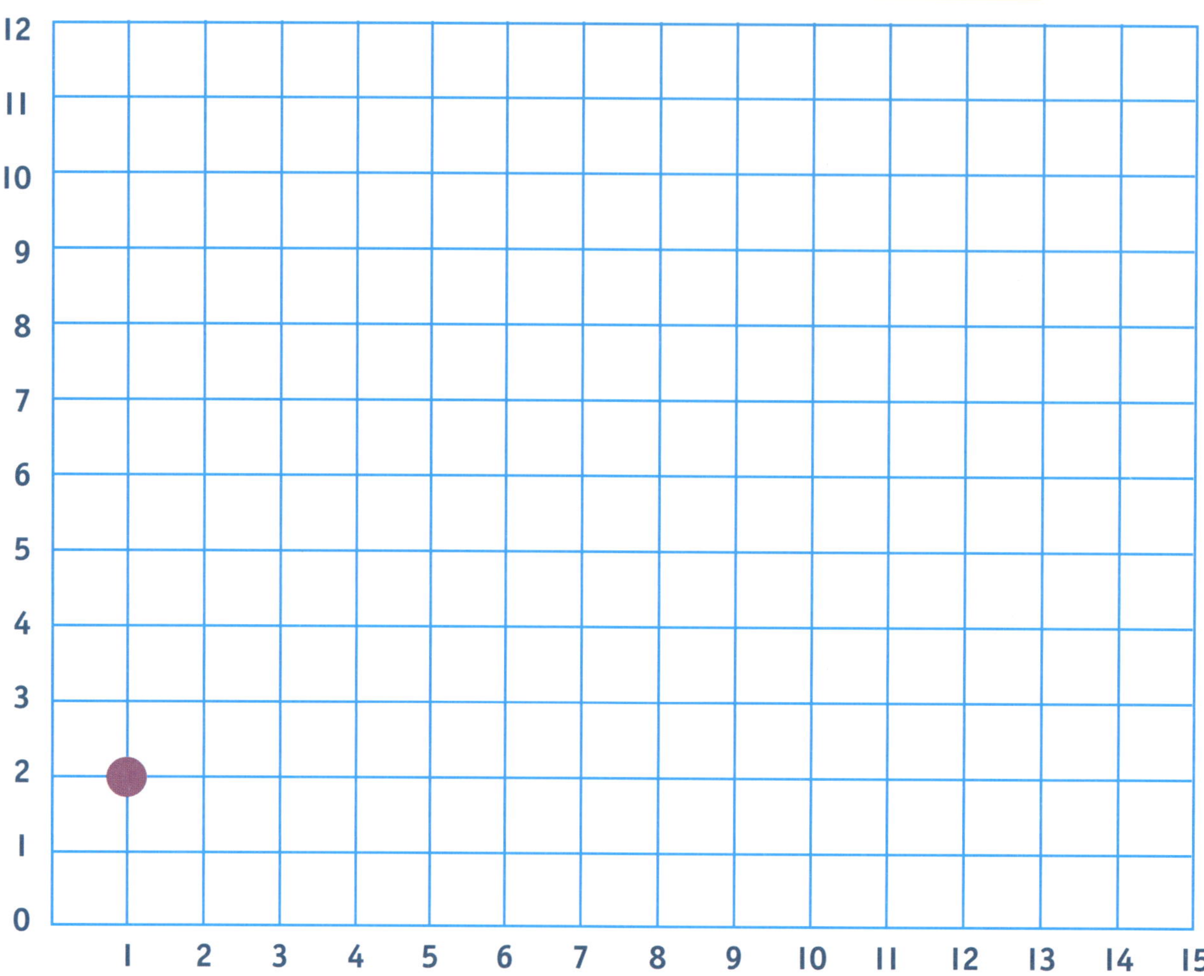

1 Draw large purple dots at:
a (1, 9) b (4, 1) c (8, 4) d (12, 2) e (3, 4) f (3, 7) g (8, 1)

2 Draw large yellow dots at:
a (4, 7) b (9, 10) c (1, 3) d (6, 4) e (12, 0) f (2, 1) g (1, 8)

3 Draw large green dots at:
a (2, 11) b (8, 7) c (2, 4) d (7, 4) e (6, 1) f (11, 3) g (10, 10)

4 Draw large pink dots at:
a (2, 7) b (8, 8) c (4, 2) d (9, 1) e (14, 3) f (7, 2) g (4, 4)

5 Draw large blue dots at:
a (8, 10) b (11, 9) c (3, 1) d (8, 3) e (13, 1) f (14, 4) g (4, 3)

6 Draw large red dots at:
a (4, 11) b (8, 9) c (1, 2) d (7, 1) e (13, 2) f (11, 4) g (9, 4)

7 Join the dots to find the word. ______________________

 AC9M5SP02 Space **MA3-GM-01** Geometric measure A • Position: Explore the Cartesian coordinate system

Unit 19 Shape and position

Position 

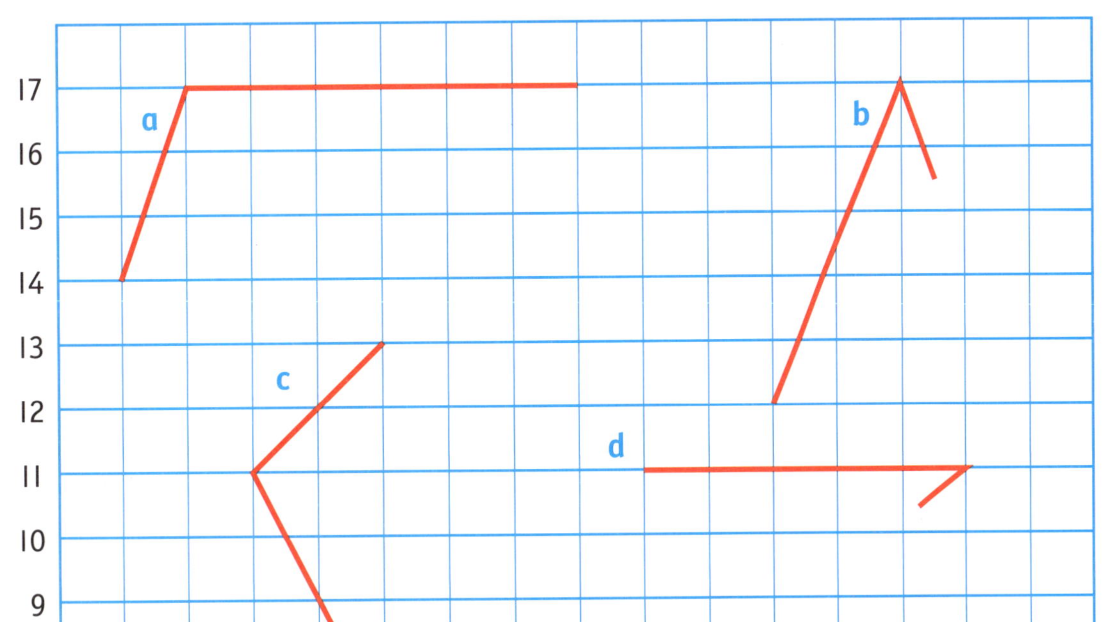

1 Join the ends of the two lines to the point. Name the shape made.

a (10, 14) ____________________

b (15, 12) ____________________

c (7, 11) ____________________

d (9, 7) ____________________

e (3, 8) ____________________

f (13, 2) ____________________

Remember to read the bottom number first, the side number second.
bottom → (4, 10) ← side

Draw a diagram

On centimetre square paper make up some shapes of your own. Swap with a friend.

Mastery Checklist

I can: ☐ use a grid to locate places on a map
☐ plot coordinates on a grid.

Unit 20 Column graph

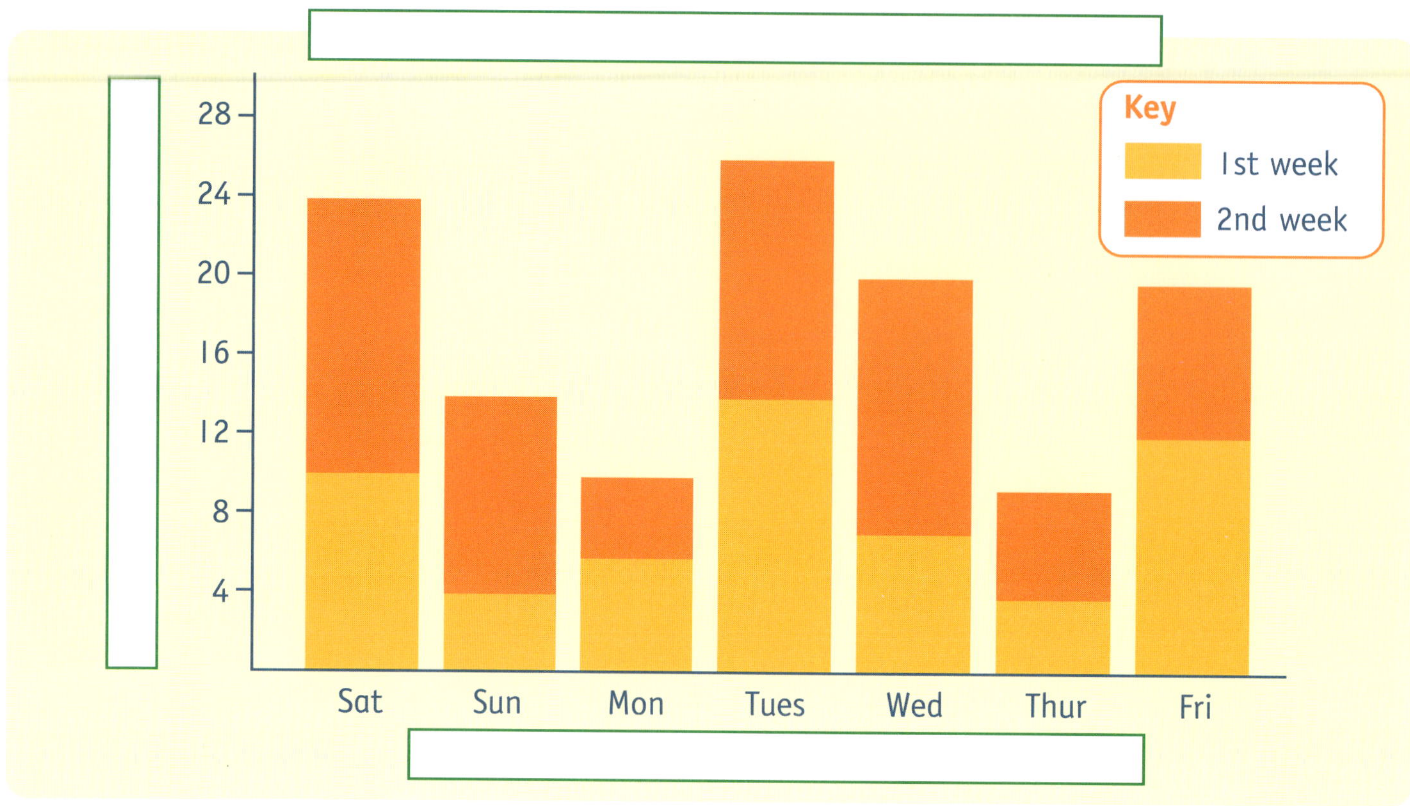

Look carefully at the graph.

1 In what way is it different? ______

______

2 What does the key tell you? ______

______

3 What could this graph be about? ______

4 Write a heading.

5 Label the two axes.

6 How else could you represent this information? ______

______

7 Write some questions for your graph.

a ______

b ______

c ______

d ______

e ______

8 Name other topics that could be shown this way.

______

Unit 20 Horizontal column graph

The Sports teacher at Pascal Primary asked the students to select the sport they would most like to play. This is her graph of the results.

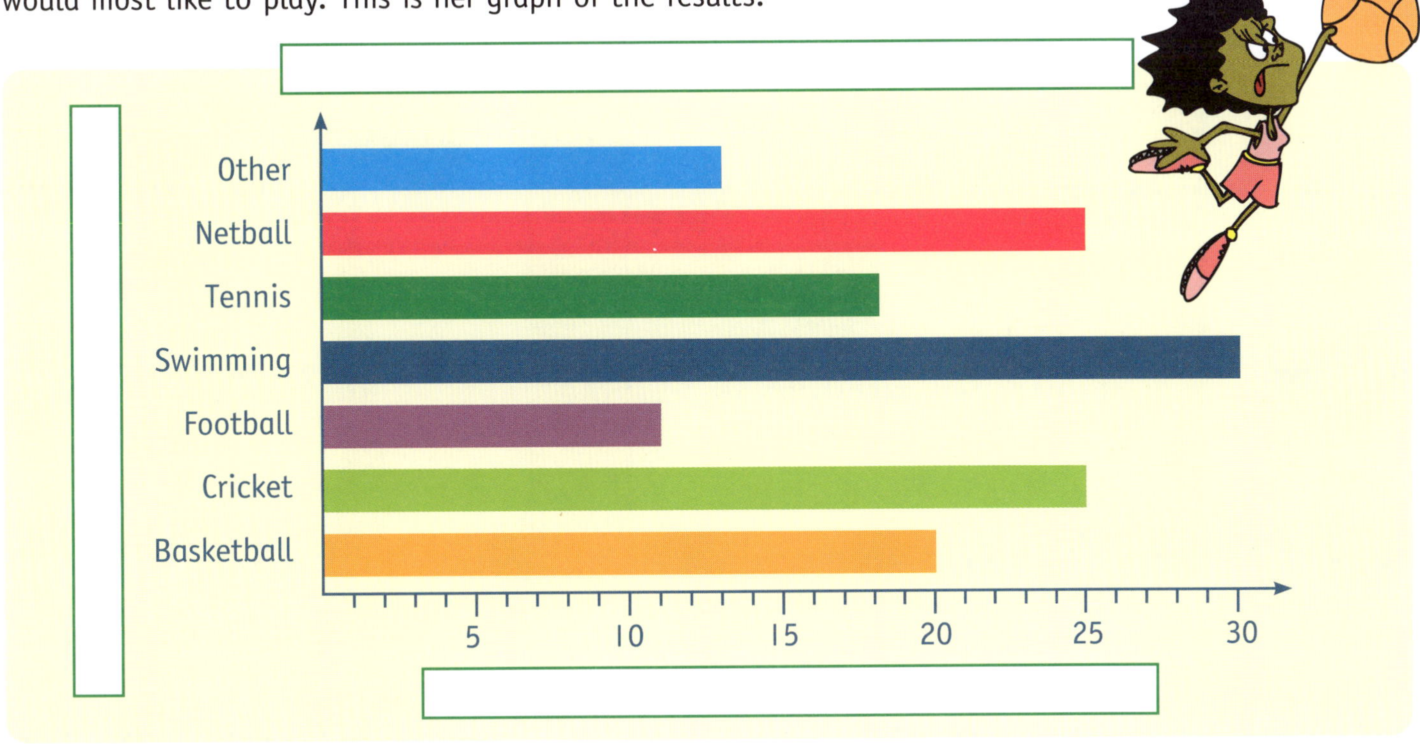

1 Give the graph a title and label both axes.

2 What sports could be included in **other**? ______________________

3 Write two ways the teacher might use this information.

a ______________________

b ______________________

4 Survey your class on their 5 favourite sports and draw a horizontal column graph to show their choices. Remember the labels.

Sport	Tally	Total

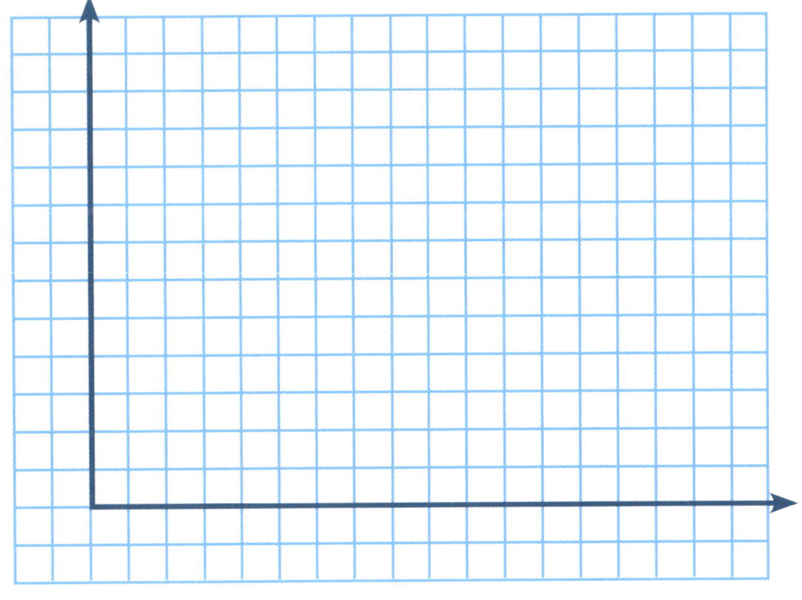

Unit 20 Gathering data

BOYS	GIRLS
JACK	ROBYN
JOHN	SU-LIN
AARON	ROBERTA
KIM	ANNABELLE
PAN	CERI
SEAN	CHIKA
ALWYN	HANA
YUSUF	SUSAN
SIRAAG	HEIDI
PIERRE	AMANDA

Dr Teachemall has a class of 20 children. Their names are displayed on a wall chart. He has asked them to work out which letters are used and how often each appears.

1 Complete this table using tally marks.

LETTER	TOTAL	LETTER	TOTAL	LETTER	TOTAL	LETTER	TOTAL
A		H		O		V	
B		I		P		W	
C		J		Q		X	
D		K		R		Y	
E		L		S		Z	
F		M		T			
G		N		U			

2 Which letter(s) is:

a used most often? ________ b used least often? ________ c not used at all? ________

3 How many letters are used altogether? ________

4 What is the average number of letters in a name? ________

5 Dr Teachemall says, "Boys' names are always longer than girls' names."

Comment on this statement. ____

____

6 Why would Dr Teachemall set the class this task? ____

____

Unit 20 Representing data

1 Draw a graph to show Dr Teachemall's information. Give the graph a title and label the axes.

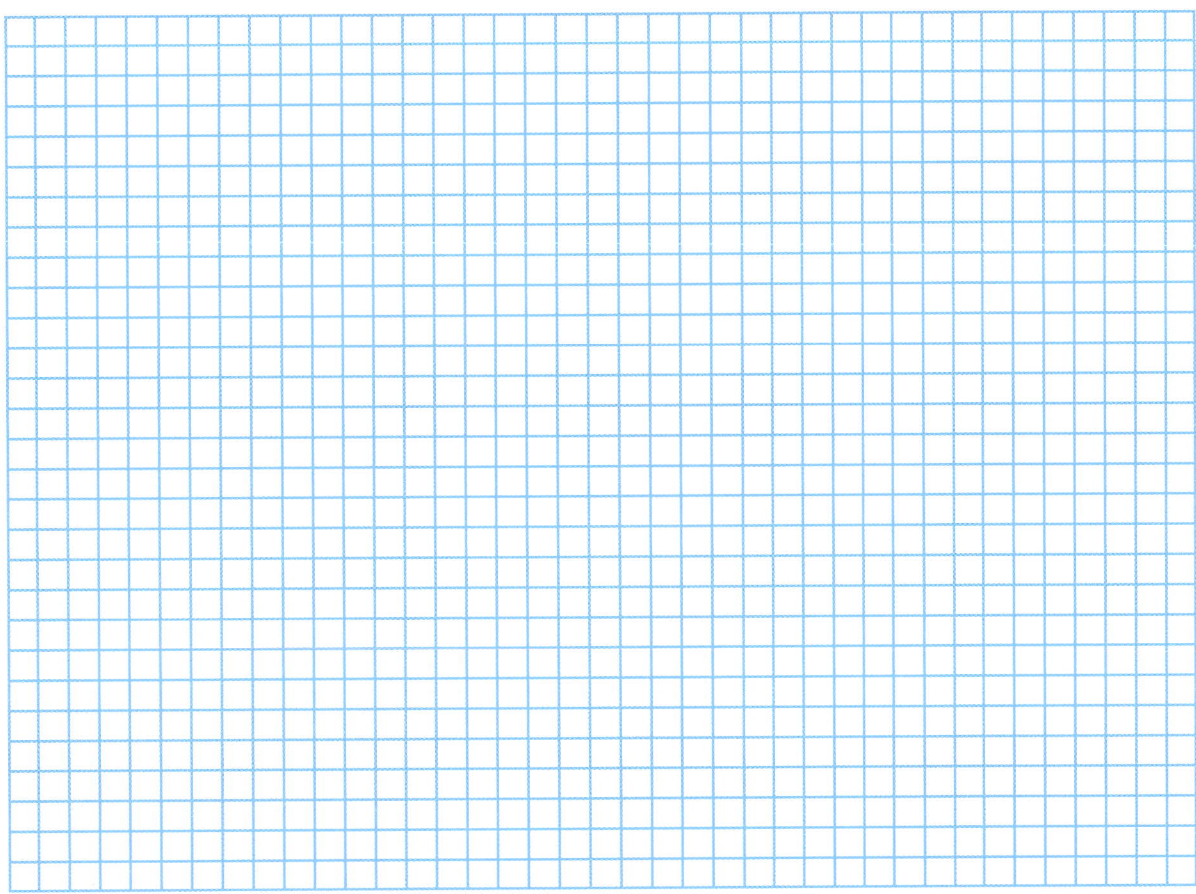

2 Write two questions you could ask about this graph.

a ______________________________

b ______________________________

3 Repeat this exercise in your class.

LETTER	TOTAL	LETTER	TOTAL	LETTER	TOTAL	LETTER	TOTAL
A		H		O		V	
B		I		P		W	
C		J		Q		X	
D		K		R		Y	
E		L		S		Z	
F		M		T			
G		N		U			

survey the class

Mastery Checklist I can:
- ☐ interpret a stacked column graph
- ☐ draw a horizontal column graph
- ☐ collect data and use tally marks to record it in a table
- ☐ choose the best type of graph to present data.

Revision Term 2

1 What is the place value of the 5? p 60

a 5876·329 ______

b 873·245 ______

c 643 009·853 ______

2 0·893 expanded is: p 60

______

______

3 p 64

$$\begin{array}{r} 684 \\ 25 \\ +\ 356 \\ \hline \end{array}$$

4 p 64

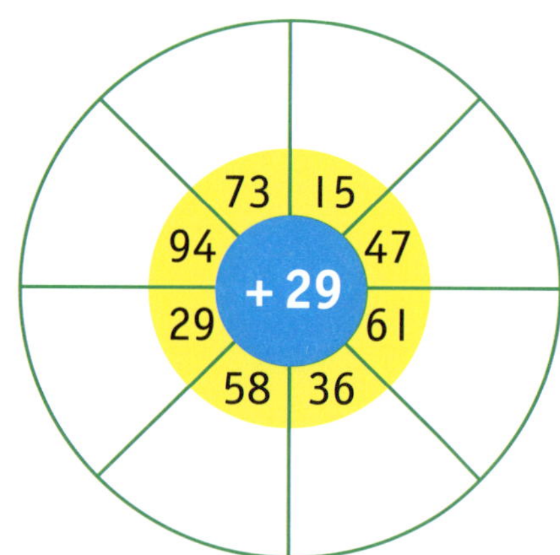

5 p 65

a
$$\begin{array}{r} 4815 \\ +\ 4978 \\ \hline \end{array}$$

b
$$\begin{array}{r} 528 \\ 3759 \\ +\ 75 \\ \hline \end{array}$$

6 p 67

a Share 580 birds between 10 cages.

b Share 760 pencils between 8 classes.

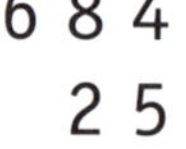

7 p 68

a $5\overline{)85}$ b $3\overline{)747}$

8 John picked 819 oranges to put into 7 tubs. How many in each tub? p 68

9 p 70

a Write the number coloured.

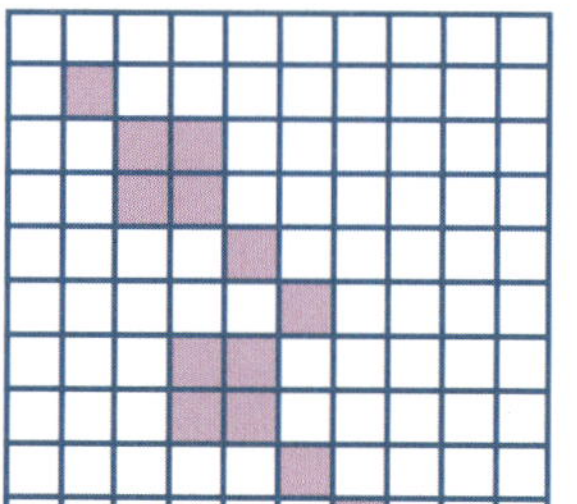

$\frac{\_\_\_}{100}$ = 0·____

b

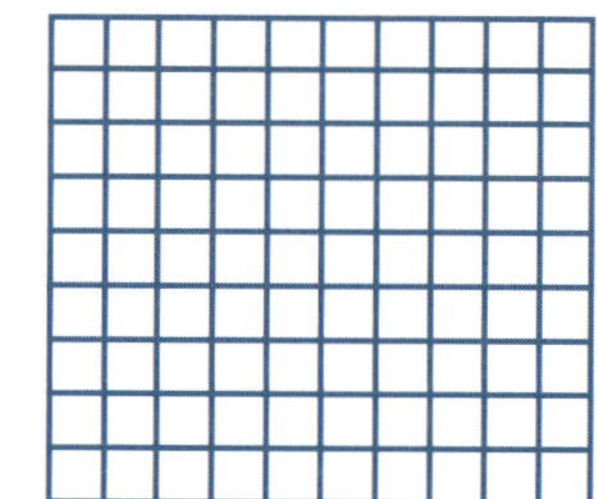

Colour 20%

10 Complete. p 71

a $\frac{99}{100}$ = ____ %

b 10% = $\frac{\square}{10}$

c 75% = $\frac{\square}{4}$

d $\frac{1}{5}$ = ____ %

11 p 77

a
$$\begin{array}{r} 8{\cdot}4 \\ 3{\cdot}8 \\ +\ 7{\cdot}7 \\ \hline \end{array}$$

b
$$\begin{array}{r} 8{\cdot}7 \\ -\ 4{\cdot}3 \\ \hline \end{array}$$

c
$$\begin{array}{r} 6{\cdot}52 \\ -\ 2{\cdot}87 \\ \hline \end{array}$$

12 p 78

a
$$\begin{array}{r} 4{\cdot}07 \\ \times\ 6 \\ \hline \end{array}$$

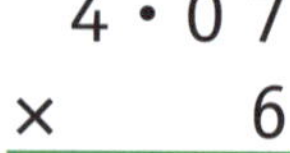

b
$$\begin{array}{r} 15{\cdot}2 \\ \times\ 4 \\ \hline \end{array}$$

Revision Term 2

13 a Measure the length and width. p 84

b Perimeter = ______________________

c Area = ______________________

14 Would you use m² or ha to measure the area of a: p 86

a farm? _____ b National Park? _____

c cafe? _____ d tennis court? _____

15 This field is 1 ha.
What could be its width and length? p 87

width ________

length ________

16 These models were built using cubic centimetre blocks. Write the volume. p 89

a

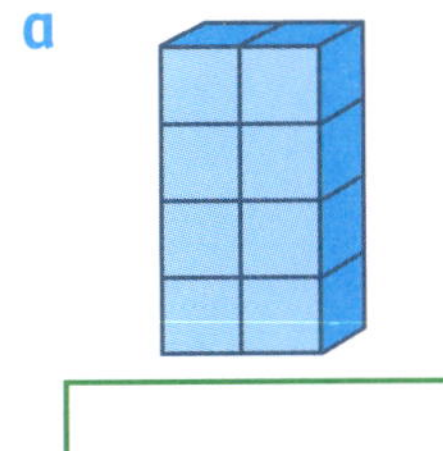

b

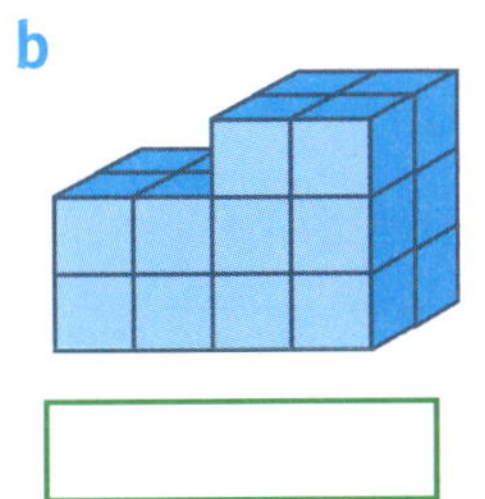

p 91

17 Circle the items with the greater volume.

a 2 shoe boxes or 6 Base 10 thousands

b a school bus or 2 family cars

c 5 Maths books or 2 house bricks

18 Write in 24-hour time. p 94

a 7:15 pm ________ b 3:42 am ________

19 Write in am or pm time. p 94

a 1128 ______________________

b 2210 ______________________

20 How much time has passed? p 95
Answer in hours and minutes.

a 06:00 to 11:45 ______________________

b 11:35 to 20:45 ______________________

c 9:58 to 13:12 ______________________

21 Draw spots at: p 98

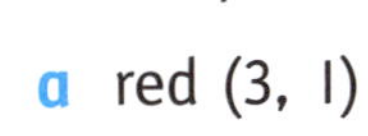

a red (3, 1)

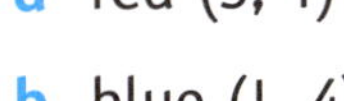

b blue (1, 4)

c green (4, 2)

d black (2, 5)

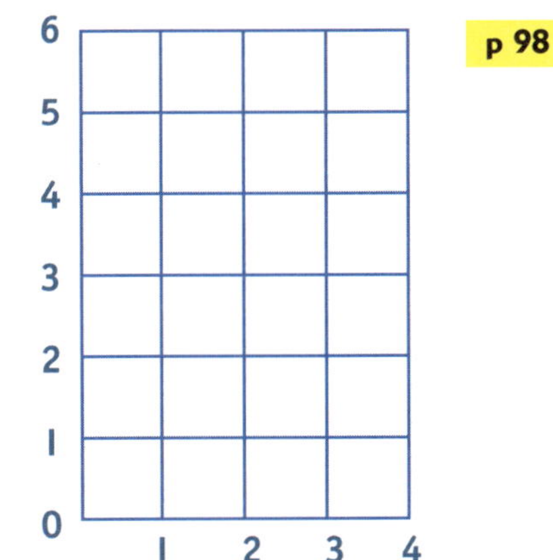

22 On Monday the canteen drew this graph about the sandwiches they made. p 102

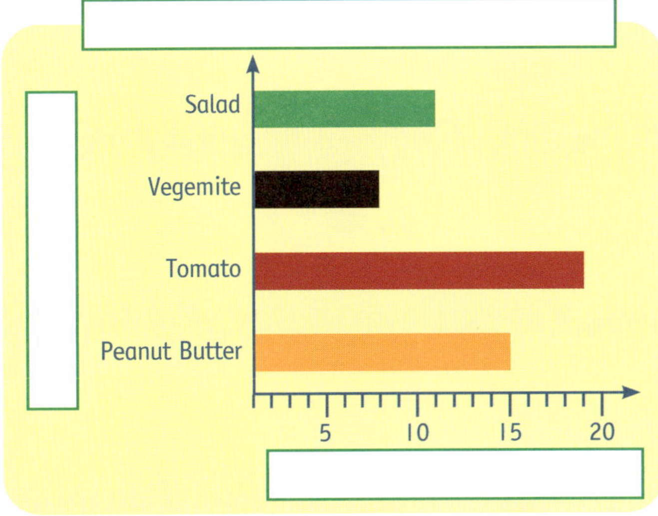

a Give the graph a title.

b Label the axes.

c Write two questions you could ask about the graph.

____

____

____

____

____

Unit 21 Addition

4-digit trading

Simon has 12 608 points.

Kim has 8094 points.

Jay has 5619 points.

Points Awards

Award	Points
Mystery flight	4455 points
Holiday	6341 points
Luggage	1753 points
Computer	2809 points
Lamp	1196 points
Watch	5015 points
Chess set	2098 points

Simon, Kim and Jay gather award points by using their credit cards. They have decided to trade some points for awards.

1 How many points are needed to claim:

a the holiday and luggage? ____________

b the flight and watch? ____________

c the computer and lamp? ____________

d the chess set and watch? ____________

e the holiday, watch and computer? ____________

f the flight, luggage and lamp? ____________

g the lamp, chess set and computer? ____________

h the flight and holiday? ____________

i the four items which need the lowest points? ____________

j the four items which need the highest points? ____________

Working

Unit 21 Addition and subtraction

Checking

Use + to check − algorithms.
eg 96 − 47 = 49
Check: 47 + 49 = 96

Use − to check + algorithms.
eg 107 + 35 = 142
Check: 142 − 35 = 107

Look at page 106.

Use addition to check these answers.

1 How many points does Simon have left if he buys:

a the holiday and luggage? ______

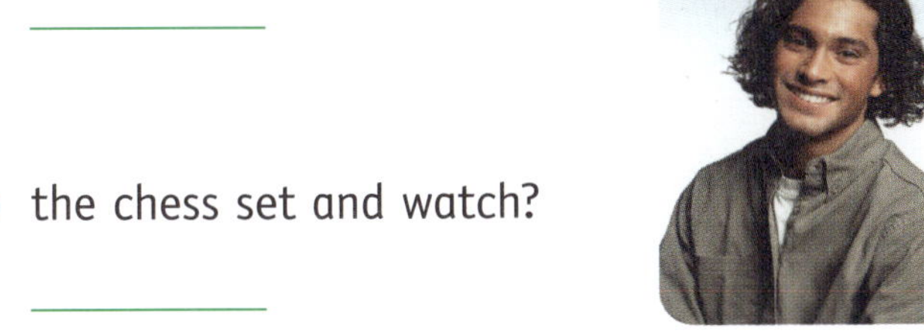

b the chess set and watch? ______

c the flight, luggage and lamp? ______

2 How many points will Kim have left if she buys:

a the computer and lamp? ______

b the flight, luggage and lamp? ______

3 a What three items can Jay buy?

______

______

b How many points will he have left? ______

Algorithm	Check

Working

Challenge!

a How many points are needed for all seven awards?

b If you earn 1 point for every $5 you spend, how much must you spend to save enough points to claim all seven awards?

Unit 21 Using addition and subtraction

1 Estimate first. Use your estimation to check your answer.

a	b	c	d
7605	8	47	921
472	607	3524	84
+ 83	+ 95	+ 6	+ 639
____	____	____	____
Est. ____	Est. ____	Est. ____	Est. ____

e	f	g	h
219	2307	364	32
6	5715	96	759
+ 5420	+ 22	+ 7	+ 4653
____	____	____	____
Est. ____	Est. ____	Est. ____	Est. ____

2 Use the inverse operations to check your answers.

a Jeremy saved 916 pens and was given 1275 by Grandma. How many does he have now?

____

Working	Check

b Deb's book has 608 pages. She has read 239. How many more does she have to read?

____

Working	Check

c On the farm there were 3702 sheep. Joe sold 395 to Bea who already owned 1454. How many do they have now?

Joe ____ Bea ____

Working	Check

Work backwards

Solly loves playing marbles. On Saturday he lost 97 to Will, gave 125 to his brother and was given 230 by Grandad. He now has 433.

How many did he have Saturday morning? ____

Mastery Checklist I can:

- ☐ add 4-digit numbers
- ☐ subtract to check addition answers
- ☐ estimate to check addition answers.

AC9M5N08 • AC9M5N09 Number **MA3-AR-01** Additive relations A • Apply efficient mental and written strategies to solve addition and subtraction problems • Use estimation and place value understanding to determine the reasonableness of solutions

Unit 22 Money multiplication

The Santos are planning a big party with lots of food and prizes galore.

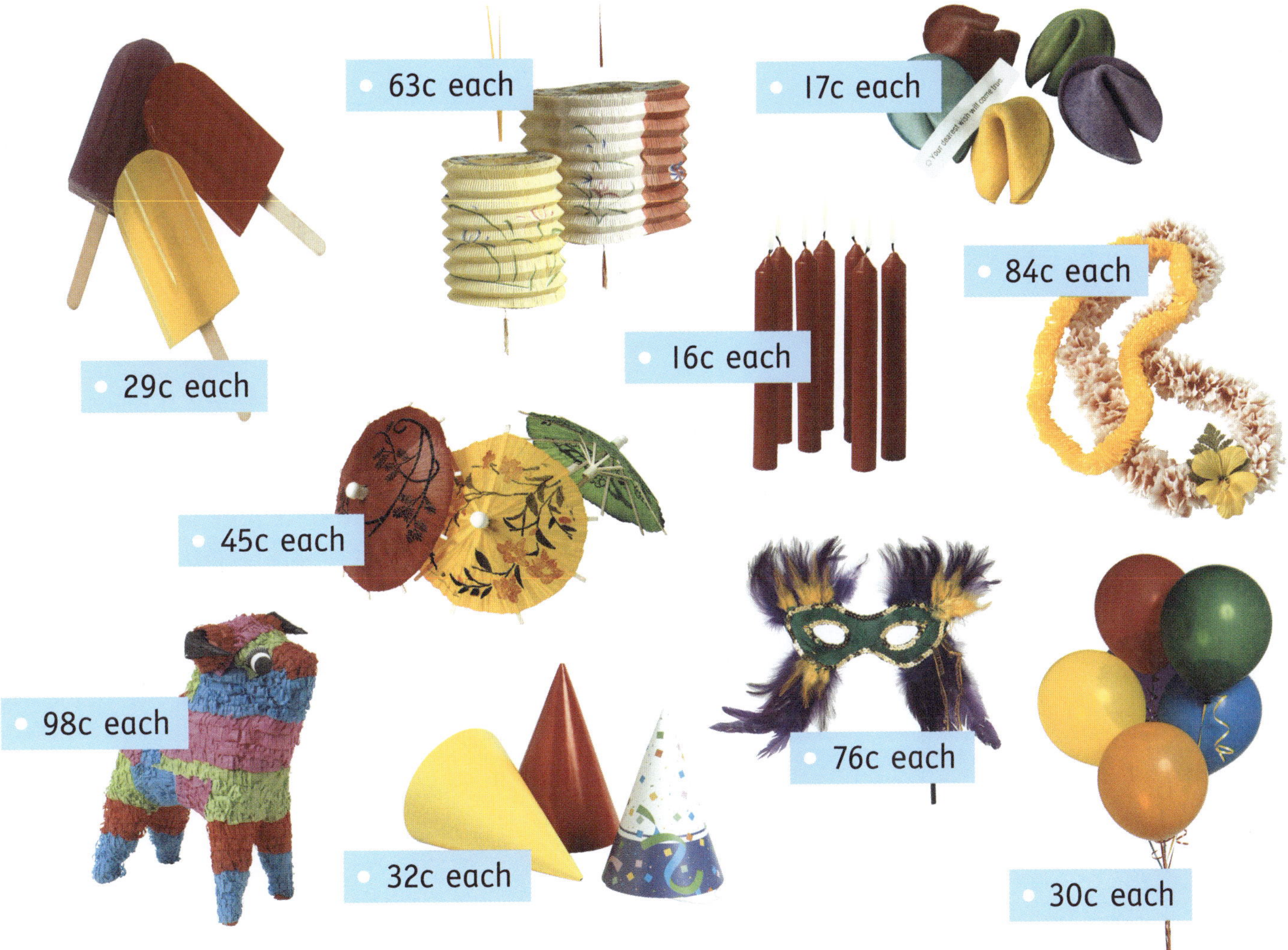

63c each

17c each

84c each

16c each

29c each

45c each

98c each

76c each

32c each

30c each

Work out these costs.

1 Buy 10 each of the:

a iceblocks. b fortune cookies. c pinatas. d hats.

2 Buy 20 each of the:

a umbrellas. b candles. c hats. d masks.

3 Buy 30 each of the:

a lanterns. b leis. c masks. d balloons.

4 Buy 50 each of the:

a umbrellas. b iceblocks. c candles. d balloons.

Unit 22 Multiplication algorithms

Use the prices on page 109.

1 Use the extended form to work out these.

Find the cost of:

a 5 iceblocks.

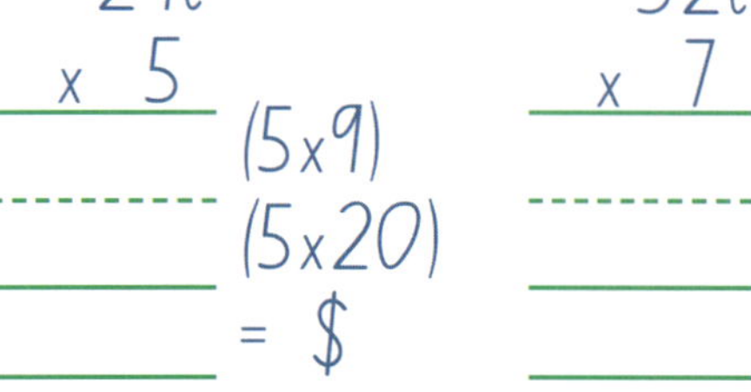

b 7 party hats.

c 8 leis.

d 6 masks.

e 8 cookies.

Multiplication

Extended form

$$\begin{array}{r} 68c \\ \times \quad 7 \\ \hline 56 \ (7 \times 8) \\ +\ 420 \ (7 \times 60) \\ \hline 476c = \$4.76 \end{array}$$

Contracted form

$$\begin{array}{r} {}^{5}68c \\ \times \ 7 \\ \hline 476c = \$4.76 \end{array}$$

trade number goes here

Money

Remember the signs.

47c × 30 = 1410c
= $14.10

58c × 8 = 464c
= $4.64

2 Use the contracted form to work out these.

Find the cost of:

a 3 pinatas.

b 9 candles.

c 4 umbrellas.

d 7 lanterns.

e 8 masks.

f 9 balloons.

g 5 leis.

3 Read all your answers. Circle any that don't make sense. Rework them.

Did your answers change? ____________

Trial and error

Sam bought 3 of one item and 4 of another. The total cost was $3.91.

What did he buy? [ ] and [ ]

Unit 22 Three-digit multiplication

1 a

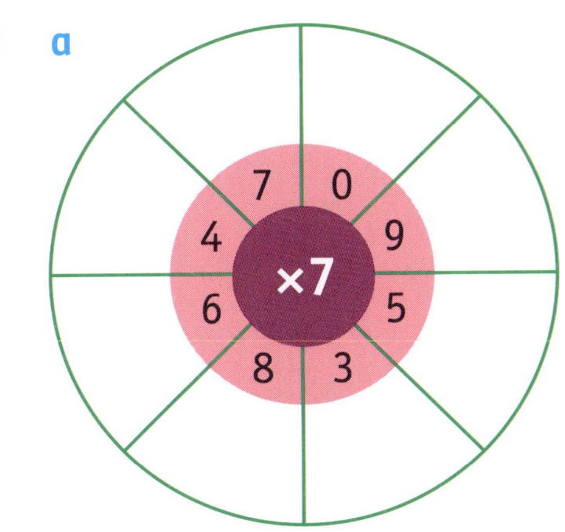

b

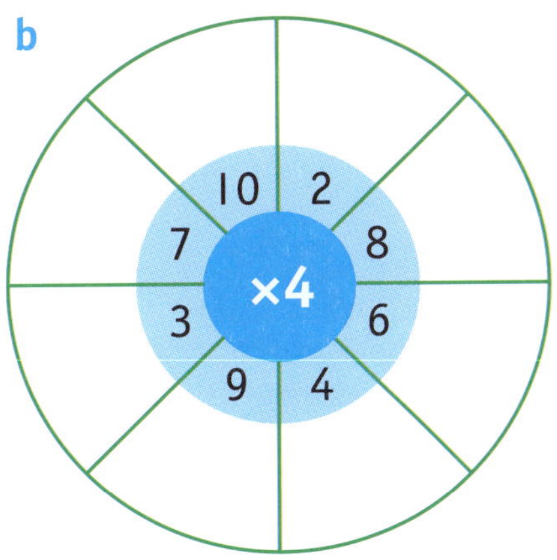

c

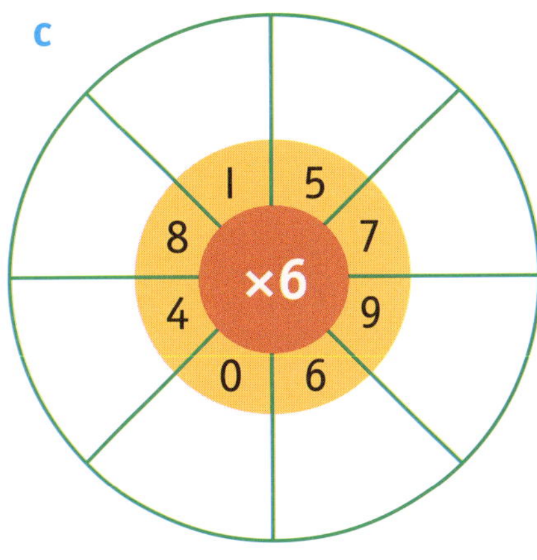

2 Circle the errors. Write the correct numerals in red.

a 67 × 9 = 606

b 81 × 5 = 486

c 95 × 5 = 425

d 46 × 4 = 174

e 30 × 6 = 186

3 a 723 × 3 = ____

b 815 × 6 = ____

c 936 × 4 = ____

d 268 × 7 = ____

e 519 × 8 = ____

f 457 × 5 = ____

g 641 × 9 = ____

h 392 × 2 = ____

Multiplying 3-digit numbers

$^{3}7^{1}62 \times 5 = 3810$

4 a 103 × 7 = ____

b 970 × 3 = ____

c 508 × 8 = ____

d 460 × 9 = ____

e 690 × 6 = ____

f 302 × 0 = ____

g 890 × 5 = ____

h 750 × 4 = ____

Challenge!

a 3 725 061 498 × 7 = ____

b 6 029 475 138 × 9 = ____

Unit 22 Multiply larger numbers

1 Use the extended form to work out these 4-digit × 2-digit multiplications.

a

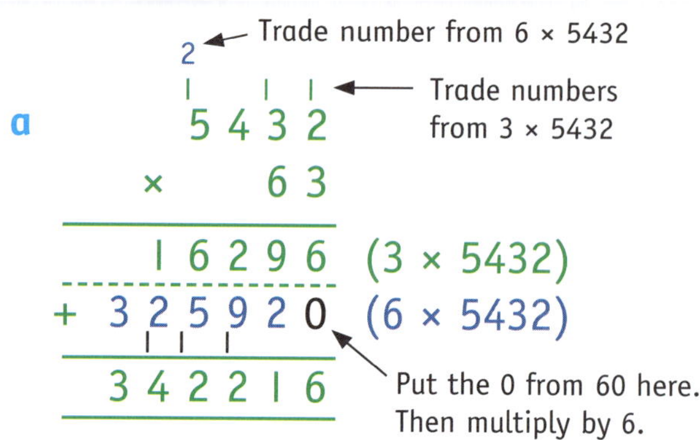

b

```
  6 4 9 8
×     2 5
---------

+       0
---------
```

c

```
  2 9 0 3
×     4 9
---------

+       0
---------
```

d

```
  9 3 7 3
×     2 4
---------

+       0
---------
```

e

```
  9 7 7 0
×     6 8
---------

+       0
---------
```

f

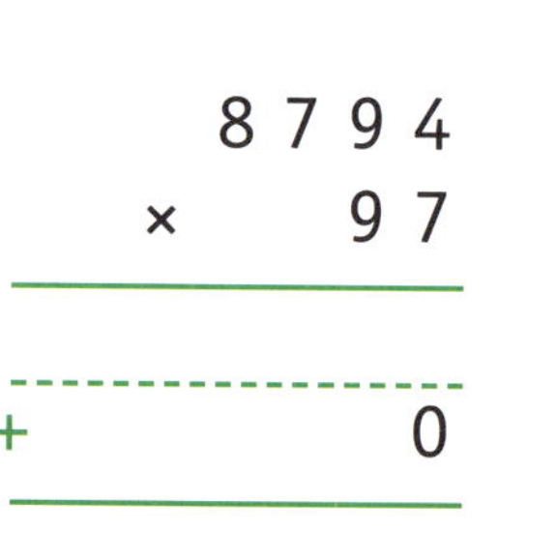

g

```
  9 5 2 4
×     3 7
---------

+       0
---------
```

h

```
  8 1 9 5
×     2 6
---------

+       0
---------
```

Mastery Checklist I can:
- ☐ multiply money amounts
- ☐ use algorithms to multiply
- ☐ multiply 3-digit numbers
- ☐ multiply 4-digit numbers.

Problem solving

Keeping up supplies

You can use a calculator.

1 Mrs Jackers needs 70 to 100 new stickers for her class. She can spend $20. She needs three different designs. Each design has 10 stickers on a card. Help her make the decision and spend as close to $20 as possible.

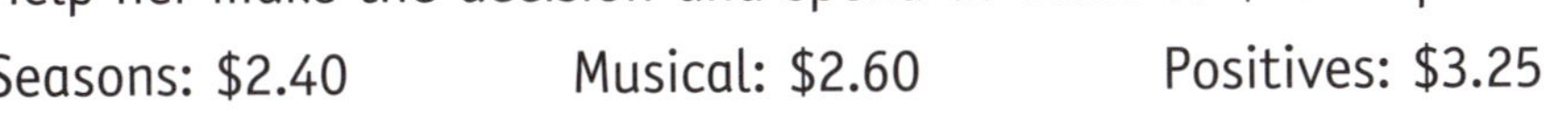

Seasons: $2.40 Musical: $2.60 Positives: $3.25
Sports: $1.90 Reminders: $2.50

Show your working.

2 Jacko wants to keep a supply of cards on hand for special events in his family. He has $50 to spend on cards and wants four different designs. Help him to spend as close to $50 as possible and total the amount he spends.

Desert Birds: $2.70 ea Fuzzies: $3.65 ea Far Out: $2.25 ea
Reef Life: $1.90 ea Champions: $5.20 ea

Show your working.

3 Handyman Aya needs to upgrade her stock of nails and screws for her handywoman jobs. She can spend $100. She needs a few packs of each size of nails and screws. How many of each size can she buy to spend all, or almost all, of her money?

50 mm nails: $2.40 35 mm screws: $3.10
75 mm nails: $2.80 40 mm screws: 3.45
100 mm nails: $2.95 50 mm screws: $3.60

Show your working.

I can solve problems by:

☐ multiplying amounts of money ☐ writing algorithms.

Unit 23 Division

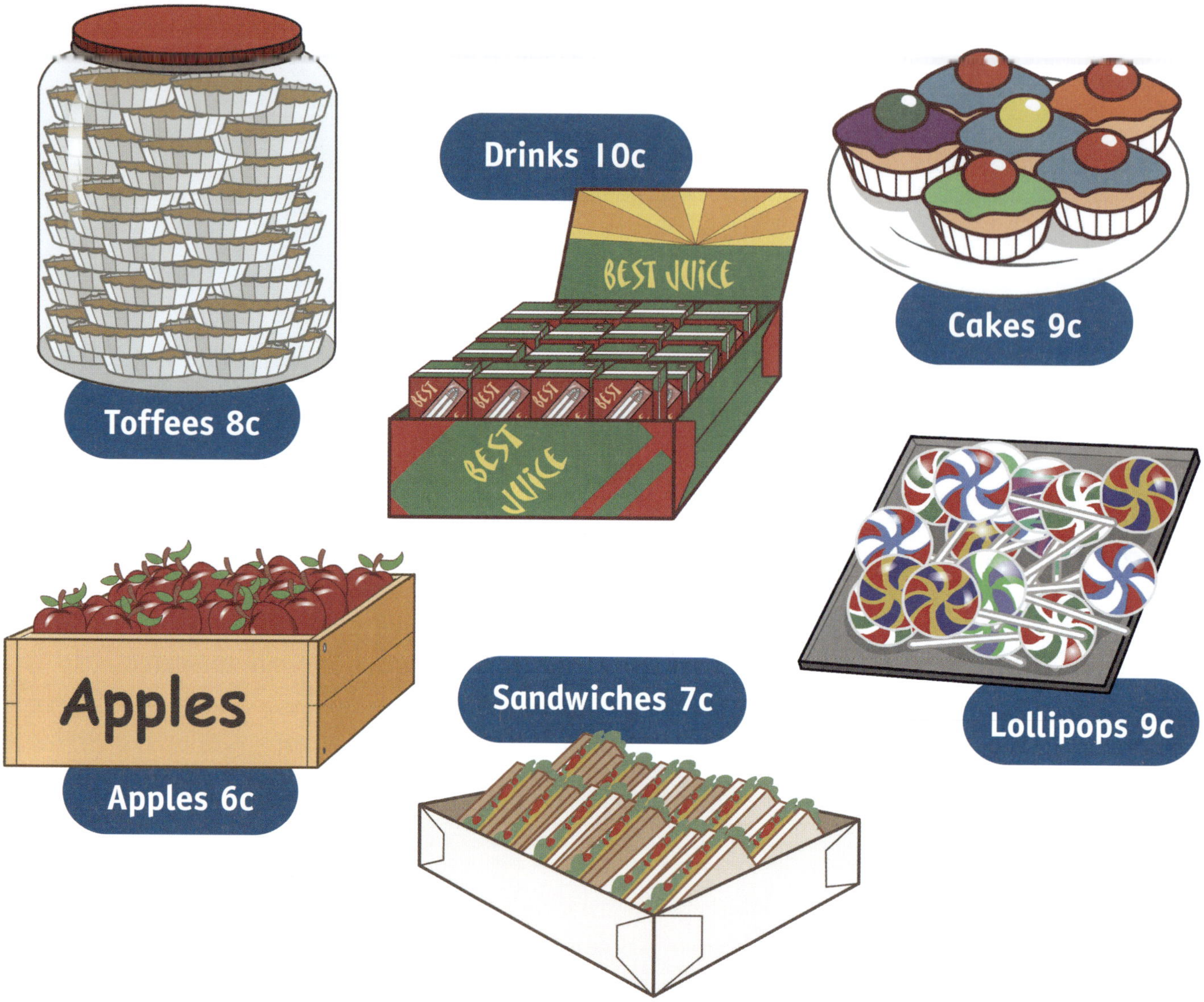

Remainders

Toffees 8c

Drinks 10c

BEST JUICE

Cakes 9c

Apples

Apples 6c

Sandwiches 7c

Lollipops 9c

During a class gala day the children were able to buy cheap food.

1 How many apples can you buy with:

a 55c?______ b 30c?______ c 40c?______ d 20c?______ e 50c?______

2 How many cakes can you buy with:

a 20c?______ b 45c?______ c 55c?______ d 85c?______ e 75c?______

3 How many toffees can you buy with:

a 65c?______ b 80c?______ c 75c?______ d 60c?______ e 35c?______

4 How many sandwiches can you buy with:

a 65c?______ b 35c?______ c 50c?______ d 30c?______ e 25c?______

5 Write 3 combinations of drinks and lollipops you can buy with 80c?

a ____________ b ____________ c ____________

Unit 23 Division signs and zero

Division signs

÷ eg 10 ÷ 5 = 2

) eg $4\overline{)12}$ = 3

1 Write the answers.

a

	35	63	7	42	14	56	70	21	49	28
÷ 7										

b

	24	4	36	8	20	28	12	40	16	32
÷ 4										

c

	36	72	45	90	27	81	54	18	63	9
÷ 9										

2 Rewrite using the) sign and then work out the answers.

a 74 ÷ 3

$3\overline{)74}$

b 59 ÷ 4

c 795 ÷ 5

d 837 ÷ 6

e 920 ÷ 8

f 765 ÷ 9

g 624 ÷ 4

h 907 ÷ 7

3

a $4\overline{)836}$

b $5\overline{)549}$

c $3\overline{)692}$

d $7\overline{)914}$

e $6\overline{)582}$

f $8\overline{)965}$

g $9\overline{)658}$

h $5\overline{)706}$

i $4\overline{)839}$

Remember to use zero.

$$\begin{array}{r} 109 \\ 6\overline{)654} \end{array}$$

Challenge!

The answers to three division problems are: **172**, **309** and **460 r 5**.
What could the division algorithms be?

Unit 23 Remainders

Estimate
78 ÷ 4
Estimate 80 ÷ 4 = 20

372 ÷ 6
Estimate 360 ÷ 6 = 60

Remember An estimate is NOT an exact answer.

1 Estimate these answers.

	Estimate
a 69 ÷ 6	
b 83 ÷ 4	
c 103 ÷ 5	
d 218 ÷ 3	
e 637 ÷ 8	

	Estimate
f 572 ÷ 7	
g 941 ÷ 9	
h 365 ÷ 2	
i 827 ÷ 4	
j 295 ÷ 8	

Writing remainders as fractions

$4\overline{)33}$ = 8 r1 or $8\frac{1}{4}$

$7\overline{)296}$ = 42 r2 or $42\frac{2}{7}$

2 Estimate first. Write the remainders as fractions.

a $3\overline{)97}$ Est. ______

b $5\overline{)84}$ Est. ______

c $7\overline{)68}$ Est. ______

d $4\overline{)595}$ Est. ______

e $7\overline{)802}$ Est. ______

f $6\overline{)921}$ Est. ______

g $8\overline{)807}$ Est. ______

h $3\overline{)891}$ Est. ______

i $5\overline{)354}$ Est. ______

j $9\overline{)528}$ Est. ______

k $8\overline{)495}$ Est. ______

3 You have 504 assorted balls to put into equal groups. How many equal groups can you make?
eg *2 equal groups of 252.*

Unit 23 Average

To find the average add all the scores and divide by how many scores there are.

The average of 3, 7, 9 and 5 is (3 + 7 + 9 + 5) ÷ 4 = 6

1 Find the average of each set of scores.

a 8, 7, 5, 11, 4 ________ b 16, 14, 10, 24 ________

c 21, 18, 12 ________ d 4, 2, 11, 16, 9, 5 ________

e 18, 31, 19, 10, 12, 17, 26 ________

2 a In the term spelling tests Don scored 8, 7, 5, 9, 9, 10, 9, 4, 7, 8.
What was his average score? ☐

b Julia loved marshmallows. During one week she ate 27 on Monday, 13 on Tuesday, 43 on Wednesday, only 2 on Thursday, 12 on Friday, 19 on Saturday and 24 on Sunday.
What was the average number per day? ☐

c The ages of 8 pups are 7 months, 11 months, 22 months, 12 months, 5 months, 13 months, 20 months and 6 months.
What is their average age? ☐

d Jay has to post some parcels.
They weigh 9 kg, 1 kg, 8 kg, 13 kg and 17 kg.
What is their average mass? ☐

e During the wet season we measured the rain on ten consecutive days:
8 mm, 12 mm, 3 mm, 17 mm, 16 mm, 16 mm, 9 mm, 8 mm, 11 mm, 5 mm.
What was the average daily rainfall? ☐

f Rosa counted the flowers on each rose bush in her garden.
This was the result: 7, 11, 4, 9, 8, 3, 2, 10, 9, 7 and 7.
What was the average number per bush? ☐

3 Write 2 instances where you would use a average.

a ____

b ____

Mastery Checklist I can:
- ☐ divide money amounts
- ☐ divide 3-digit numbers that have remainders
- ☐ estimate division answers
- ☐ write remainders as fractions.

Problem solving

Read, plan, work, check

Solve these problems. Estimate first.

A printer prints out 8 pages each minute.
How long will it take to print 184 pages?
Est. 25
What? minutes How? 184 ÷ 8
Answer = 23 minutes

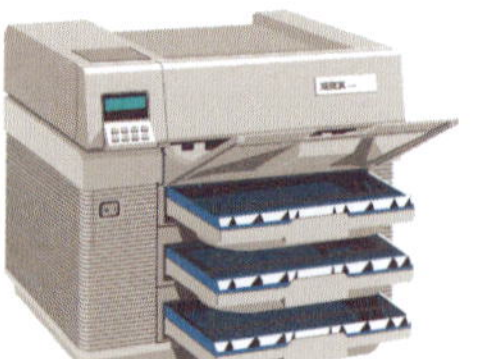

Working

$$8\overline{)184}$$ 23 remainder working: 24

1 **a** A ticket to a show costs $9. How many tickets can be bought for $380? Est. ____________
What? ____________ How? ____________
Answer = ____________

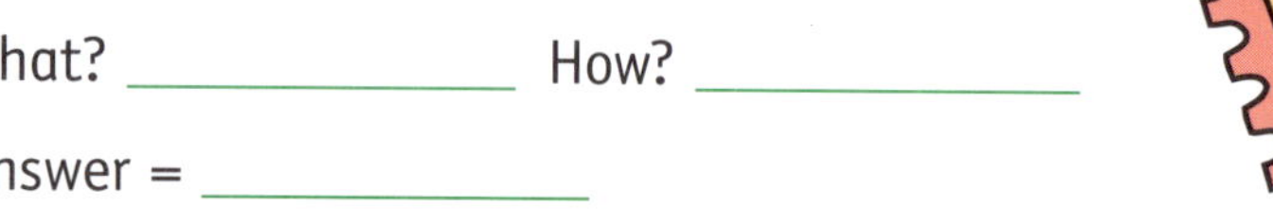

b How much change is there? Est. ____________ What? ____________
How? ____________ Answer = ____________

2 **a** Eight slices can be cut from each cake. If 264 slices are needed, how many cakes must be bought? Est. ____________
What? ____________ How? ____________
Answer = ____________

b If 284 slices are needed, how many cakes should be bought? Est. ____________
What? ____________
How? ____________ Answer = ____________

3 A carpenter has 531 table legs.
How many tables can he make?
Est. ____________ What? ____________
How? ____________ Answer = ____________

4 A bunch of flowers costs $7. How many bunches can be bought for $413? Est. ____________
What? ____________ How? ____________
Answer = ____________

I can solve problems by:
☐ estimating and dividing ☐ writing algorithms.

 AC9M5N07 • AC9M5N08 Number MAO-WM-01 Working mathematically • choosing and applying mathematical techniques to solve problems • MA3-MR-01 Multiplicative relations A • Represent and solve division problems with whole number remainders • Select and apply strategies to divide a number with 3 or more digits by a one-digit divisor

Unit 24 Equivalent fractions

A B C D E F G H I J K L

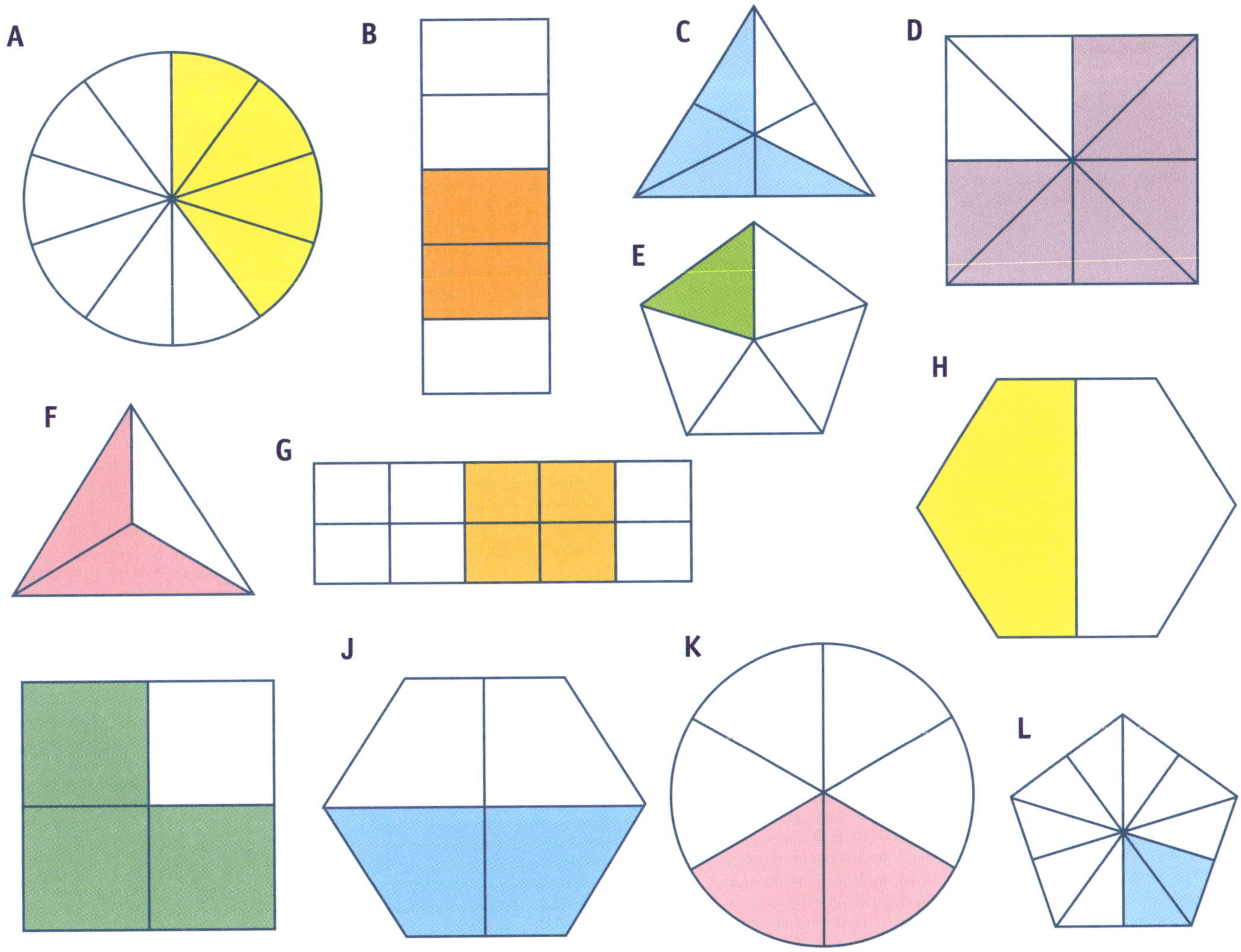

1 Name the fraction coloured in each shape.

A ______ B ______ C ______ D ______ E ______ F ______

G ______ H ______ I ______ J ______ K ______ L ______

2 Name fractions that are the same size.

a A = ______ b B = ______ c C = ______ d D = ______ e E = ______ f H = ______

3 Name the equal fractions.

a $\frac{4}{10}$ = ______ b ______ c ______ d ______ e ______ f ______

4 a Look carefully at the equal fractions.

b Write a comment about what you can see. ______________________

____

____

5 Write four different fractions that are equal to $\frac{1}{2}$. ______ ______ ______ ______

Unit 24 Making equivalent fractions

1 Make equivalent fractions for each diagram on page 119 by multiplying the numerator and the denominator by 4.

a $\frac{4}{10} = \frac{4 \times 4}{10 \times 4} = \frac{16}{40}$	b $\frac{2}{5} = \frac{2 \times 4}{5 \times 4} =$	
c	d	
e	f	
g	h	i
j	k	l

Remember $\frac{2}{5}$ 2 ← **numerator**, 5 ← **denominator**

To make equivalent fractions

- **multiply the numerator and the denominator by the same number.**
  eg $\frac{1}{3} = \frac{1 \times 5}{3 \times 5} = \frac{5}{15}$

OR

- **divide the numerator and the denominator by the same number.**
  eg $\frac{4}{8} = \frac{4 \div 4}{8 \div 4} = \frac{1}{2}$

2 Divide to make the smallest equivalent fraction.

a $\frac{5}{20} = \frac{5 \div 5}{20 \div 5}$	b $\frac{6}{30} =$	c $\frac{5}{10} =$
d $\frac{15}{40} =$	e $\frac{8}{28} =$	f $\frac{20}{90} =$

3 Circle the equivalent fractions.

a $\frac{2}{3}, \frac{3}{6}, \frac{4}{6}$ b $\frac{6}{12}, \frac{5}{8}, \frac{1}{2}$ c $\frac{2}{5}, \frac{6}{15}, \frac{4}{12}$ d $\frac{1}{4}, \frac{1}{8}, \frac{2}{16}$

e $\frac{3}{9}, \frac{1}{3}, \frac{6}{12}$ f $\frac{7}{8}, \frac{10}{12}, \frac{5}{6}$ g $\frac{10}{20}, \frac{6}{10}, \frac{3}{5}$ h $\frac{2}{4}, \frac{3}{6}, \frac{4}{8}$

4 a $\frac{15}{20} = \frac{3}{\square}$ b $\frac{24}{32} = \frac{\square}{4}$ c $\frac{27}{30} = \frac{\square}{10}$ d $\frac{28}{36} = \frac{7}{\square}$

e $\frac{21}{56} = \frac{3}{\square}$ f $\frac{90}{100} = \frac{\square}{10}$ g $\frac{16}{18} = \frac{8}{\square}$ h $\frac{20}{50} = \frac{10}{\square} = \frac{\square}{5}$

Unit 24 Ordering fractions

1 a Colour each fraction.

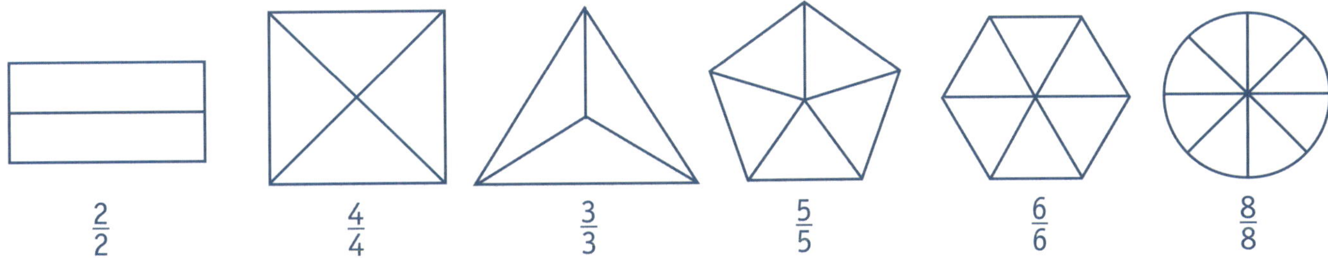

$\frac{2}{2}$ $\frac{4}{4}$ $\frac{3}{3}$ $\frac{5}{5}$ $\frac{6}{6}$ $\frac{8}{8}$

b How much of each shape did you colour? __________

c Complete: If a fraction is equal to 1, the numerator and the denominator ____________________.

2 a $1 = \frac{\square}{10}$ b $1 = \frac{7}{\square}$ c $\square = \frac{9}{9}$ d $1 = \frac{\square}{56}$ e $1 = \frac{100}{\square}$

3 Colour.

a 

$1\frac{1}{2}$

b 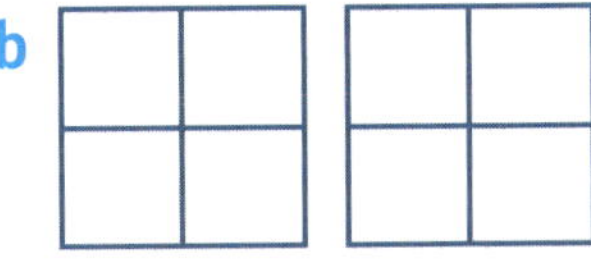

$1\frac{3}{4}$

c 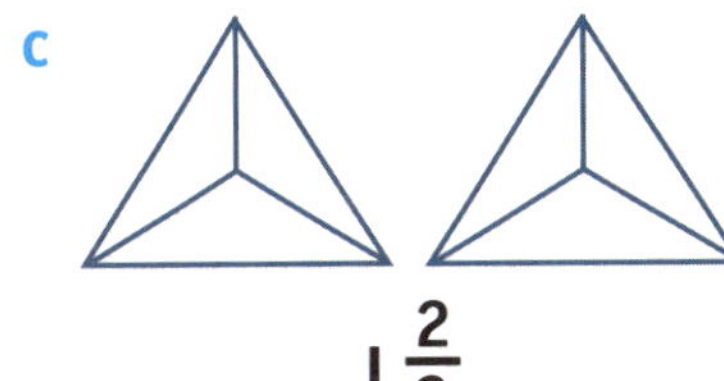

$1\frac{2}{3}$

d

$2\frac{1}{5}$

e 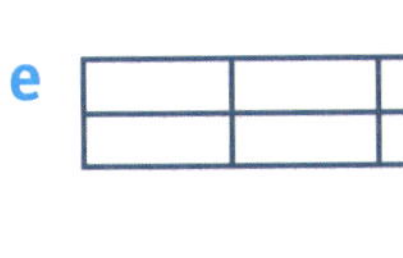

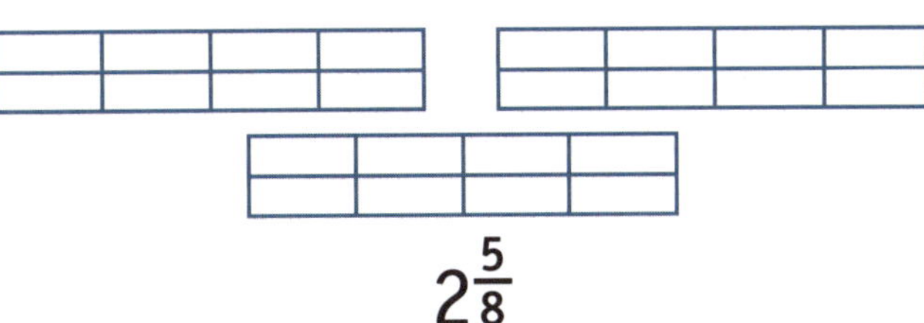

$2\frac{5}{8}$

4 Place these fractions on the number line.

a $2, 1\frac{1}{4}, \frac{1}{4}, 1\frac{3}{4}$ 0 — 1 — 2

b $1\frac{1}{2}, \frac{2}{3}, 2\frac{1}{4}$ 0 — 1 — 2 — 3

Challenge! Order from smallest to largest: $\frac{3}{4}, 1\frac{1}{2}, \frac{1}{5}, \frac{7}{10}, \frac{5}{6}, 1\frac{1}{3}, \frac{2}{3}, 1\frac{3}{4}, \frac{1}{12}$

Mastery Checklist I can:

- ☐ write the fraction coloured in a shape
- ☐ identify equivalent fractions
- ☐ colour to show mixed numbers
- ☐ order fractions on a number line.

Problem solving

Fractions

1 Five kids have a chocolate bar each for their snack. They have eaten some when they decide to compare how much each has left. Johnno has five eighths of his left, Simon has four fifths of his left, Jed has two thirds left, Phil has seven tenths and Gorgio has three quarters left. Simon is happy because he says he has the most left. Is he right?

Colour fractions and compare.

2 Millie, Molly and Mandy are having a sleepover and drinking hot chocolate before bed. After the movie, Milly has one half of hers left, Molly has two thirds left and Mandy has five sixths left. Milly becomes very upset when she realises she has the least left. One of the others can solve the problem by giving Milly some of hers and then they will all have the same amount of hot chocolate left. How will they do this? Hint: use sixths.

I can solve problems by:

☐ understanding fractions ☐ drawing diagrams.

Unit 25 Number sentences

A
I am thinking of a number so that when I double it and add 9, the answer is 23.

B
I am thinking of a number so that when I halve it and subtract 8, the answer is 5.

C
I am thinking of a number so that when I multiply it by 6 and add 2, the answer is 56.

D
I am thinking of a number so that when I add 7 and then divide by 3, the answer is 11.

E
I am thinking of a number so that when I subtract 9 and then multiply by 9, the answer is 81.

F
I am thinking of a number so that when I multiply by 7 then divide by 4, the answer is 14.

Each child is thinking of a special number.

1 Write a number sentence to find each special number. Call the number ■, eg ■ + 5 = 7, ■ = 2

A ______________________ **B** ______________________

C ______________________ **D** ______________________

E ______________________ **F** ______________________

2 Write special number problems for a friend to solve.

Unit 25 Problems and number sentences

Algebra 1 

1 Match a number sentence from the coloured box with a story and answer the problem.

a Andy rides his bike 15 km to school and 15 km home each day. Jake says that's 5 km more than he rides to school and back. How far does Jake ride his bike?

_______________ _____

b Three baby elephants have slurped up 20 L of water each. The mother elephant has drunk all her water, but needs 15 L more to equal the baby elephants' total. How much has the mother elephant drunk?

_______________ _____

c Seven children have donated $6 each to their class's charity. Their friends are not impressed and say that is half their total donation. How much have the friends donated?

_______________ _____

d Six cyclists in a relay have ridden 15 km each. Three riders wish to do the same number of km in a relay. How far will they each have to ride to cover the same distance?

_______________ _____

A 3 × 2 × 14 = ? × 2 × ? **B** 3 × ? = 6 × 15 **C** 250 − 55 = ? − 5

D 3 × 20 = ? + 15

E ? ÷ 2 = 7 × 6 **F** 72 ÷ ? = 4 × 2 **G** 15 × 2 = ? + 5

e While I saved $250, my neighbour saved hard as well. I then spent $55 and had the same amount as she had after she spent only $5. How much had my neighbour saved?

_______________ _____

f I read for 3 hours a day for 2 days and read 14 pages an hour. Mum read on the same days, for more hours but she read fewer pages. How long did she read each day and how many pages did she read?

_______________ _____

g Our netball club attracted 72 players in my age group. We formed into groups consisting of 4 pairs of children of equal ability. How many groups did we make?

_______________ _____

2 Write a story for this pair of equivalent number sentences. 50 − ? = 3 × 16

____

____

____

Unit 25 What is my value?

1 What is my value?

a ■ + 6 = 18 − 3
■ = ______

b 8 × ■ = 45 + 11
■ = ______

c ★ ÷ 9 = 4 × 2
★ = ______

d 53 + 24 = ▲ × 11
______ = ▲

e 90 ÷ 9 = 17 − ✷
______ = ✷

f 36 + 8 = ✦ × 4
______ = ✦

g ★ + 37 = 100 − 19
★ = ______

h 94 − ✳ = 38 + 17
✳ = ______

i 7 × 3 = 63 ÷ ▲
______ = ▲

j 86 − 59 = ■ ÷ 2
______ = ■

k 204 ÷ 4 = ★ + 21
______ = ★

l 147 ÷ ✳ = 73 − 52
✳ = ______

2 Rewrite using inverse operations to find the value of ■.

Addition is the inverse of subtraction. Division is the inverse of multiplication.

a ■ + $\frac{1}{4}$ = 2
■ = $2 - \frac{1}{4}$
= ______

b ■ − 2·3 = 1·8
■ = 1·8 + ______
= ______

c ■ × 3 = 7·8

■ = ______
= ______

d ■ ÷ 5 = 3·4
■ = ______
= ______

e ■ − $\frac{1}{5}$ = $\frac{3}{5}$
■ = ______
= ______

f ■ + 7·63 = 10·25
■ = ______
= ______

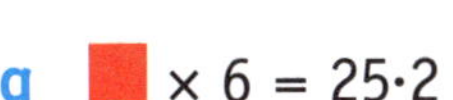
g ■ × 6 = 25·2

■ = ______
= ______

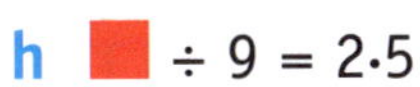
h ■ ÷ 9 = 2.51
■ = ______
= ______

i ■ + $\frac{3}{8}$ = $3\frac{5}{8}$
■ = ______
= ______

j ■ − $1\frac{1}{4}$ = $2\frac{1}{2}$
■ = ______
= ______

3 Substitute the values into the questions to check your answers in question 2.

a $1\frac{3}{4} + \frac{1}{4} = 2$ true
b ______
c ______
d ______
e ______
f ______
g ______
h ______
i ______
j ______

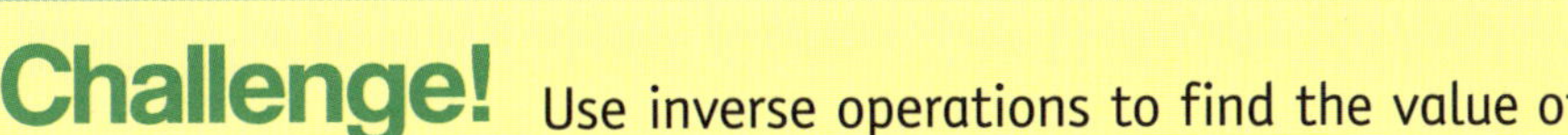

Challenge! Use inverse operations to find the value of ★.

a 2 × ★ + 94 = 108 ______

b 288 ÷ 9 = 64 − 4 × ★ ______

Unit 25 Pattern tables

A

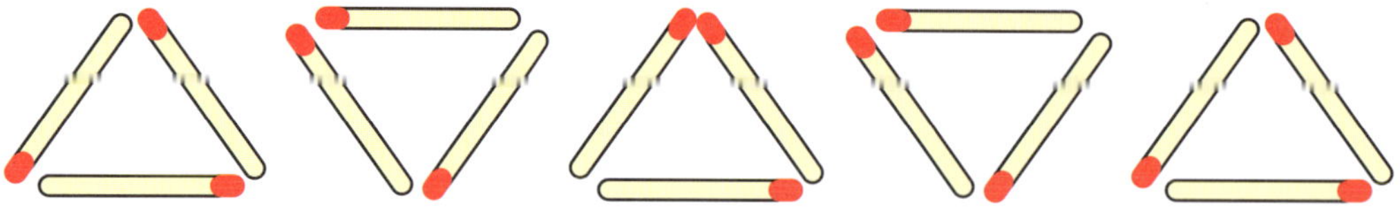

B

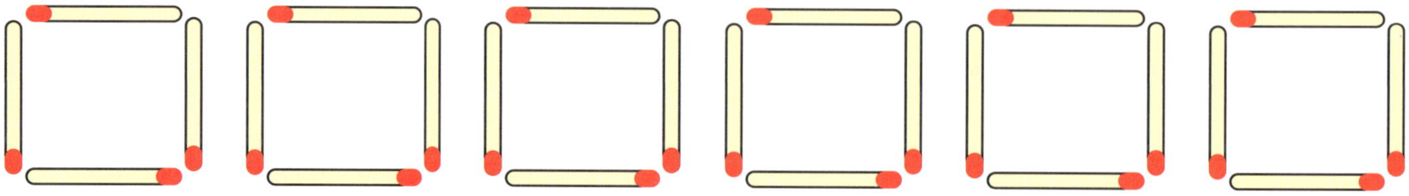

C

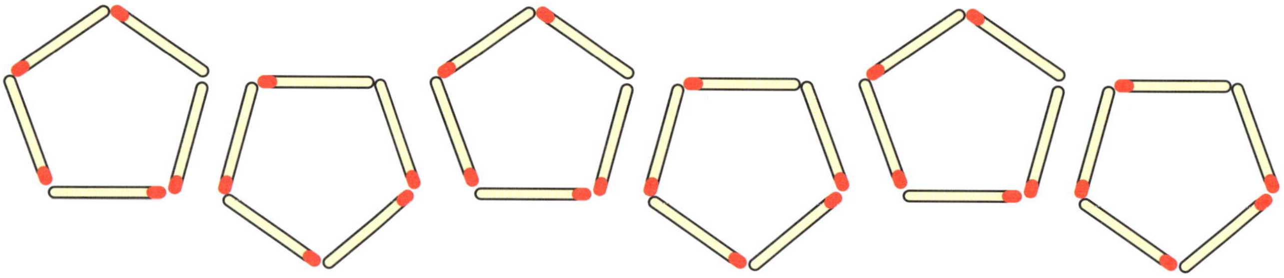

D

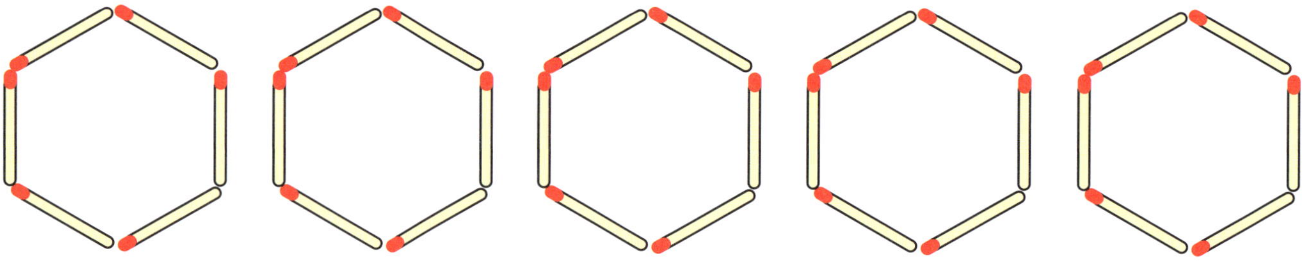

Fill in the table for each pattern.

A

Number of shapes										
Number of sticks										

B

Number of shapes										
Number of sticks										

C

Number of shapes										
Number of sticks										

D

Number of shapes										
Number of sticks										

Unit 25 Patterns in words

Use the patterns on page 126.

1 Describe each pattern in words.

A ______

B ______

C ______

D ______

2 Write the rule for each pattern.

A ______

B ______

C ______

D ______

3 For each pattern, write the value of the:

a 15th number. A ______ B ______ C ______ D ______

b 20th number. A ______ B ______ C ______ D ______

c 100th number. A ______ B ______ C ______ D ______

4 a Draw a pattern using octagons.

b Fill in the table for your pattern.

Number of shapes										
Number of sticks										

c Describe your pattern in words. ______

______

d Write the rule for your pattern. ______

e What is the value for the 20th shape? ______ the 50th shape? ______

Mastery Checklist I can:
- ☐ write a number sentence to match a story
- ☐ find the missing value
- ☐ complete pattern tables
- ☐ make my own shape pattern.

Playground Marking

Investigation 3

measure a 10 m square

Draw a 10 m square on the playground using measuring and drawing tools.

What are the tools you use?

Write the procedure for drawing the square.

What area does the square take up?

Name the types of triangles that can be drawn inside this square without measuring angles.

How do you draw the triangles?

 AC9M5M01 • AC9M5M02 Measurement **MAO-WM-01** Working mathematically • choosing and applying mathematical techniques to solve problems • communicating thinking and reasoning coherently and clearly • **MA3-2DS-01 • MA3-2DS-02** Two-dimensional spatial structure A • 2D shapes: Classify two-dimensional shapes and describe their properties • Two-dimensional spatial structure A • Area: Calculate the areas of rectangles using familiar metric units

Playground Marking

Investigation 3

Invent a game based on the square and the triangle shapes within it.

Write the rules and how to play it here.

You need to measure 20 m on the playground to place the wickets and the creases on the field for a game of cricket. Only use what you have naturally, ie your body.

Write how you do it.

use body measures

Now use a measuring tape to check your length. Were you close to 20 m? Explain.

List three or more times when you would use the measuring tape instead of your body.

To carry out these tasks, I need to:

- ☐ understand the properties of a square
- ☐ solve the problem of drawing a square on a playground
- ☐ know how much space a 10 m square takes up
- ☐ know how to apply measurements of my body to real-life measurement
- ☐ work cooperatively with a partner or group.

I enjoyed this task!

☆☆☆☆☆

Revision

1 What combination of strawberries and apples will cost exactly 95c?

Strawberries 7c

Apples 8c

9 strawberries and 8 apples	9 strawberries and 4 apples	8 strawberries and 9 apples	8 strawberries and 4 apples
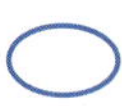			

2 Jallana wants this rug which requires 2850 reward points.

She only has 1768 points.

How many more points does she need?

982	1082	4618	118
			◯

3

$$6\overline{)636} = ?$$

131	101	106	16
◯	◯	◯	◯

4

What fraction is coloured?

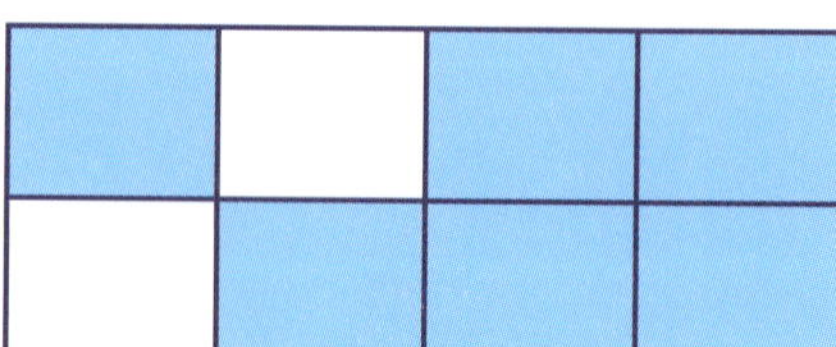

$\frac{1}{4}$	$\frac{1}{2}$	$\frac{3}{4}$	$\frac{2}{8}$
	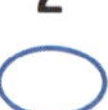		◯

Revision

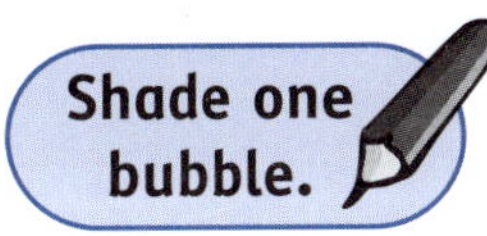

5 Which number sentence matches the story?

A roller-coaster ride costs $12 for one adult and half as much for one child. It costs $36 altogether for Jack and his children to ride the roller-coaster.

How many children does Jack have?

$\$12 \times ? + \frac{1}{2} = \$36$	$\$36 - \$12 \div ? = \$6$	$\$12 + (\$12 \div 2 \times ?) = \$36$	$\$36 \div 2 + \$12 = ?$
○	○	○	○

6

$$\begin{array}{r} 9\,3\,8\,2 \\ \times \quad 4\,9 \\ \hline \\ + \qquad 0 \\ \hline \\ \hline \end{array}$$

459 187	459 718	495 781	495 718
○	○	○	○

7

$$\begin{array}{r} 5\,6 \;\; r4 \\ 7\overline{)3\,9\,{}^{4}6} \end{array}$$

What would be the remainder as a fraction?

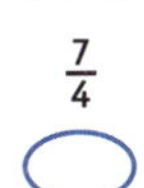
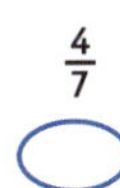

$\frac{7}{4}$	56	7	$\frac{4}{7}$
○	○	○	○

---

8 Which fraction could be placed in the box on the number line?

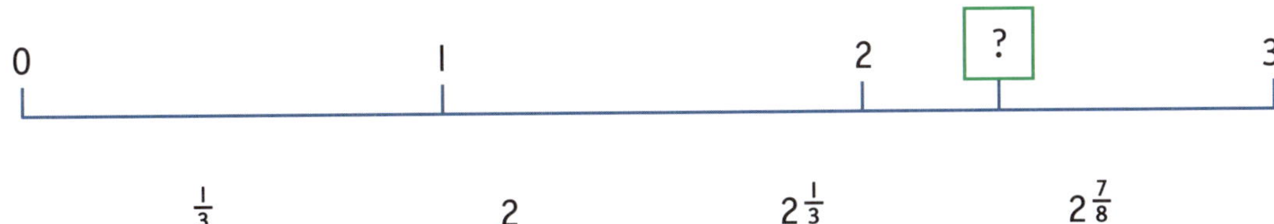

$\frac{1}{3}$	2	$2\frac{1}{3}$	$2\frac{7}{8}$
○	○	○	○

9

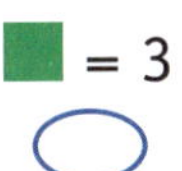

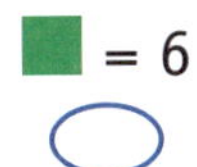

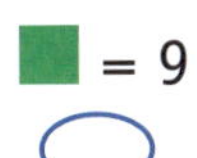

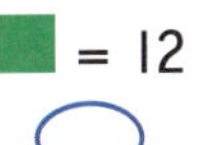

Unit 26 Measuring lengths

Area

1 Measure the dimensions of each shape.
Write the measurements on the shape.

2 Find the area of each coloured shape.

a A = 1 x 2 + 4 x 2
= 2 + 8
= ______ cm²

b A = ______ + ______
= ______
= ______

c A = ______ + ______
= ______
= ______

d A = ______
= ______
= ______

e A = ______
= ______
= ______

3 Find the perimeters.

a P = ______ + ______ + ______ + ______ + ______ + ______
= ______

b P = ______ + ______ + ______ + ______ + ______ + ______
= ______

Unit 26 Perimeter rules

I Find the perimeter for each square.

a
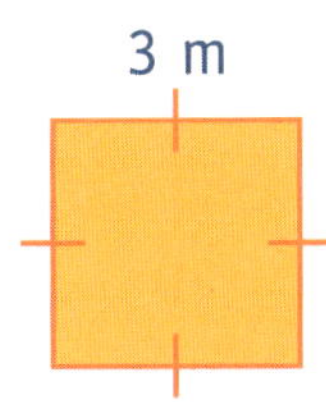

b
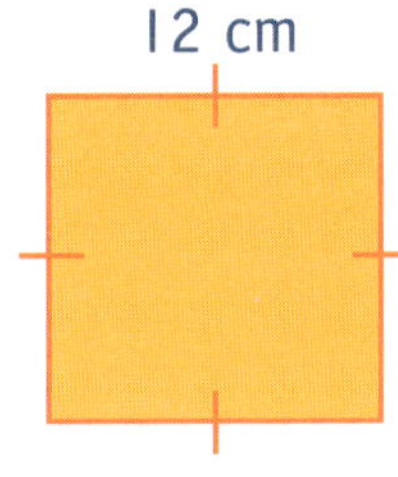

c
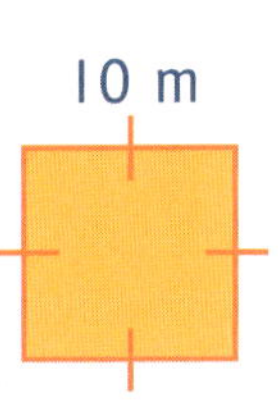

d
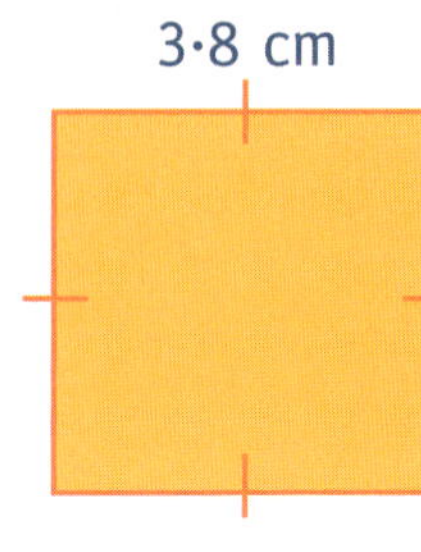

P = P = P = P =

e Write the rule for finding the perimeter of a square.

2 Find the perimeter for each rectangle.

a
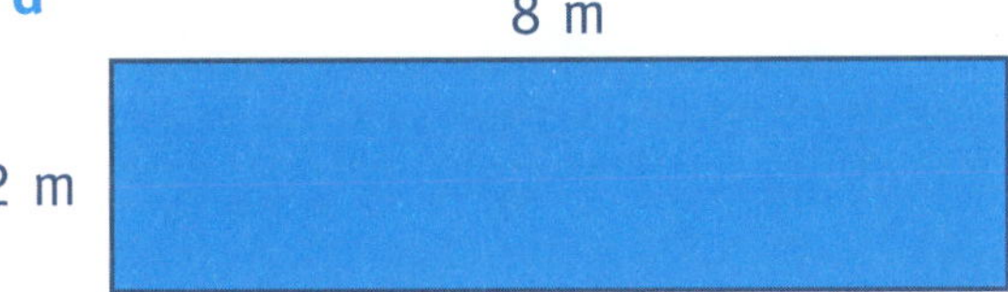

b
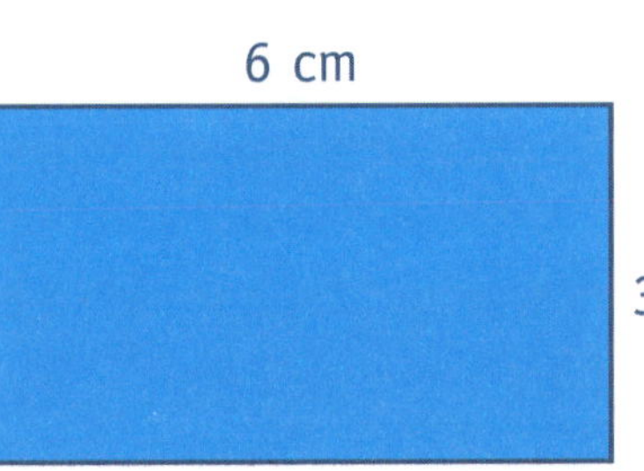

c

d
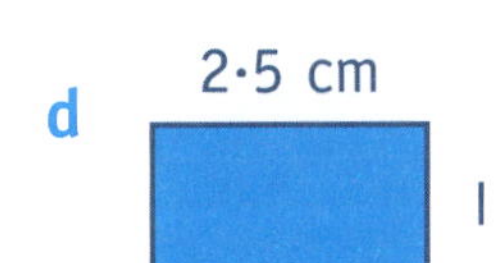

1 cm

a P =  b P =  c P =  d P = 

e Write the rule for finding the perimeter of a rectangle.

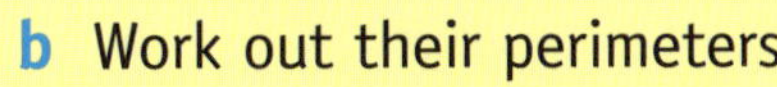

3 a Chen has to fence his swimming pool area. It is 12·36 m long and 7·45 m wide.
How much fencing will he need?

b Chai is putting ribbon around the edge of 2 birthday cards she is making. Each card is 14·6 cm long and 7·8 cm wide.
How much ribbon does she need?

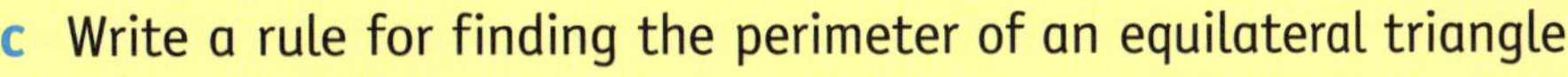

Challenge!

a Draw several equilateral triangles.
b Work out their perimeters.
c Write a rule for finding the perimeter of an equilateral triangle.
d Repeat for isosceles triangles.

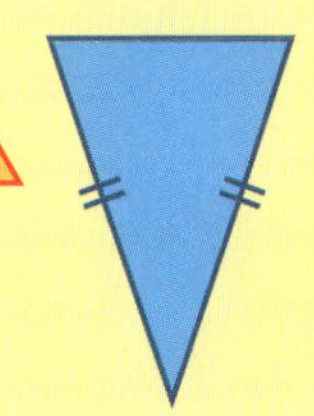

Mastery Checklist

I can:
- ☐ measure shapes to find the area and perimeter
- ☐ find the rule to calculate perimeter for squares and rectangles.

Unit 27 Mass – g, kg and t

Large loads are measured in tonnes.
1000 kg = 1 tonne (t)

1 What items, weighing tonnes, might be carried in each load?

a Plane: 3 tonnes ______________________

b Forklift: 1 tonne ______________________

c Train: 10 tonnes ______________________

d Truck: 6 tonnes ______________________

e Semitrailer: 8 tonnes ______________________

2 Say whether each item is measured in grams (g), kilograms (kg) or tonnes (t).

a pumpkin [ ]

b can of food [ ]

c watermelon [ ]

d van [ ]

e family sedan [ ]

f book [ ]

g suitcase [ ]

h kiwi fruit [ ]

Unit 27 Large masses

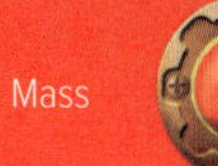

1000 kg = 1 t

1 Use page 134.
Write the mass of each load in kilograms.

a Plane ______ b Train ______ c Forklift ______ d Truck ______

e Semitrailer ______ f Train + Plane ______

g Truck + Semitrailer ______ h Plane + Forklift ______

2 Write the following in tonnes and suggest what each one may be, eg 2000 kg = 2 t pumpkins.

a 9000 kg ______

b 1000 kg ______

c 10 000 kg ______

d 4000 kg ______

e 15 000 kg ______

f 20 000 kg ______

3 Arrange the following in order, lightest to heaviest.

a 5000 kg, 50 t, 50 kg, 5500 kg ______

b 3 t, 300 kg, 30 t, 30 000 kg ______

c 800 kg, 8000 g, 80 000 kg, 8 t ______

d 1000 t, 10 000 kg, 1000 g, 100 kg ______

e 20 000 kg, 200 t, 2000 kg, 20 t ______

4 Write three objects that each of these scales can measure.

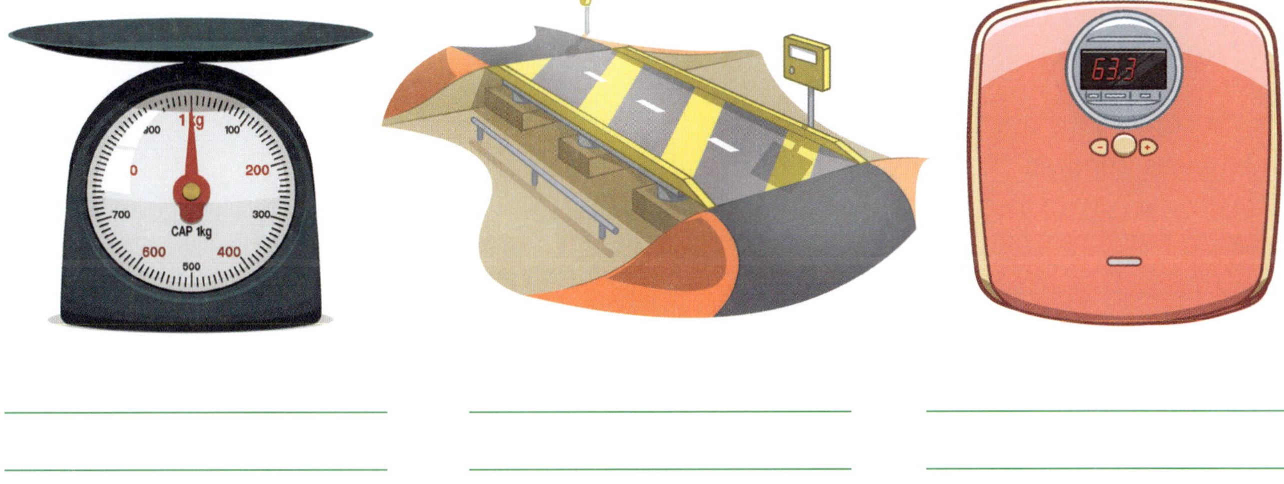

______ ______ ______

______ ______ ______

______ ______ ______

Unit 27 Grams, kilograms and tonnes

1 Which unit of measure is used to record each mass correctly?

a 4·5 ______

b 6 ______

c 1·2 ______

d 60 ______

e 80 ______

f 1·5 ______

g 150 ______

h 0·6 ______

2 Complete the following. Use the words tonnes, kilograms or grams.

a Ned used 5 ______ of gravel in his driveway after the rain.

b Mum asked me to buy a 30 ______ packet of spice for her baking.

c Dad was sure he had lost 3 ______ after two weeks of training for the marathon.

d The truck weighed 4 ______ with a load and 1.5 ______ empty.

e After the floods, there were many ______ of debris in the streets.

3 Write these sentences correctly.

a I have grown 3 kilograms in height since my last birthday.

______

b Our class donated 50 metres of canned food to the Charity Food Drive.

______

______

c My cat leapt 2 grams to catch that cockroach.

______

______

Mastery Checklist I can:
- ☐ choose the best unit to measure mass
- ☐ convert tonnes to kilograms
- ☐ compare and order masses.

Problem solving

Working with mass

estimate mass, measure to check

1 Work in a group of 4. What do you think is the average mass of your school bags?

Estimate the mass of the bag that you think is the closest to the average of your group.

Record it here.

Estimated mass of _______________'s bag:

Estimate the masses of the other bags in the group.

Estimated masses:

Weigh those bags on a bathroom scale.

Masses:

Find the average of the masses.

Total mass +	Average mass ÷	Bag of average mass

Whose bag was closest to the average? _______________

2 Zara's backpack has a mass of 13 kg. She takes out three objects with masses of 1262 g, 2098 g and 1140 g.

What is the mass of her backpack now?

Challenge!

Find out what the following terms mean in the trucking world.

Tare:

Aggregate:

I can solve problems by:

☐ understanding mass and using division ☐ writing algorithms.

A

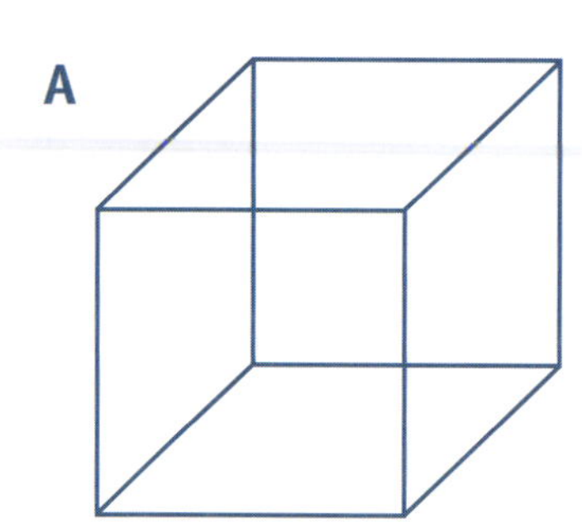

B

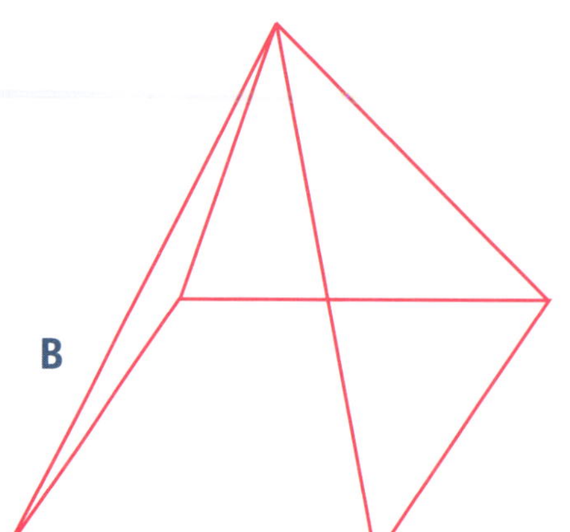

C

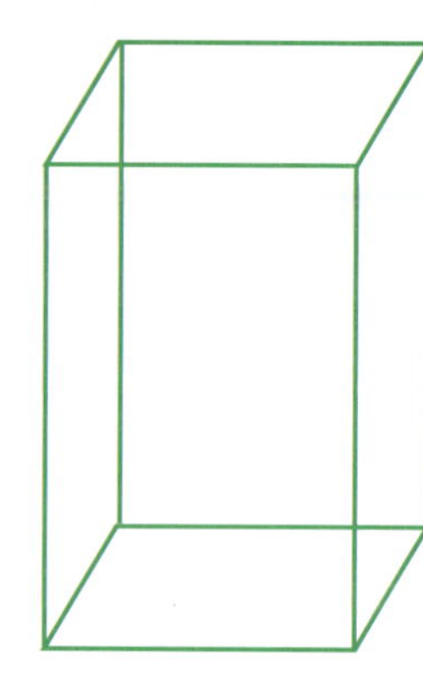

D

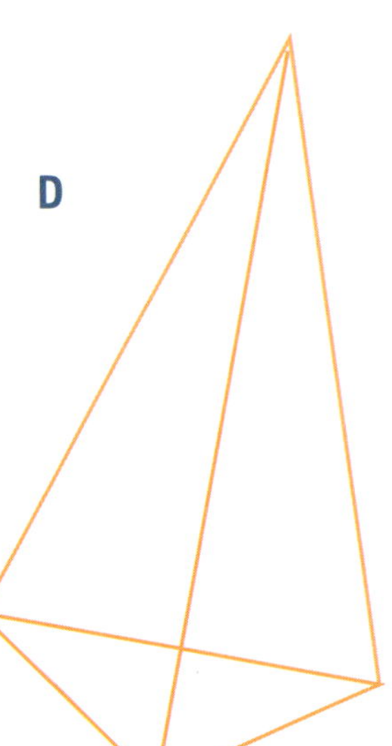

E

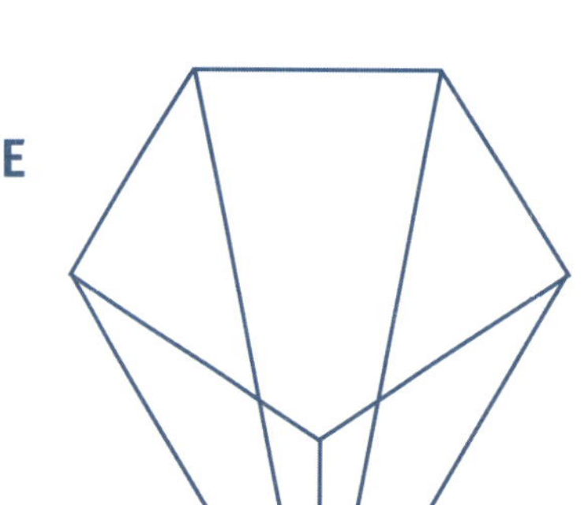

F

G

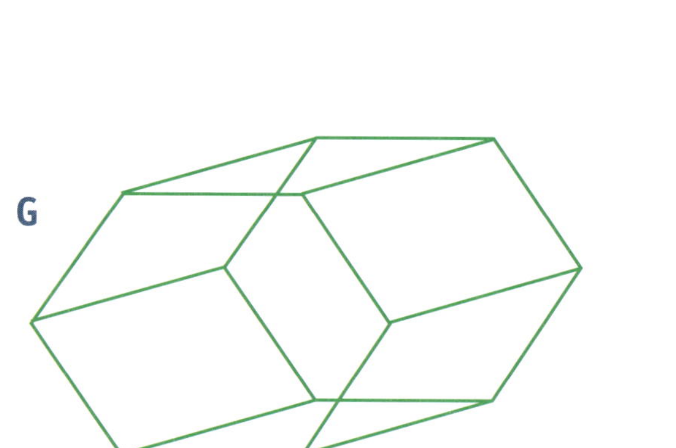

1 Name the 3D objects.

A __________ B __________ C __________

D __________ E __________ F __________

G __________

2 Write the letter of the 3D object that matches each net.

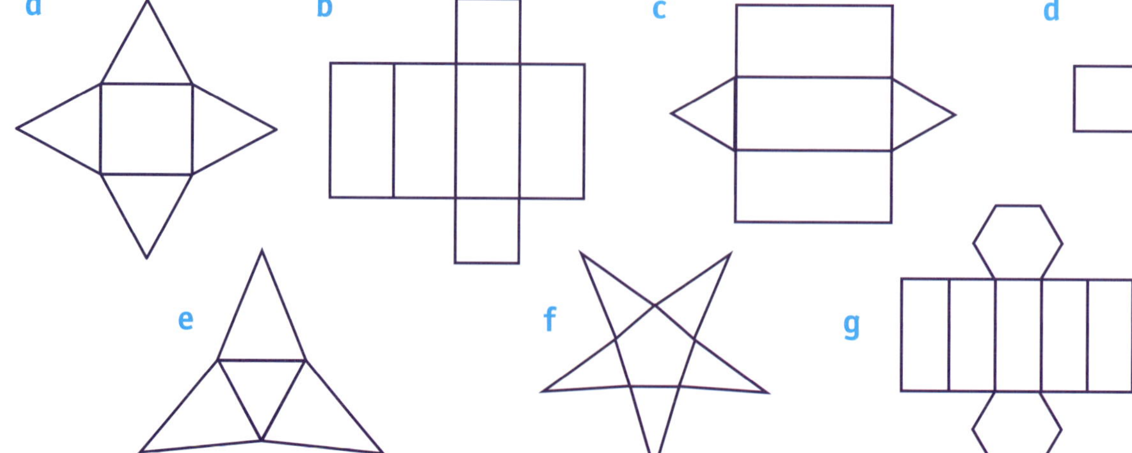

Unit 28 Comparing 3D objects

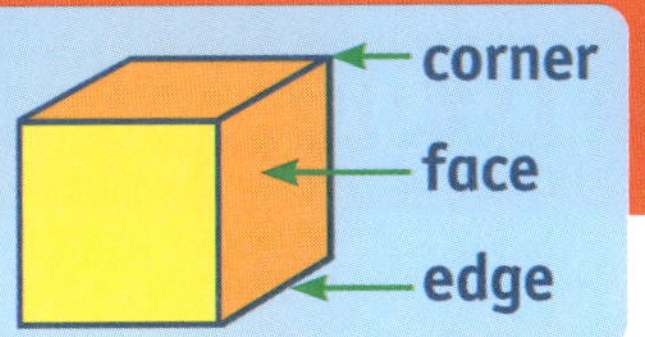

1 Complete the table for each 3D object on page 138.

Name	Number of faces	Number of edges	Number of corners
A			
B			
C			
D			
E			
F			
G			

2 Compare objects **B** and **E** and fill in the table.

Name	Things that are similar	Things that are different

Comment ______________________________

____

3 Compare objects **C** and **F** and fill in the table.

Name	Things that are similar	Things that are different

Comment ______________________________

____

Unit 28 3D objects

A 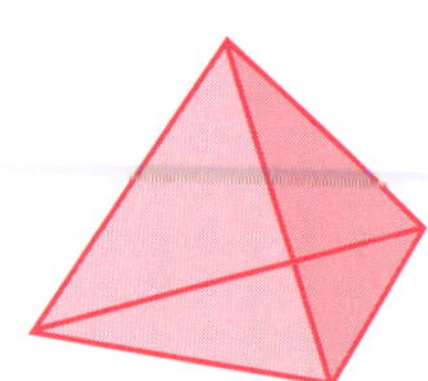

B 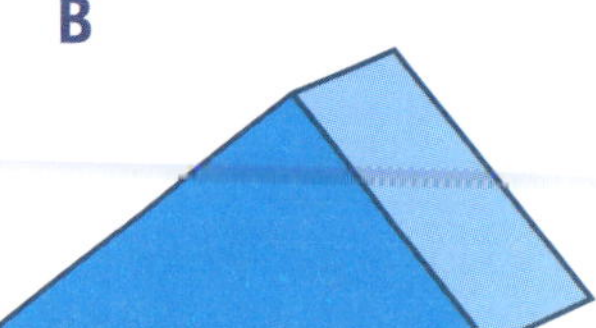

C 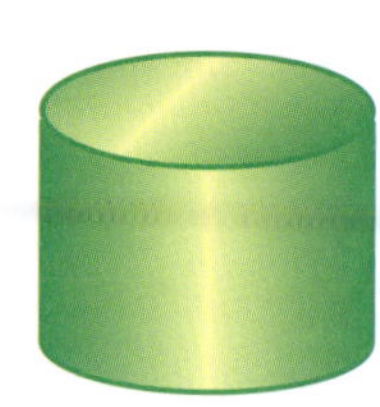

D 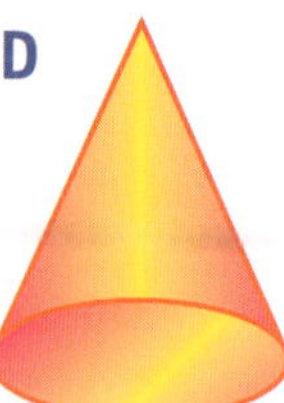

1 Name each solid.

A ______________________ B ______________________

C ______________________ D ______________________

2 Draw a net for each solid. Label each net as **A**, **B**, **C** or **D**.

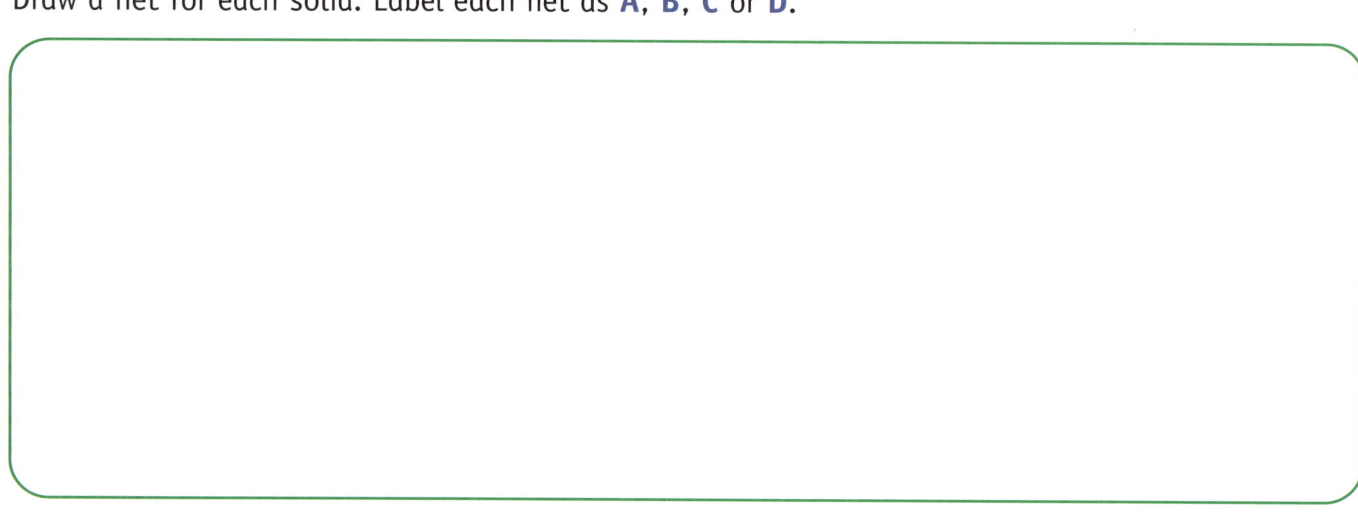

3 Draw pyramids. Join the top vertex to each corner.

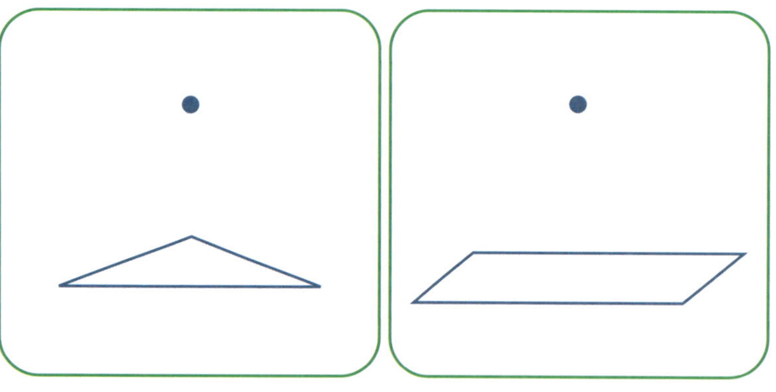

4 Draw the net of this pyramid.

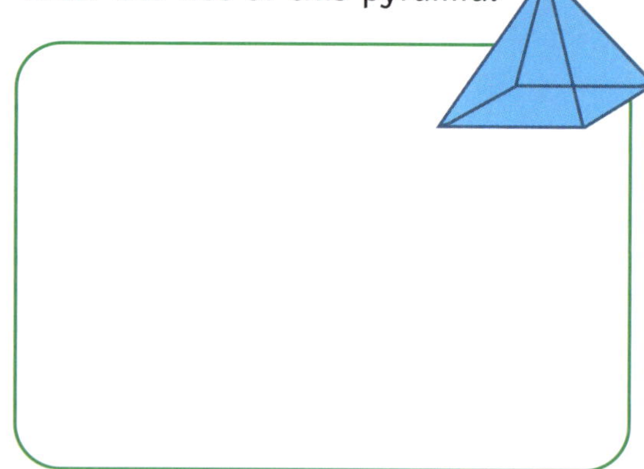

Challenge! Which of these is not the net of an open rectangular prism?

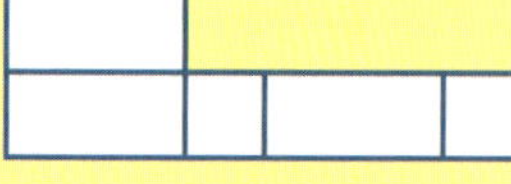

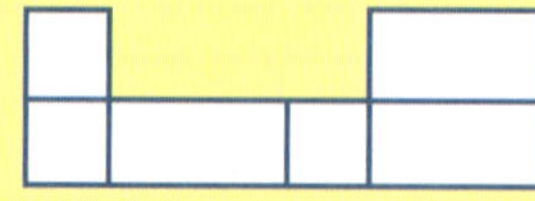

Mastery Checklist I can:

- ☐ connect 3D objects to their nets
- ☐ count faces, edges and corners of 3D objects
- ☐ compare 3D objects to things that are similar and different
- ☐ draw 3D objects and their nets.

AC9M5SP01 Space **MA3-3DS-01** Three-dimensional spatial structure A • 3D objects: Compare, describe and name prisms and pyramids • Connect three-dimensional objects with two-dimensional representations

Unit 29 Types of triangles

1 Write the measurements on the sides of **A**, **B**, **C** and **D**.

A Equilateral triangle

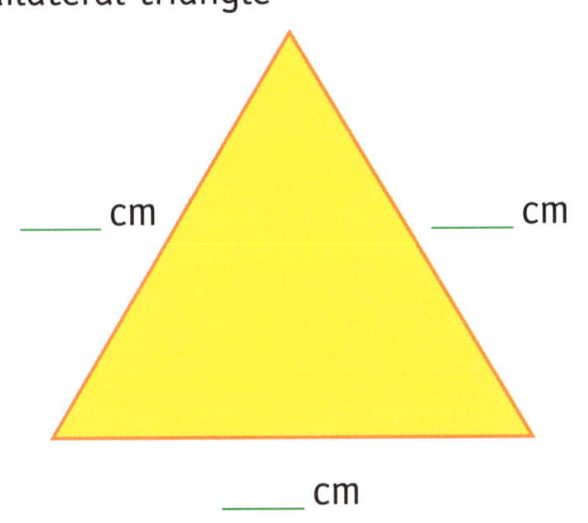

B Isosceles triangle

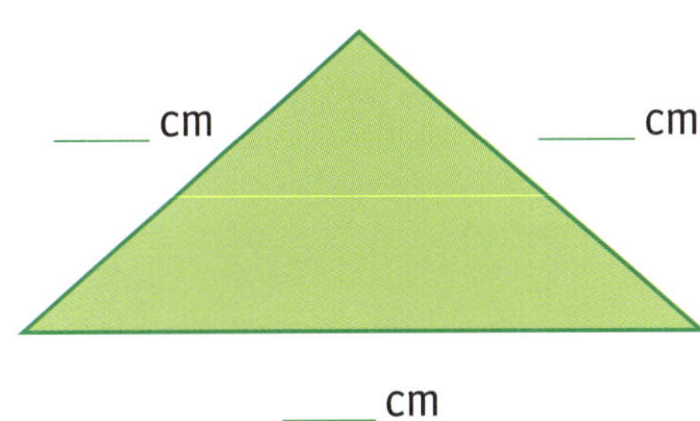

C Scalene triangle

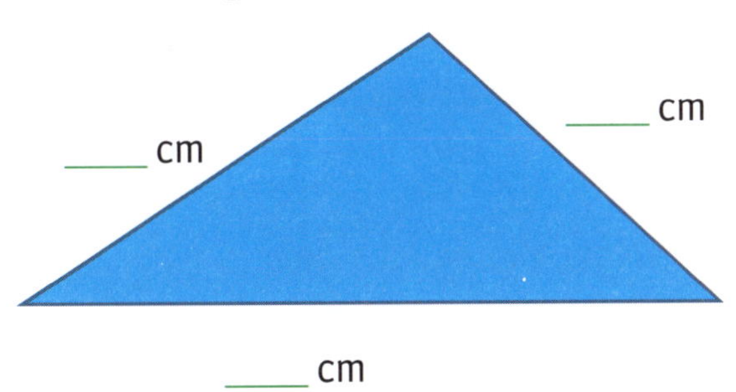

D Right-angled triangle

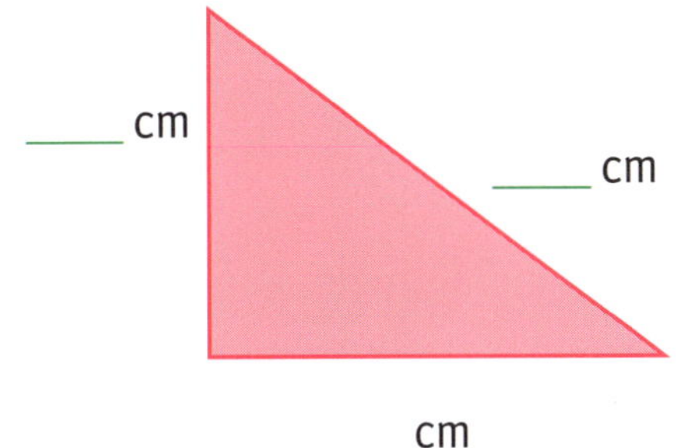

2 Complete these statements.

a An equilateral triangle has ____________ equal sides.

b An isosceles triangle has ____________ equal sides.

c A scalene triangle has ____________ equal sides.

3 A right-angled triangle has __________ right angle.

4 Use your ruler and a pair of compasses to draw:

a an equilateral triangle.

b an isosceles triangle.

Unit 29 Measuring triangles

2D shapes

1 Prove that this is an isosceles triangle by measuring the angles with a protractor.

a It has ____________ sides.

b It has ____________ angles.

c Its two equal angles are ____________ the two equal sides.

d Mark the equal angles.

e Mark the equal sides.

2 Prove that this is an equilateral triangle by measuring the angles with a protractor.

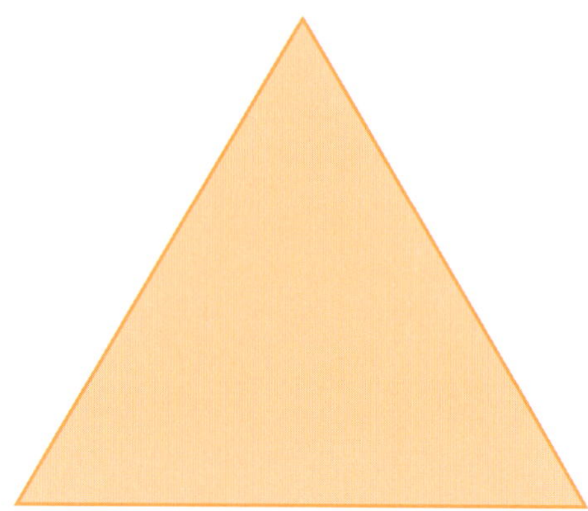

a It has ______ ____________ sides.

b It has ______ ____________ angles.

c Each of the angles are ______ degrees.

d Mark the equal angles.

e Mark the equal sides.

3 Prove that this is a right-angled triangle by measuring the angles with a protractor.

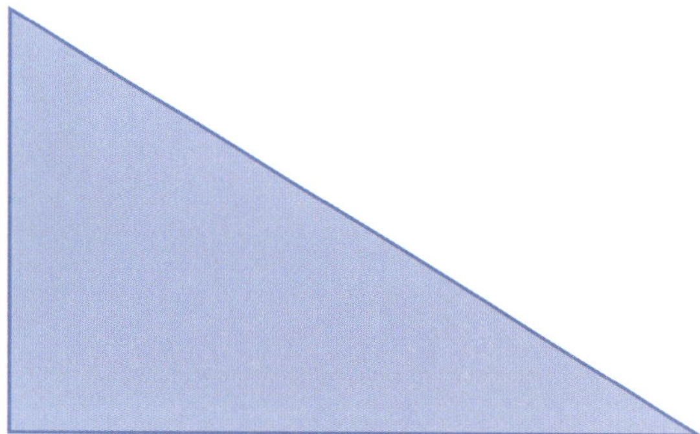

a This triangle contains a ____________ ____________.

b The other two angles measure ______° and ______°. They are ____________ angles.

c If this triangle is reflected and placed against itself, the shape will be a ____________.

4 Prove that this is a scalene triangle by measuring the angles with a protractor.

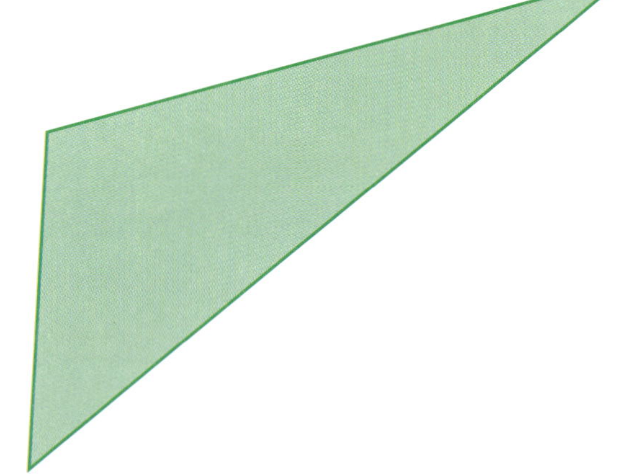

a This triangle has ______ ____________ ____________.

b This triangle has ______ ____________ ____________.

c The angles measure ______°, ______° and ______°.

Unit 29 Symmetry of shapes

1

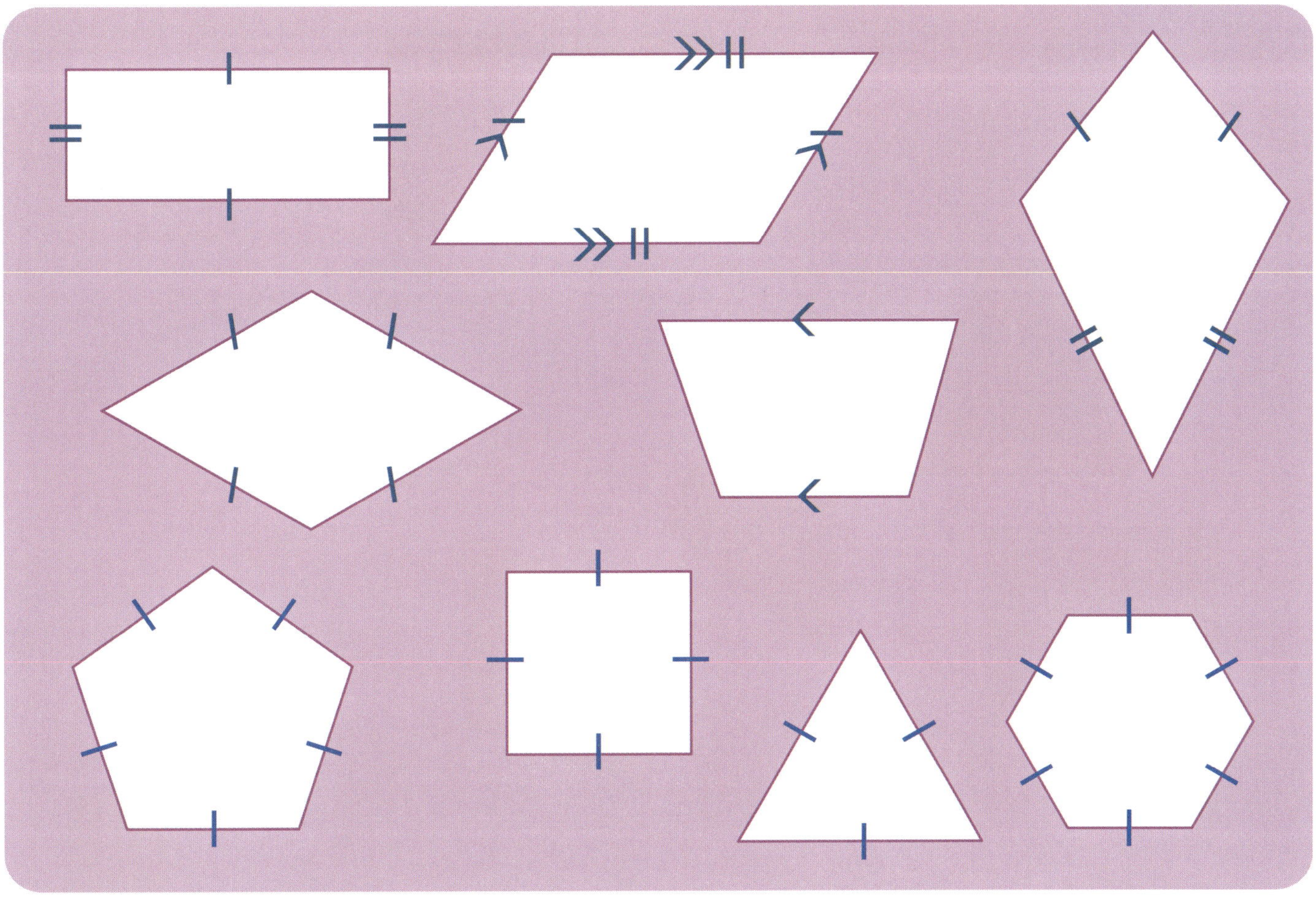

a Draw the axes of symmetry on these shapes.

b Name the shape with no axis of symmetry. ____________________

c Name the shapes with one axis of symmetry. ____________________

d Name the shapes with two axes of symmetry. ____________________

e True or false? The axes of symmetry are also diagonals on all quadrilaterals. ____________

2 Draw three different composite shapes that each have one line of symmetry.

A composite shape is made up of 2 or more 2D shapes joined together:

Challenge! Draw all the special quadrilaterals.
Label them clearly and write all their properties.

Unit 29 Special quadrilaterals

A B C D E F G H I J K L M N O P

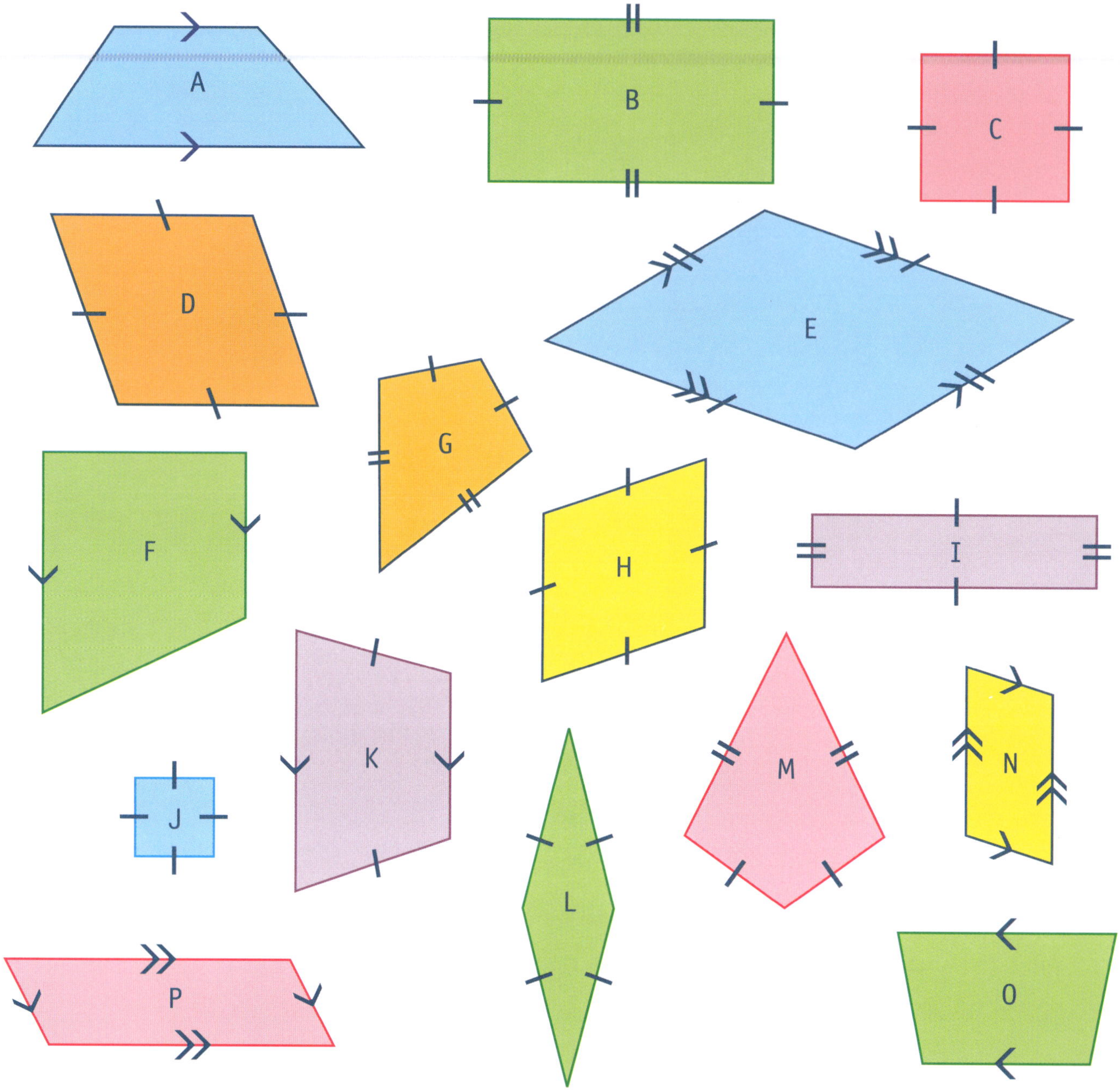

Place each quadrilateral in the correct column using its letter.

Square	Rectangle	Rhombus	Kite	Parallelogram	Trapezium

Mastery Checklist I can:
- ☐ identify different types of triangles
- ☐ identify symmetry in polygons
- ☐ identify different types of quadrilaterals.

Unit 30 Angle sum

Angles

1 a Measure each angle in the triangle.

b Add the angles. ________

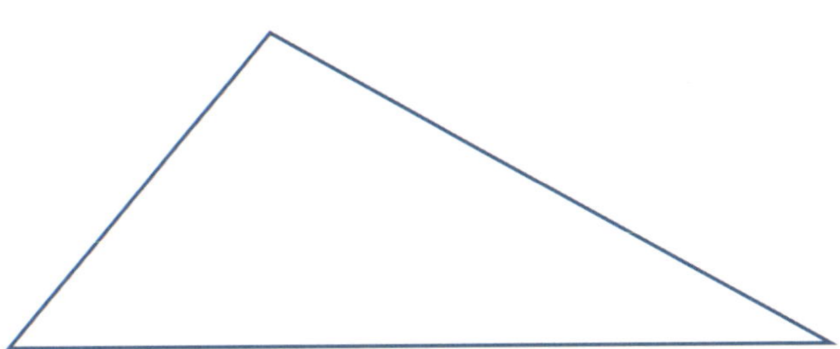

2 a Measure each angle.

b Add the angles. ________

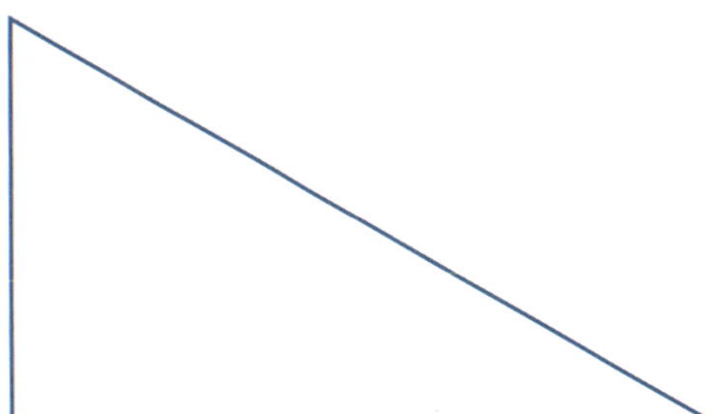

3 Complete. The sum of the angles in a triangle is ________ .

4 Find the missing angles.

a

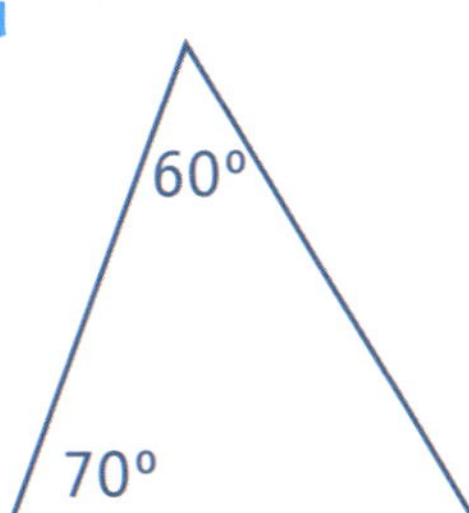

b

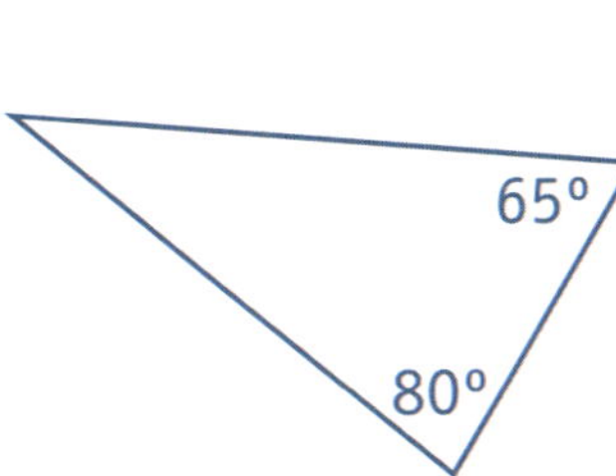

c

10°

130°

d

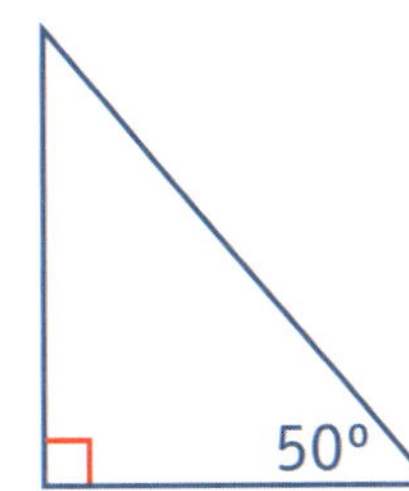

5 Measure each angle in both quadrilaterals.
Add the angles for each quadrilateral.

a

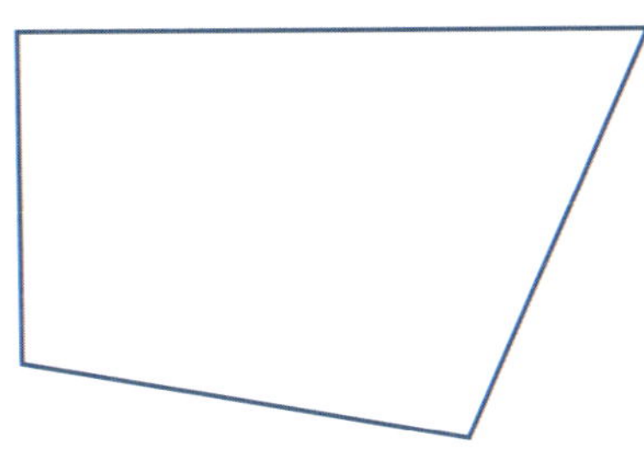

Sum of angles ________

b

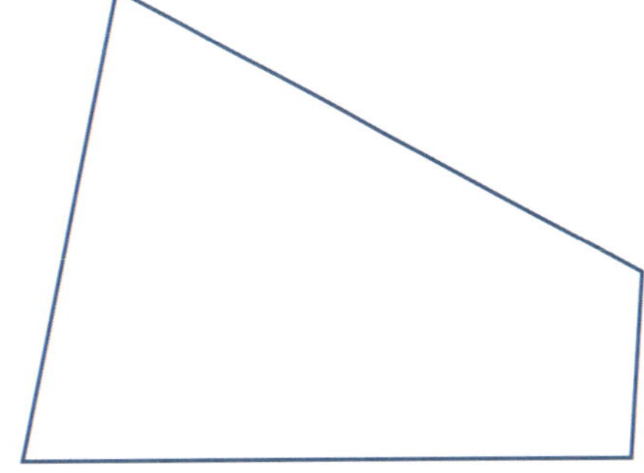

Sum of angles ________

c Complete. The sum of the angles in a quadrilateral is ________ .

Draw a diagram

1 On plain paper draw a large pentagon and a hexagon and measure their angles.

2 Find the sum of their angles.

3 What is the size of one angle in a regular pentagon and a regular hexagon?

Unit 30 Angles

Complementary angles add to 90°.

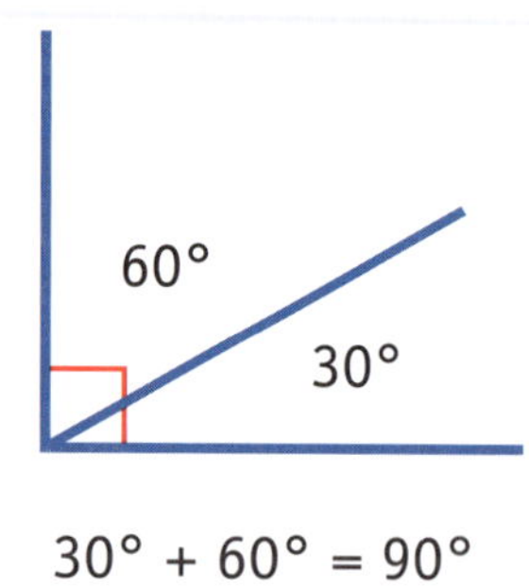

$30° + 60° = 90°$

Supplementary angles add to 180°.

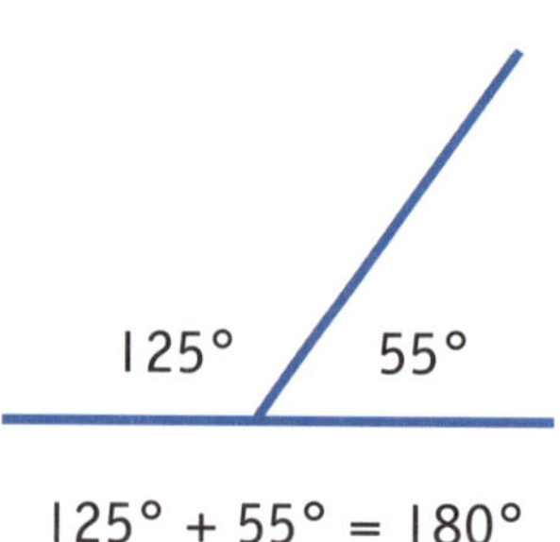

$125° + 55° = 180°$

Revolutions add to 360°.

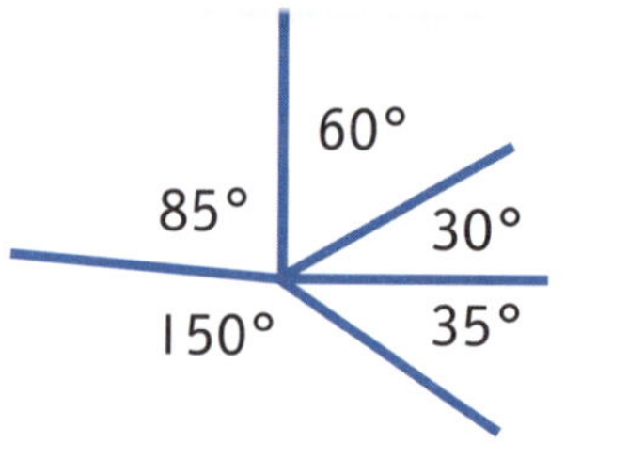

$60° + 30° + 35° + 150° + 85° = 360°$

1 Write the missing values for the complementary angles.

a

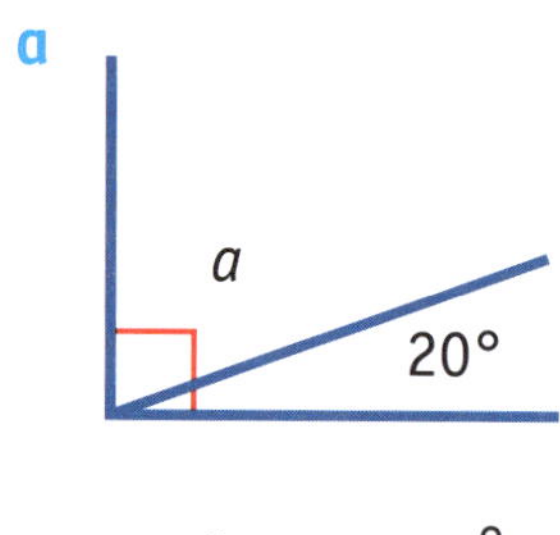

a = ______°

b

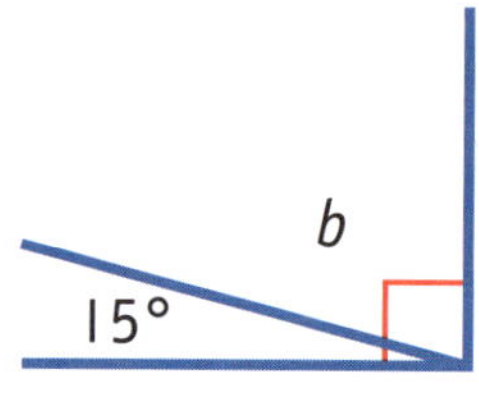

b = ______°

c

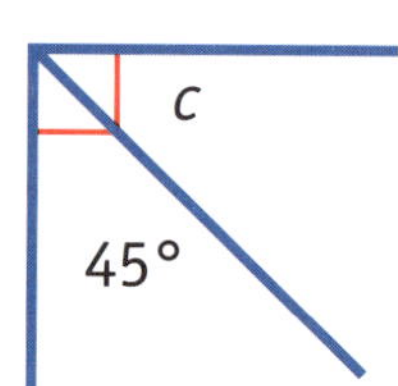

c = ______°

d

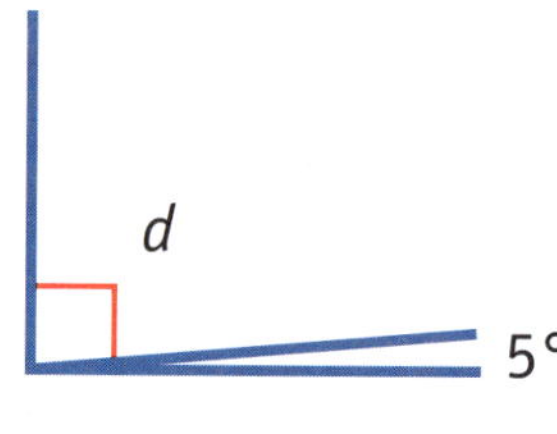

d = ______°

2 Write the missing values for the supplementary angles.

a

e
143°

e = ______°

b

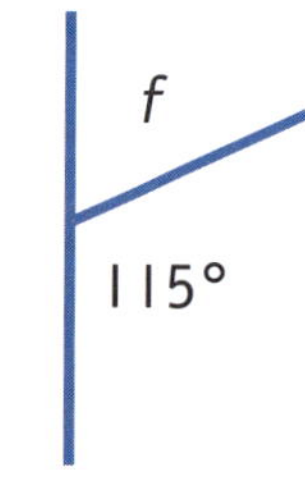

f = ______°

c

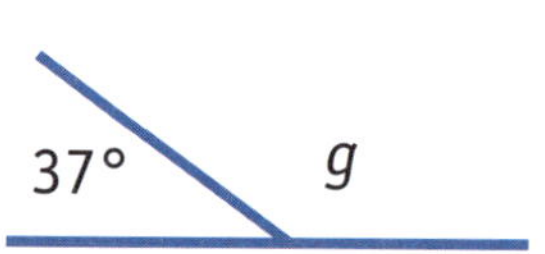

g = ______°

d

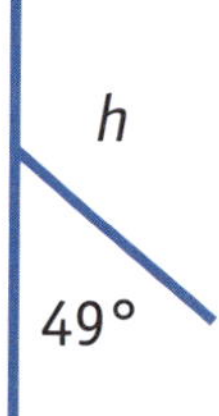

h = ______°

3 Write the missing values for the revolutions.

a

60°
120°
i
110°

i = ______°

b

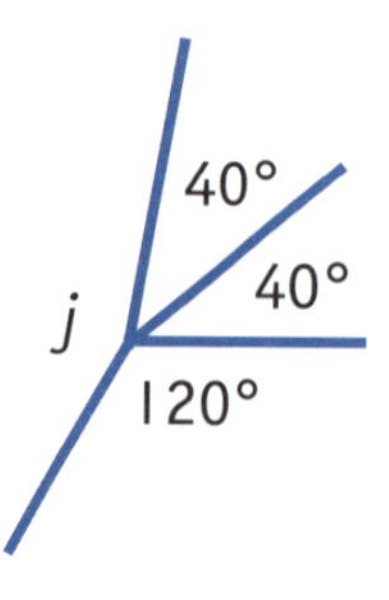

j = ______°

c

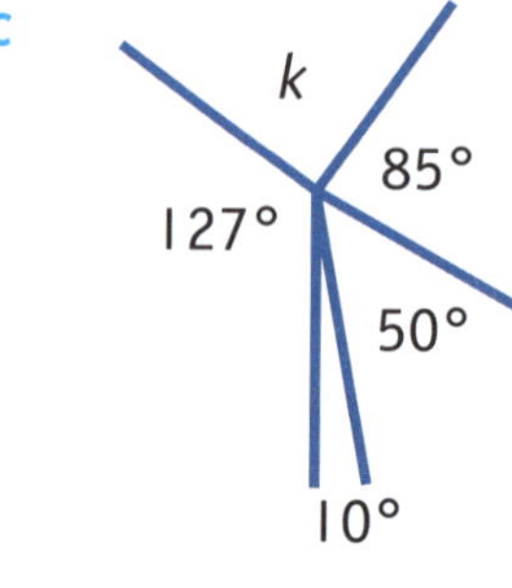

k = ______°

d

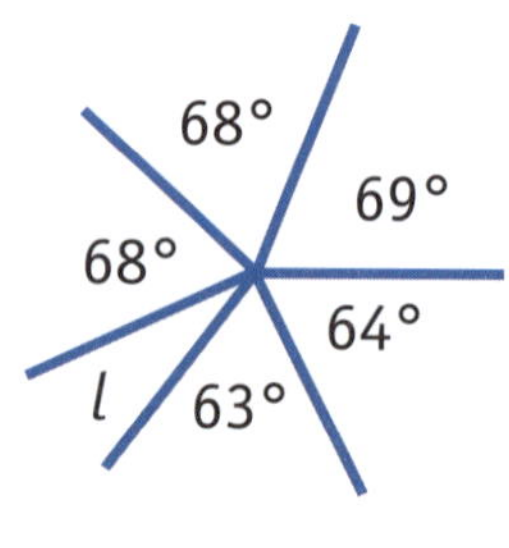

l = ______°

AC9M5M04 Measurement **MA3-GM-03** Geometric measure B • Angles: Investigate angles on a straight line and angles at a point
• Angles: Investigate the relationships formed by the intersection of straight lines

Unit 30 Angle problems

Answer these angle problems. Draw a diagram to help you work out each one.

1 In a right-angled triangle, one angle is 30°.

What are the other two angles?

____

2 Two angles are complementary and exactly the same size. What size is each angle?

____

3 Two angles are supplementary and exactly the same size. What size is each angle?

____

4 Angle a = 60°, b = 120°, c = 90° and d = 30°. Which two angles add to give 120°?

____

5 Jai is measuring angles that form a revolution. The angles are 25°, 45°, 62°, 115° and 103°.

What is the size of the last angle?

____

Is it acute or obtuse?

____

6 Angle P is half the size of angle Q. Angle Q is 70°. What size is angle P?

____

Mastery Checklist I can:

- ☐ identify complementary and supplementary angles
- ☐ identify revolutions
- ☐ calculate missing values
- ☐ add the angles in a triangle
- ☐ add the angles in a quadrilateral.

Unit 31 Line graphs

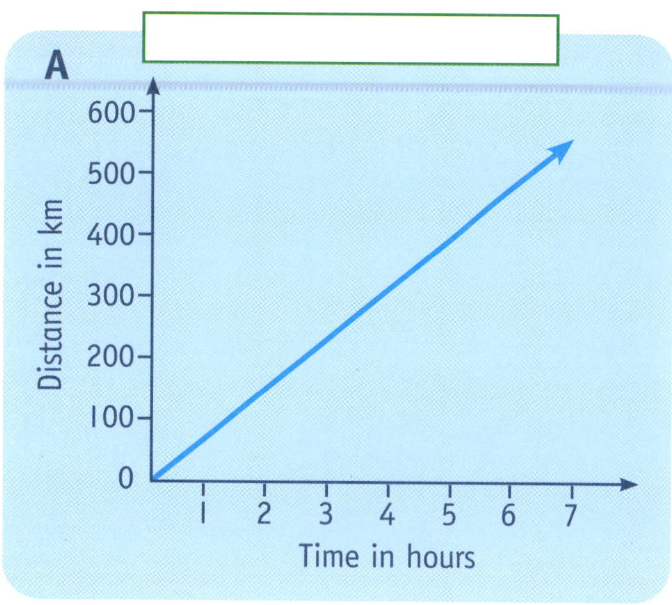

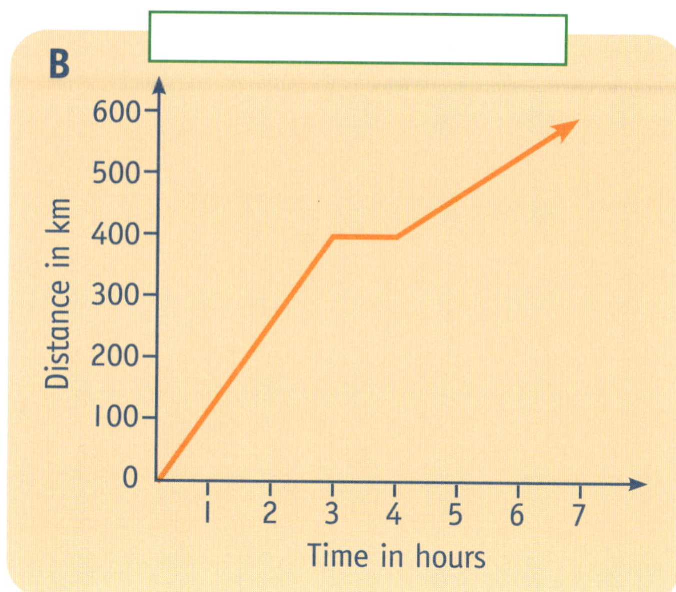

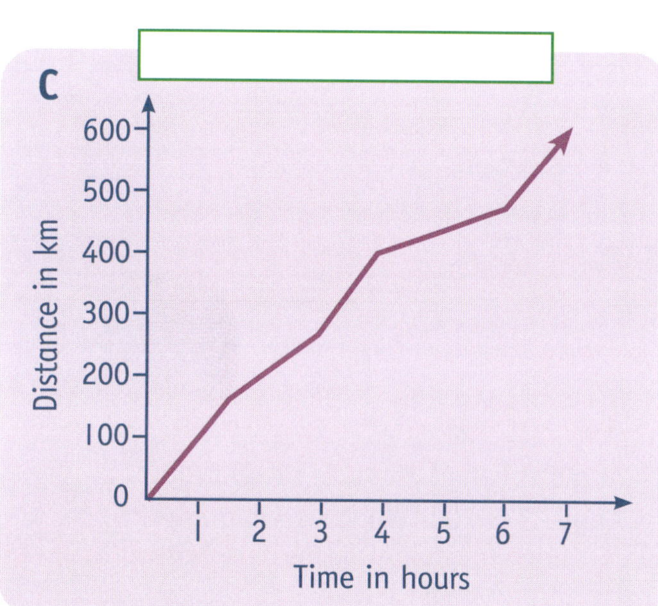

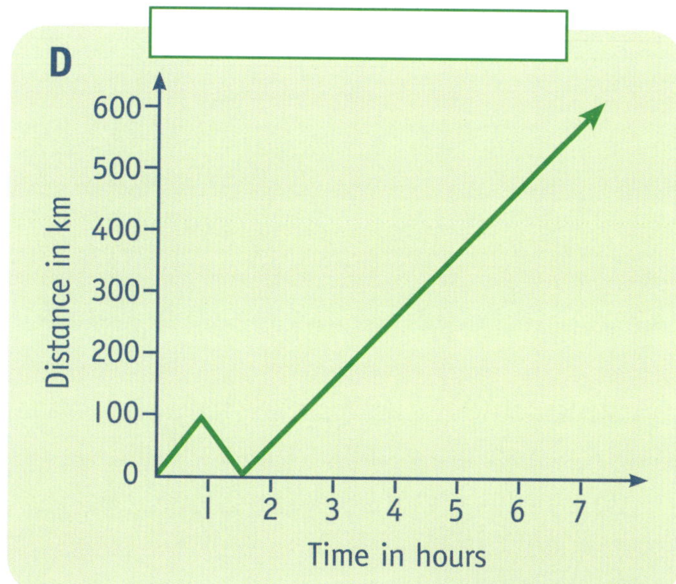

These are graphs about a holiday trip.

1 Read these stories. Which graph best tells each story?

  a We hadn't gone far when we realised we'd left the dog behind. We had to go back and get him. ____

  b We were slow sometimes, especially when we were stuck behind big trucks. But Dad worked out that our average speed was 80 km/h. ____

  c We wanted to get there quickly so Dad drove straight through at a steady speed. ____

  d Dad and Jo shared the driving. We had to go more slowly when Jo drove after lunch, as she is only a new driver. ____

2 Write a title for each graph.

Unit 31 Reading a line graph

The swimming pool manager graphed the temperature of the pool water on a cool afternoon. He wanted to find out if the heating system was working properly.

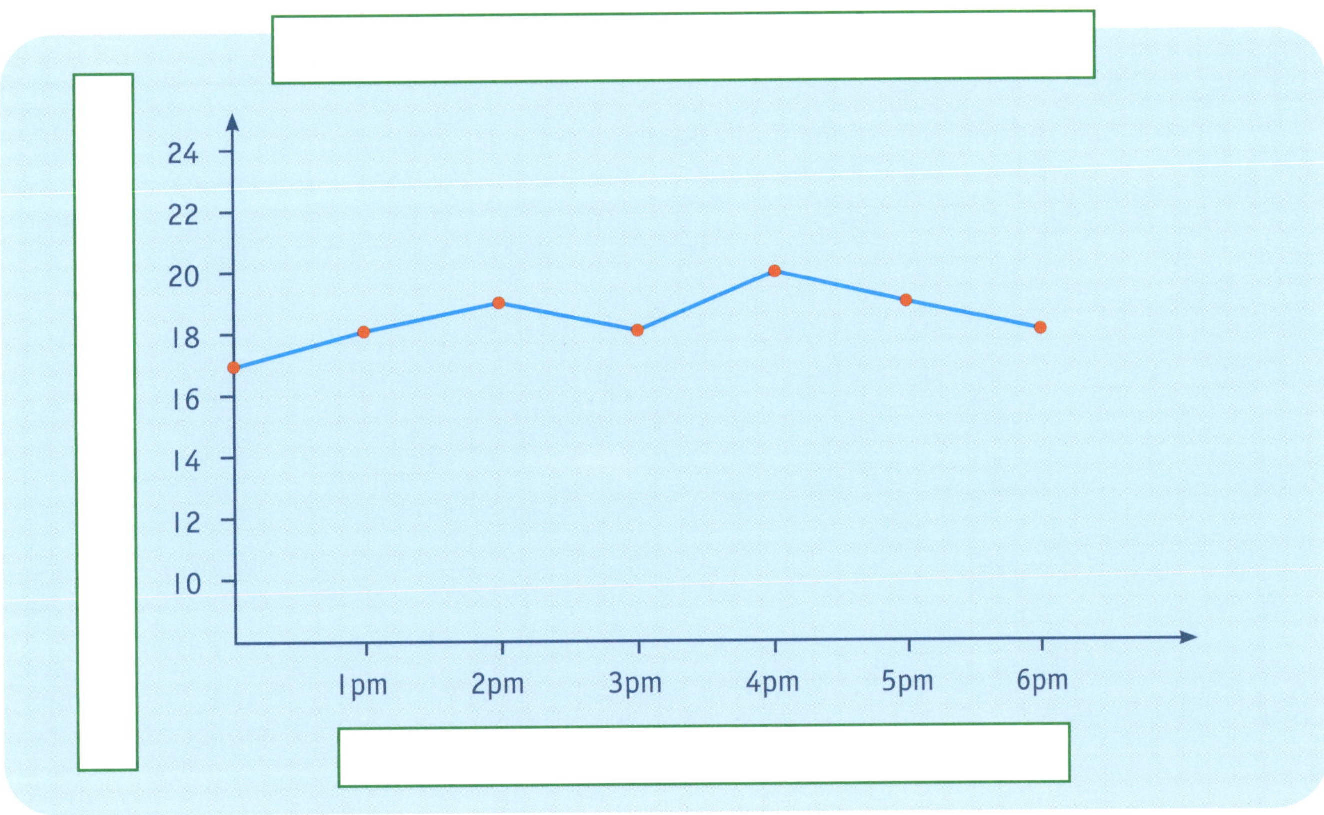

1 a Give the graph a title.

b Write the labels for both axes.

2 What is the difference between the highest temperature and the lowest temperature? ______

3 When did these extremes occur? ______

4 Between what hours was the greatest increase in temperature? ______

5 What might have caused the change between 5 pm and 6 pm? ______

6 What was the temperature at 1:30 pm? ______

7 Tick the questions that this graph can answer.

- ☐ What is the latest time the temperature was taken?
- ☐ How many people were in the pool at 12:00?
- ☐ At what time was the first temperature taken?
- ☐ When did the manager go home?
- ☐ Was the temperature too hot?
- ☐ Is the heating system controlling the heat evenly for the day?

Unit 31 Drawing a line graph

On Saturday Dan recorded the temperature every hour from 10 am to 10 pm.

Time	10 am	11 am	noon	1 pm	2 pm	3 pm	4 pm	5 pm	6 pm	7 pm	8 pm	9 pm	10 pm
Temperature	17 °C	18 °C	20 °C	21 °C	19 °C	18 °C	16 °C	16 °C	14 °C	13 °C	13 °C	12 °C	10 °C

1 Draw a line graph to show this information. Be accurate.

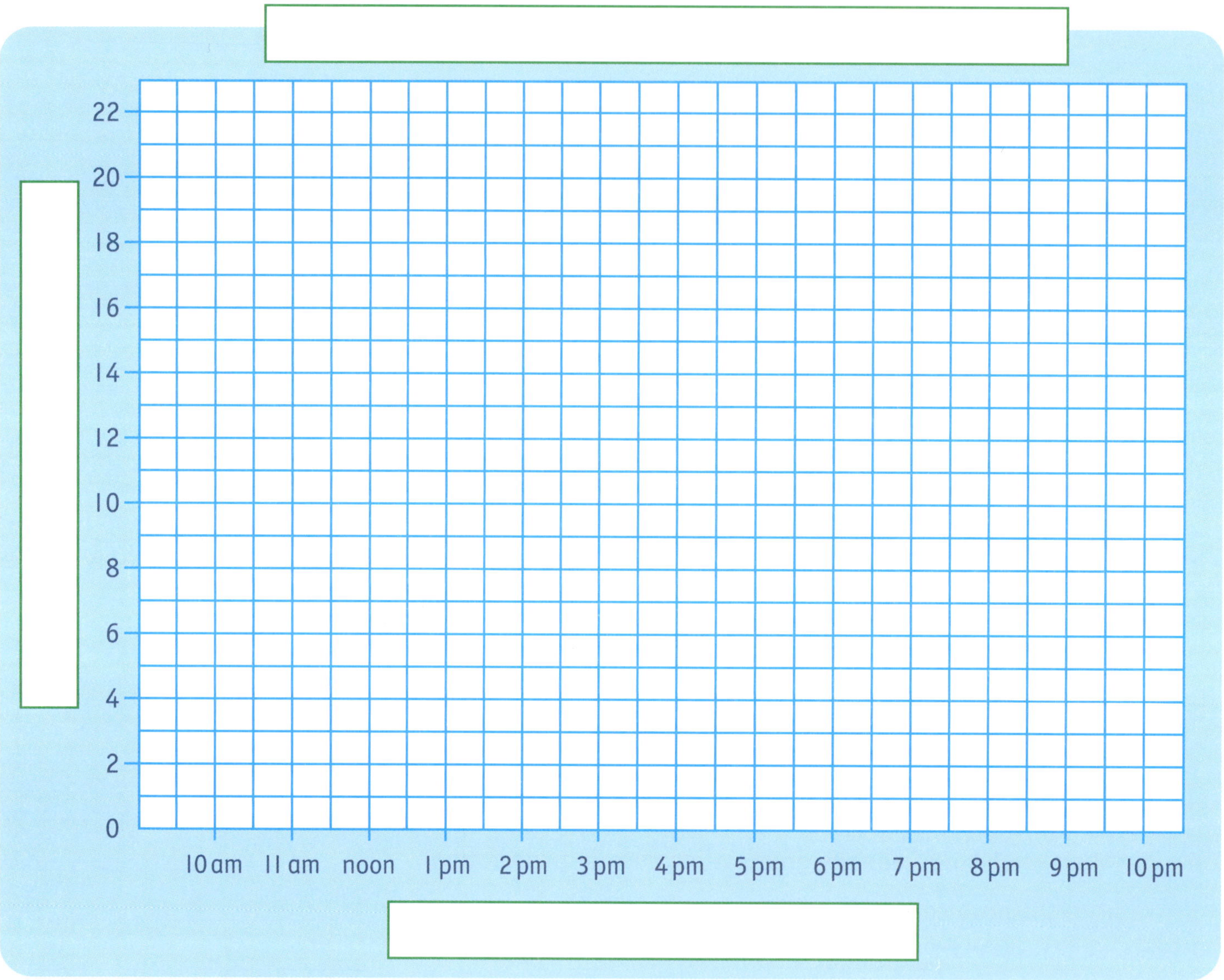

22
20
18
16
14
12
10
8
6
4
2
0

10 am 11 am noon 1 pm 2 pm 3 pm 4 pm 5 pm 6 pm 7 pm 8 pm 9 pm 10 pm

2 Write a title for the graph.

3 Label both axes.

4 What is the difference between the highest and lowest temperature? __________

Challenge!

Look online to find examples of line graphs. Print them and paste them onto cardboard. Give each a title. Make a class display.

Unit 31 Reading costs from line graphs

1 Use this line graph to find the cost of oil.

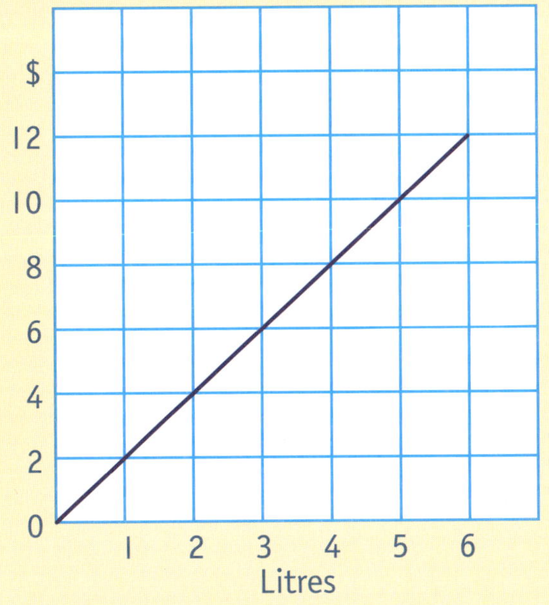

What is the cost of:

a 3 litres ______ b 2·5 litres? ______

c 4·5 litres? ______ d 0·5 litres? ______

2 Use this line graph to find the cost of rope.

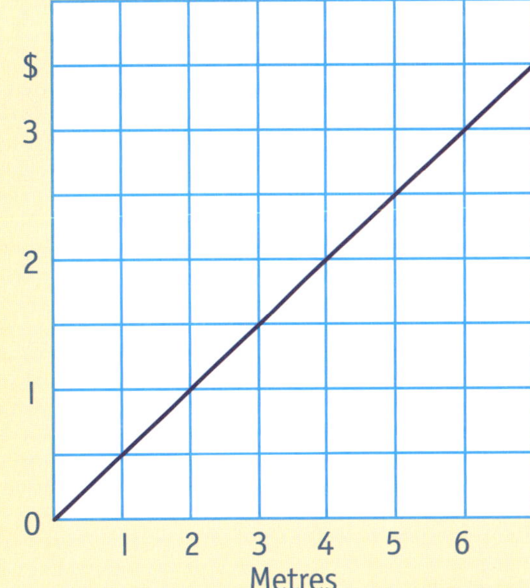

What is the cost of:

a 1 metre? ______ b 6 metres? ______

c 3 metres? ______ d 2·5 metres? ______

3 a Complete the graph which will show the cost of potatoes from 0 to 10 kg at $1.50 per kg.

b What is the cost of 5·5 kg? ______________

Mastery Checklist I can:

- ☐ match graphs to real-world events
- ☐ interpret a line graph
- ☐ draw a line graph
- ☐ answer questions about a line graph.

Revision Term 3

1 

p 107

What is the total cost of:

a shoes and a watch? ________

b microwave and watch? ________

c microwave and shoes? ________

d shoes, microwave and watch? ________

2 Estimate first then add. p 108

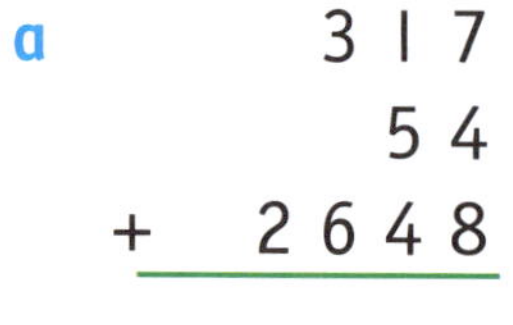
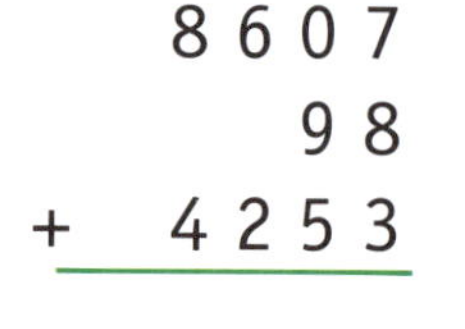

	a	b
	317	8607
	54	98
+	2648	4253
	______	______

Est. ________ Est. ________

3 Cost of: p 109

a 20 balls at 16c each. ________

b 30 sweets at 37c each. ________

c 50 cakes at 89c each. ________

4 p 111

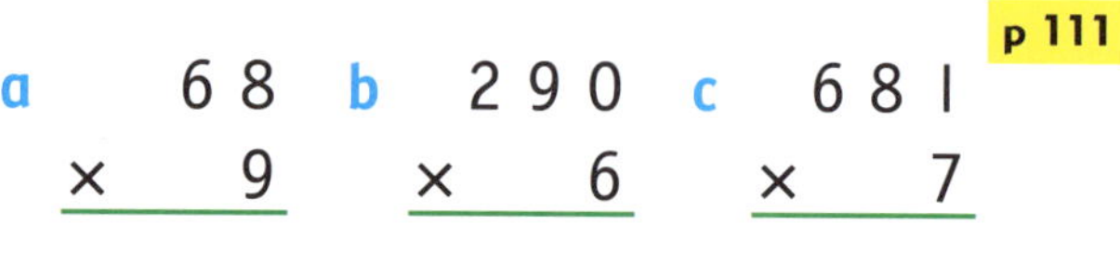

	a	b	c
	68	290	681
×	9	6	7
	______	______	______

5 p 115

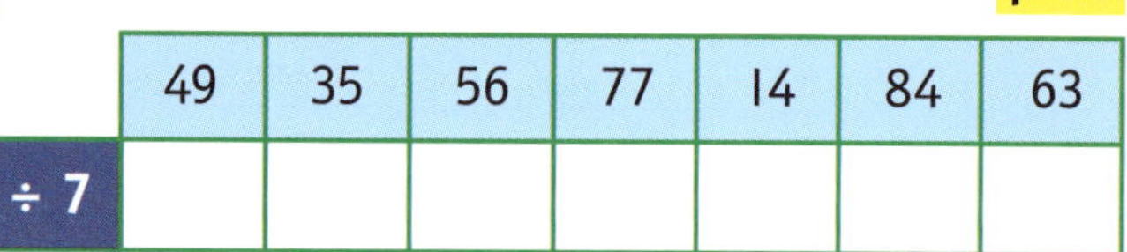

	49	35	56	77	14	84	63
÷ 7							

6 p 116

a $7\overline{)426}$

b $4\overline{)909}$

p 118

7 8 slices can be cut from each cake. If 194 slices are needed, how many cakes must be bought?

8 Name the coloured fraction. p 119

a 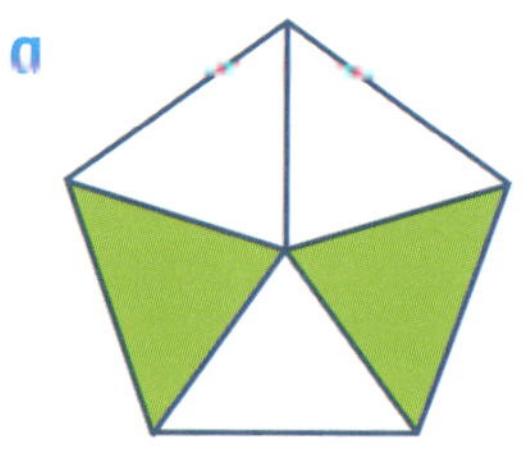

b 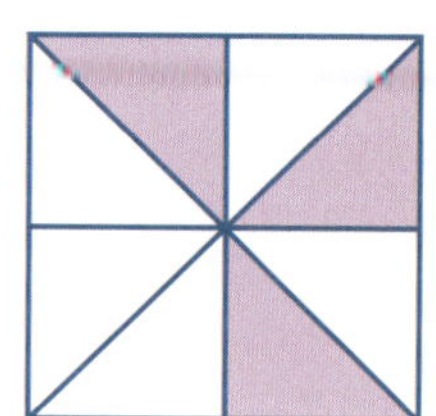

________ ________

9 Circle the equivalent fractions. p 120

a $\frac{2}{3}$, $\frac{4}{6}$, $\frac{3}{4}$ b $\frac{1}{4}$, $\frac{4}{8}$, $\frac{2}{4}$

10 Colour: p 121

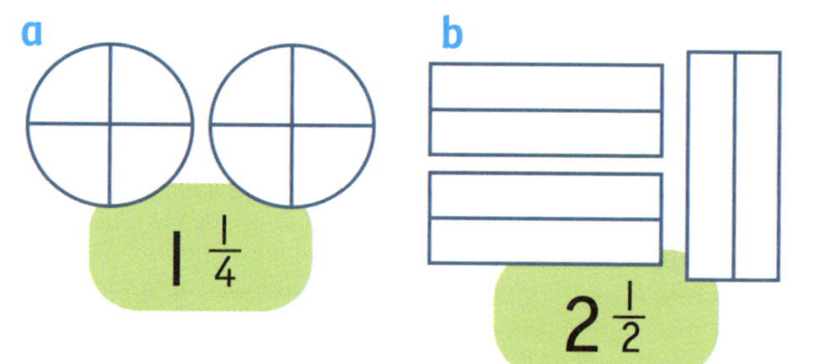

11 Write the missing values. p 125

a $22 \times 5 = \_\_ \times 10$ b $12 \times \_\_ = 2 \times 60$

c $75 \div 5 = \_\_ \times 3$ d $144 \div 12 = 24 \div \_\_$

12 p 126

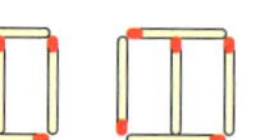
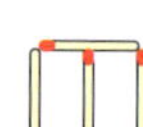
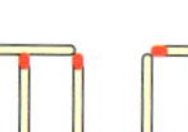

Number of shapes	2	3	4	5	10
Number of sticks					

a Fill in the table for the pattern.

b Write the pattern in words.

____

____

____

____

13 Find the perimeter and area. p 132

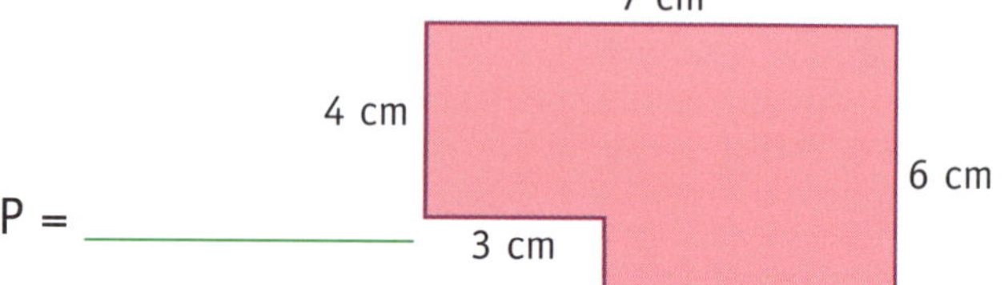

P = ________

A = ________

14 What measurement would you use to measure: p 134

a the mass of a mouse? ________

b the mass of a truck? ________

c the mass of a person? ________

d the mass of a phone? ________

e the mass of an elephant? ________

15 Change to grams. p 136

a 7 kg ________ b $10\frac{1}{2}$ kg ________

16 Use g or kg. p 136

a The mass of a dog is 15 _____.

b The mass of a box is 1 _____.

c The mass of a pencil is 10 _____.

d The mass of 1 L of water is 1 _____.

17 Describe the sides and angles in each type of triangle. p 141

a Equilateral triangle ________________

____

b Isosceles triangle ________________

____

c Scalene triangle ________________

____

18 Measure these angles. p 145

a _____ b _____ c _____

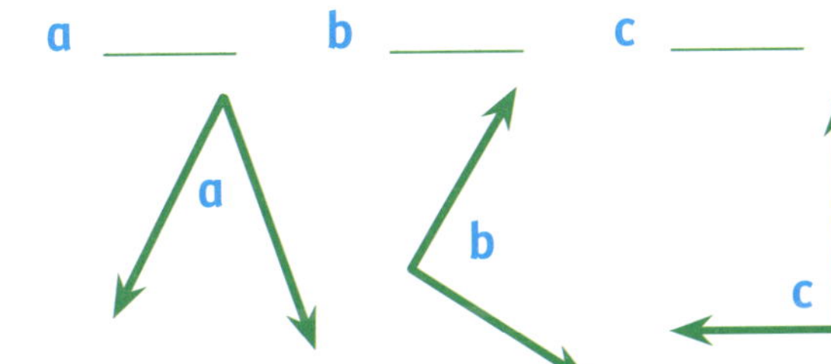

19 Find a°. p 145

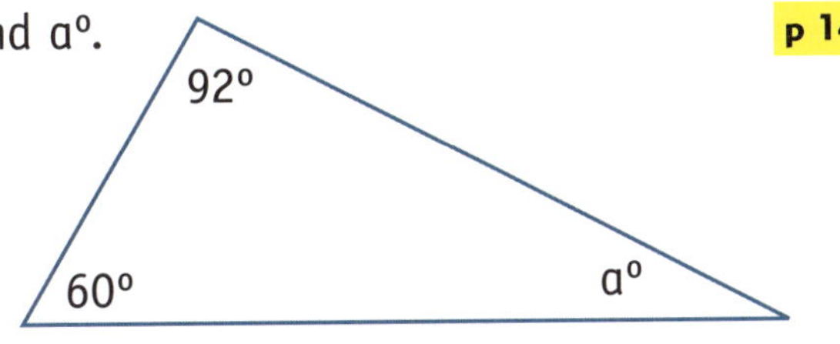

This triangle is a ________________ triangle.

20 a Draw complementary angles. Make one angle 30°. p 146

b Draw supplementary angles. Make one angle 100°.

21 A walker keeps this record of the distance he has walked from his starting point on a long walk. p 150

Time	8 am	9 am	10 am	11 am	12 pm	1 pm	2 pm
km	0	4	8	11	12	15	17

Draw a line graph to show this information.

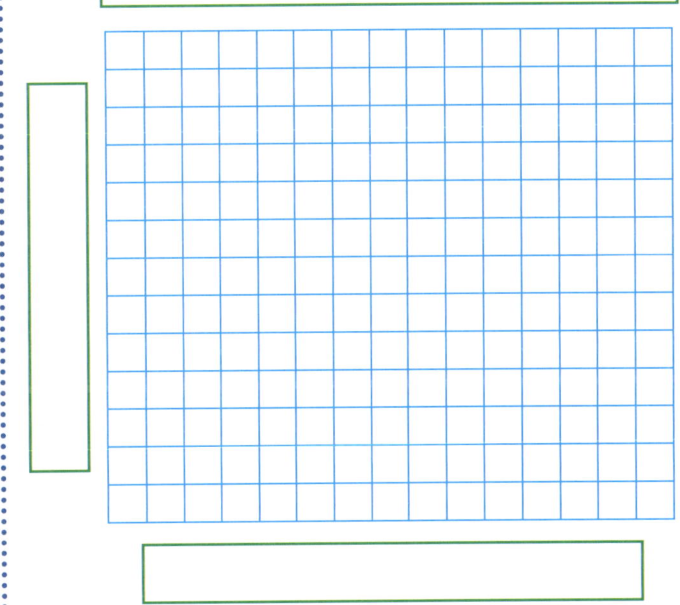

Unit 32 Matching quotients

The quotient is the answer when you divide.
Draw lines to link the three which belong together.
Colour to match.

Hint: start by estimating.

	NUMBER		DIVIDED BY		QUOTIENT
1	723	A	6	a	$73\frac{1}{2}$
2	815	B	3	b	144 r 3
3	294	C	5	c	$73\frac{1}{4}$
4	642	D	7	d	135 r 5
5	847	E	4	e	100 r 5
6	586	F	7	f	214
7	705	G	4	g	76
8	684	H	8	h	121
9	541	I	9	i	$144\frac{1}{2}$
10	590	J	9	j	121 r 1
11	867	K	6	k	$135\frac{1}{4}$
12	1090	L	8	l	$73\frac{3}{4}$

AC9M5N07 Number **MA3-MR-01** Multiplicative relations A • Represent and solve division problems with whole number remainders
• Select and apply strategies to divide a number with 3 or more digits by a one-digit divisor

Unit 32 Inverse checking

Checking

Division and multiplication are inverse operations. Check divisions by multiplying.

$$4\overline{)92}\ \ 23 \qquad \text{Check: } 23 \times 4 = 92$$

1 Check your answers by multiplying.

a $6\overline{)318}$ Check ___ ___ × 6 = ______

b $5\overline{)415}$ Check ___ ___ × 5 = ______

c $8\overline{)792}$ Check ___ ___ × 8 = ______

d $7\overline{)399}$ Check ___ ___ × 7 = ______

e $4\overline{)156}$ Check ___ ___ × 4 = ______

f $9\overline{)711}$ Check ___ ___ × 9 = ______

g $6\overline{)522}$ Check ___ ___ × 6 = ______

h $8\overline{)952}$ Check ___ ___ ___ × 8 = ______

i $3\overline{)549}$ Check ___ ___ ___ × 3 = ______

j $7\overline{)973}$ Check ___ ___ ___ × 7 = ______

k $5\overline{)875}$ Check ___ ___ ___ × 5 = ______

2 Draw lines to link factors to their numbers. Some factors belong to more than one number.

Remember

Factors divide exactly into a number.

Unit 32 Four-digit division

1 Divide this number by 2, 3, 4, 5, 6, 7, 8, 9.

Write an algorithm for each.

Before starting, predict (yes/no) whether there will be an exact answer and estimate the answer.

a  2) 7 5 0

P ______ Est. ______

b) P ______ Est. ______

c) P ______ Est. ______

d) P ______ Est. ______

e) P ______ Est. ______

f) P ______ Est. ______

g) P ______ Est. ______

h) P ______ Est. ______

2

a 3) 3 4 7 1

b 4) 5 9 3 2

c 7) 8 4 6 3

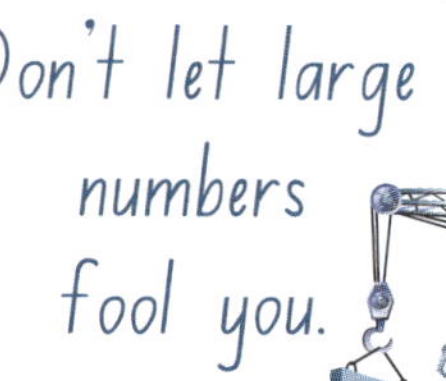

d 5) 8 9 6 0

e 6) 7 7 7 6

f 4) 7 1 9 2

g 9) 7 9 5 6

h 3) 4 8 2 7

i 7) 5 3 2 4

j 8) 4 1 3 5

k 5) 2 5 3 6

l 9) 6 6 0 0

m 4) 2 7 9 5

n 6) 6 0 0 3

Challenge! Fill in the missing numbers.

a 6) 5 ☐ 2 = 9 7

b 4) ☐ 9 2 = 2 4 ☐

c 7) 1 ☐ ☐ 1 = 1 6 ☐

Unit 32 Dividing by 10

Zuri and Summer were stocking up on kitchen items for their cafe.

1 Use this information to write the price under each item.

a They paid $78.30 for 6 oil cans.

b 9 jugs cost $86.13.

c $69.70 was the cost of 5 timers.

d They paid $76.20 for 3 sets of scales.

e 4 woks cost $84.36.

2
a $10 \overline{)70}$
b $10 \overline{)90}$
c $10 \overline{)30}$
d $10 \overline{)47}$
e $10 \overline{)59}$
f $10 \overline{)93}$

3
a $10 \overline{)150}$
b $10 \overline{)270}$
c $10 \overline{)950}$
d $10 \overline{)860}$
e $10 \overline{)392}$
f $10 \overline{)764}$
g $10 \overline{)5163}$
h $10 \overline{)4895}$

4 How much each if 10 cost:

a $50? ______
b $79? ______
c $36? ______
d $1.50? ______
e $2.80? ______
f $9.40? ______
g $11.20? ______
h $33.50? ______
i $59.10? ______
j $72.30? ______
k $123.60? ______
l $297.90? ______

Challenge!

How much did Zuri and Summer (question 1) pay altogether?

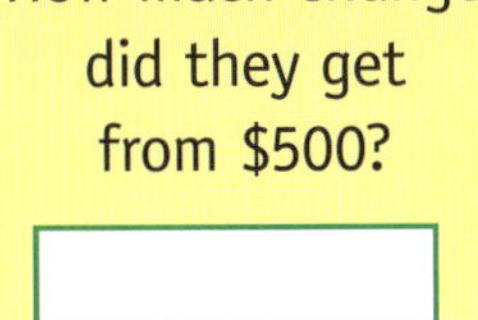

How much change did they get from $500?

Mastery Checklist

I can:
- ☐ estimate to find the quotient
- ☐ multiply to check division answers
- ☐ divide 4-digit numbers
- ☐ divide by 10.

Problem solving

Work groups

The 84 new recruits for the Arjy Barjy Army will carry out their activities in groups. Some of the activities are:

gardening duty **kitchen duty** **dining** **use of showers**
bussing to town **cleaning rooms** **training for cross country survival**

1 Divide the 84 recruits into various groupings. No one gets left out.

2 List five group activities (you can make some up), the number required for each group and the number of groups that will be made.

Activity – what and how often	Number of groups and how many in each group
Cleaning rooms – sweep, dust, empty garbage, clean bathrooms; daily.	14 groups of 6 people. Each group on duty once each fortnight.

3 Find numbers between 100 and 200 that cannot be divided into groups.

What do we call these numbers?

I can solve problems by:
☐ using division ☐ writing algorithms.

Unit 33 More addition

4-digit trading

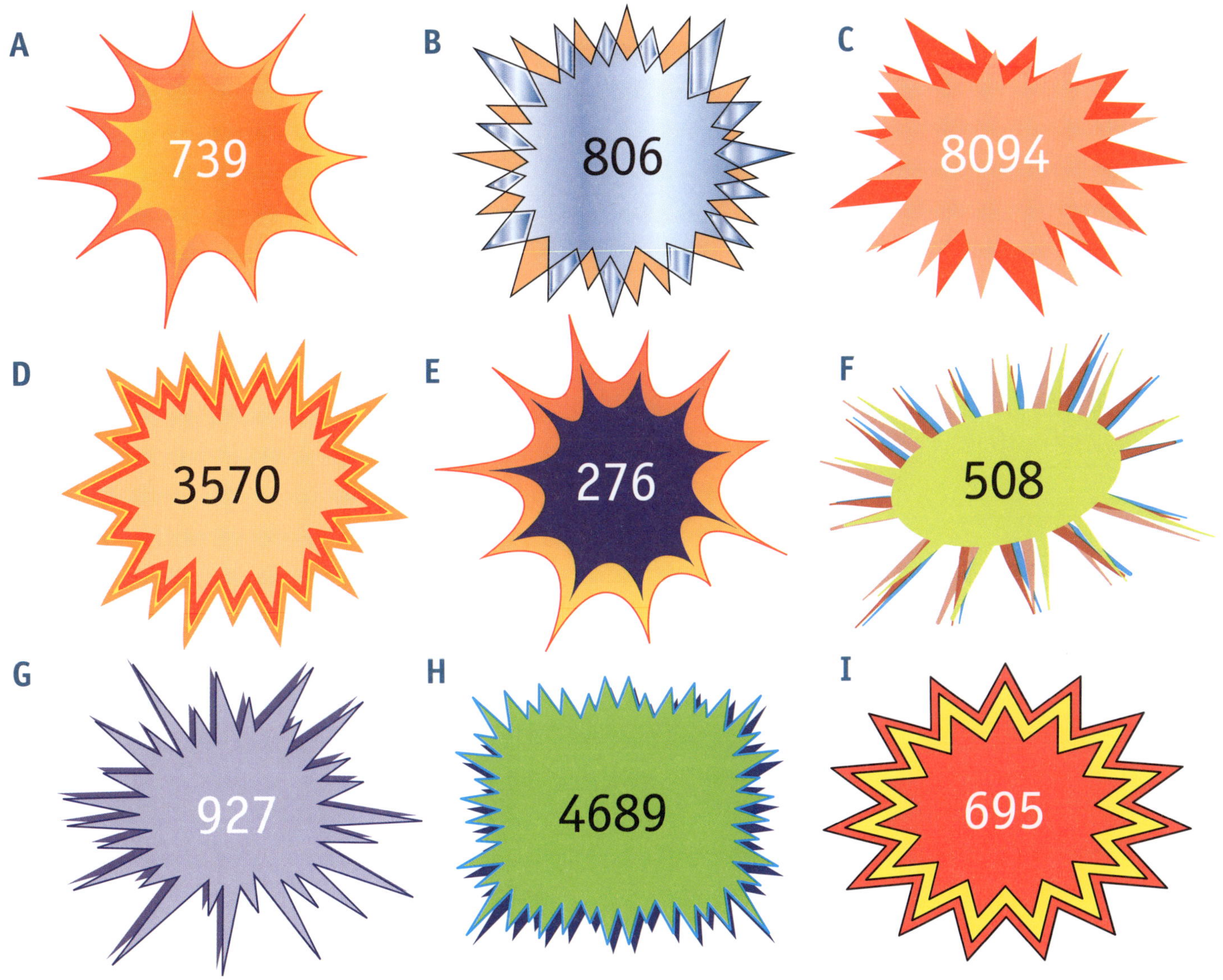

A 739

B 806

C 8094

D 3570

E 276

F 508

G 927

H 4689

I 695

1 Add.

a B + E + I = ____________

b G + F + E = ____________

c A + C = ____________

d H + D = ____________

e A + B + C = ____________

f D + E + G = ____________

g F + C = ____________

h I + H + B = ____________

i F + I + B + A = ____________

j C + D + E + G = ____________

Working

Unit 33 More subtraction

Use the numbers on page 159.

1 Change each number into dollars and cents. eg A = $7.39

A ______ B ______ C ______ D ______ E ______

F ______ G ______ H ______ I ______

2 Using the money amounts, write the algorithm, estimate the answer and then do the working.

a A – F

$	c
$7	. 3 9
– 5	. 0 8

Est. ______

b I – E

$ c

Est. ______

c G – E

$ c

Est. ______

d D – B

$ c

Est. ______

e B – I

$ c

Est. ______

f H – A

$ c

Est. ______

g C – D

$ c

Est. ______

h C – I

$ c

Est. ______

3 a Eddy had $10. He bought a hamburger for $4.16 and a drink for $2.72.

How much change did he receive?

b The gardener had 1640 daffodils for sale. 715 died in a storm but then another 396 bloomed.

How many could he sell?

Challenge!

Use all these cards to:

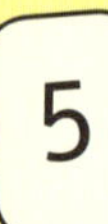

7 6 1 2 5 4 9

a make three numbers to give the highest total.

b make two numbers to give the least difference.

AC9M5N08 • AC9M5N09 Number **MA3-AR-01** Additive relations A • Apply efficient mental and written strategies to solve addition and subtraction problems

Unit 33 Money multiplication

PRICES

CART RIDE	$2.65
CABLE CAR	$1.74
NOCTURNAL HOUSE	$3.08
AQUARIUM	$4.95

Roobat School went to the zoo. Help the principal work out these prices.

1 10 children from Year 3 went:

a to the nocturnal house. ________ b to the aquarium. ________

c on a cart ride. ________ d in the cable car. ________

2 8 children from Year 4 went:

a to the nocturnal house. ________ b to the aquarium. ________

c on a cart ride. ________ d in the cable car. ________

3 6 children from Year 5 went:

a to the nocturnal house. ________ b to the aquarium. ________

c on a cart ride. ________ d in the cable car. ________

4 9 children from Year 6 went:

a to the nocturnal house. ________ b to the aquarium. ________

c on a cart ride. ________ d in the cable car. ________

Working

Unit 33 Averages

Word problems

1 Find the averages of these sets of scores.

a 4, 9, 7, 8. ______ b 5, 7, 11, 3, 9. ______

c 6, 5, 12, 6, 7, 4, 9. ______ d 27, 31, 23. ______

e 9, 13, 16, 11, 14, 12, 10, 9, 5. ______

f 22, 37, 19, 10. ______

g 9, 7, 8, 3, 6, 6, 11, 4, 8, 8. ______

h 37, 52, 31. ______ i 17, 12, 15, 11, 5. ______

j 11, 7, 9, 13, 8, 5, 15, 12. ______

Average

To find an average, total all the scores and divide by how many there are.
eg the average of 7, 9, 3, 8, 6 and 9 is 7.
(7 + 9 + 3 + 8 + 6 + 9) ÷ 6
42 ÷ 6 = 7

2 Write the averages of these as decimals.

a 7, 5, 12, 14. ______ b 11, 13, 16, 12, 11. ______ c 78, 133. ______

3 Write the averages of these scores as mixed numbers.

a 11, 13, 7, 9, 20, 8. ______ b 46, 38, 64. ______ c 15, 17, 24, 19. ______

4 a Last week in Bobsley it rained every day:
Monday 7 mm, Tuesday 11 mm, Wednesday 14 mm, Thursday 5 mm, Friday 9 mm, Saturday 6 mm and Sunday 4 mm.

What was the average daily rainfall? ______

b In the Zarde family there are 4 boys.
Daz is 4 yr 3 mth, Raz is 6 yr 2 mth, Dez is 8 yr 11 mth and Rez is 12 yr.

What is their average age? ______

c In the Vetsa family there are 4 girls.
Vas is 90 cm tall, Veat is 1 m 5 cm, Sev is 1 m 17 cm and Tav is 1 m 24 cm.

What is their average height? ______

d Work with three friends and find the average height of the four of you. ______

Working

Trial and error

The average of a set of 5 scores is 14·8.

Three scores are 9, 18, 12. The missing scores are consecutive numbers.

Write the missing numbers. [ ] [ ]

Mastery Checklist

I can:
- ☐ add 3 numbers
- ☐ subtract money
- ☐ find the average
- ☐ multiply money.

Problem solving

Travelling time

Uncle Ned and Uncle Van have to drive to a city hotel 480 km away for a meeting.

Uncle Ned's car will average 80 km/h and Uncle Van's car will average 60 km/h. They both must rest for 10 minutes every two hours.

If they want to arrive at the city hotel together, how much before Uncle Ned leaves home must Uncle Van leave?

Hint: Use a table or draw a diagram.

I can solve problems by:

☐ understanding length and time ☐ choosing the correct strategy.

Problem solving

Plan to make money

Plan to hold a class fundraising morning for your class to buy a Rainy Day Interactive Game Screen.

You have priced the screen at $2200. The school will contribute $500 to the cost if your class organises the whole event.

1 Write a list of activities for the time between 10 am and 11:30 am. Allocate people who will run the activity. Make sure there is a variety of activities and some food.

2 List the materials needed and costs for making and running the activities. Hint: get people to donate their time and the materials for this if possible.

3 Decide on prices and how much each activity expects to raise in the time.

4 Estimate how much this will raise in total. Adjust prices if you need to.

Activity/stall	People on duty	Materials needed	Prices/ amount to raise

Total expected: ____________________ Is this expectation reasonable? ____________________

Why? ____________________

____

____

I can solve problems by:

☐ using addition ☐ estimating and checking.

 AC9M5N09 Number MAO-WM-01 Working mathematically • choosing and applying mathematical techniques to solve problems • communicating thinking and reasoning coherently and clearly • **MA3-AR-01** Additive relations A • Apply efficient mental and written strategies to solve addition and subtraction problems • **MA3-MR-01** Multiplicative relations B • Select and apply strategies to solve problems involving multiplication and division with whole numbers

Unit 34 Order fractions on a number line

1 Circle the larger fraction.

a $\frac{3}{5}$ $\frac{1}{2}$

b $\frac{3}{4}$ $\frac{2}{5}$

c $\frac{7}{8}$ $\frac{1}{2}$

d $\frac{2}{5}$ $\frac{3}{4}$

e $\frac{1}{4}$ $\frac{3}{8}$

f $\frac{6}{8}$ $\frac{7}{10}$

g $\frac{1}{2}$ $\frac{3}{5}$

h $\frac{1}{4}$ $\frac{1}{8}$

2 Write the missing fractions on the number lines.

a

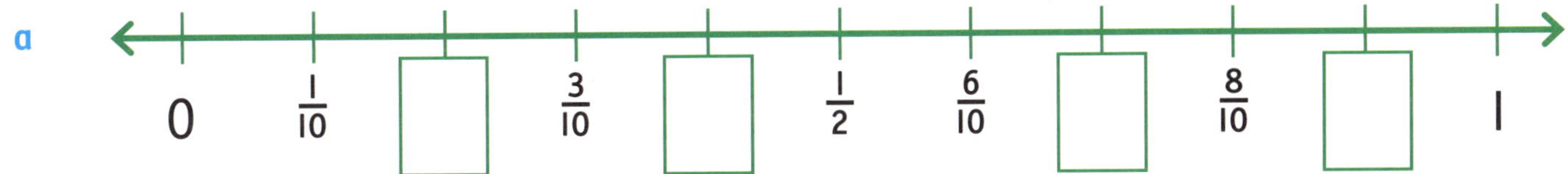

b

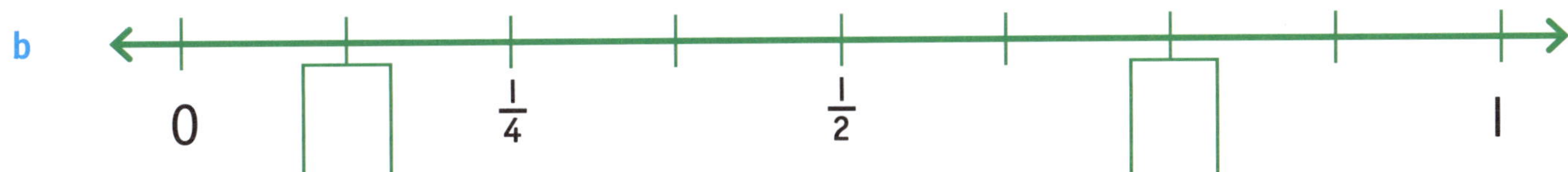

c

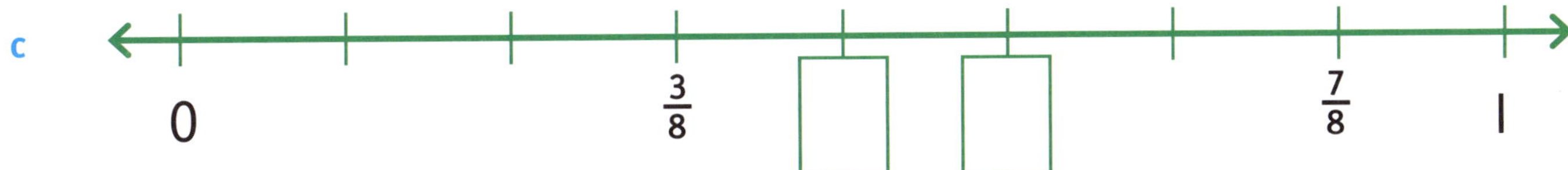

d

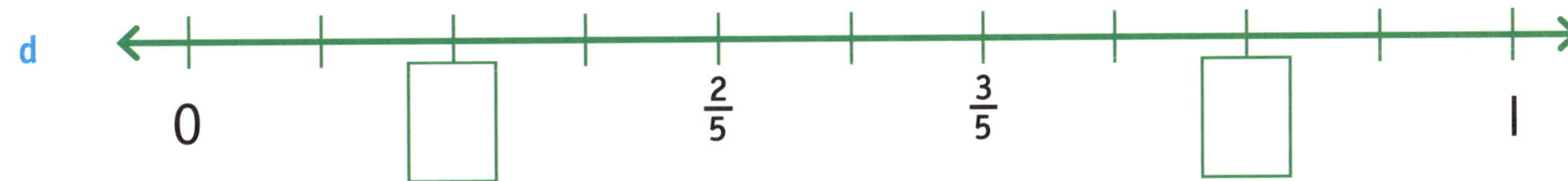

3 Draw lines to connect the fractions to the correct marks on the number line.

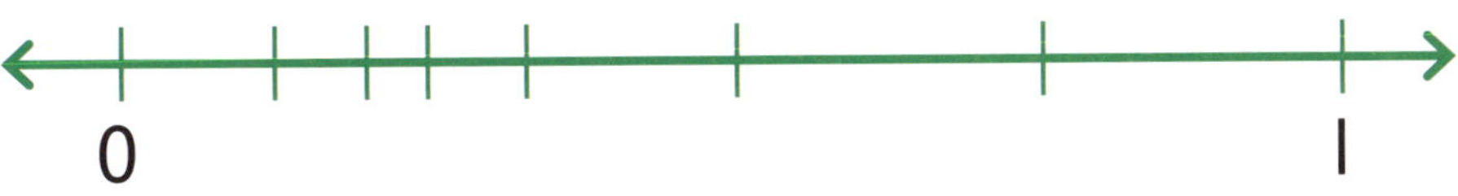

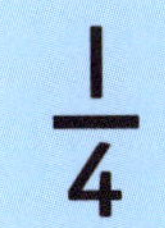

$\frac{3}{4}$ $\frac{1}{8}$ $\frac{1}{3}$ $\frac{1}{2}$

Unit 34 Recognise fractions as ÷

Looks like a division sign → ÷ $\frac{3}{4}$ ← numerator ← denominator

$3 \div 4$

$\frac{3}{4}$ represents dividing something into 4 equal parts and having 3 of those parts

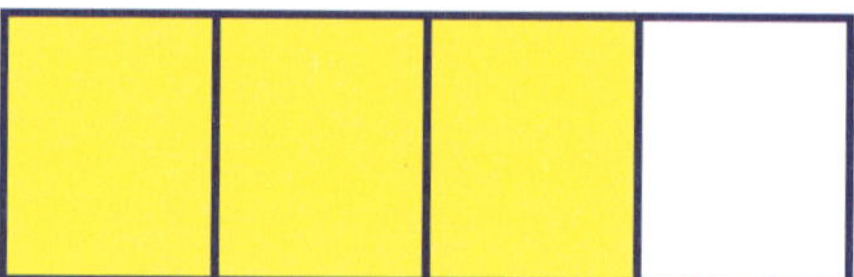

1 Draw lines to match the fractions to the correct division expressions.

a $\frac{2}{3}$	$1 \div 4$
b $\frac{3}{5}$	$2 \div 3$
c $\frac{6}{8}$	$6 \div 8$
d $\frac{1}{4}$	$4 \div 5$
e $\frac{4}{5}$	$5 \div 10$
f $\frac{5}{10}$	$3 \div 5$

2 Write the division expression for each fraction.

a $\frac{2}{3}$ $2 \div 3$ b $\frac{3}{4}$ ____________

c $\frac{1}{8}$ ____________   d $\frac{1}{5}$ ____________

e $\frac{2}{10}$ ____________   f $\frac{7}{8}$ ____________

g $\frac{9}{10}$ ____________   h $\frac{3}{8}$ ____________

3 Complete the table.

Fraction	Division	Out of
a $\frac{5}{8}$	$5 \div 8$	5 out of 8
b $\frac{1}{2}$		
c $\frac{7}{10}$		
d $\frac{4}{6}$		
e $\frac{3}{10}$		
f $\frac{1}{8}$		

Unit 34 Equivalent fractions

Equivalent fractions are different fractions that represent the same amount.

$\frac{1}{2}$ 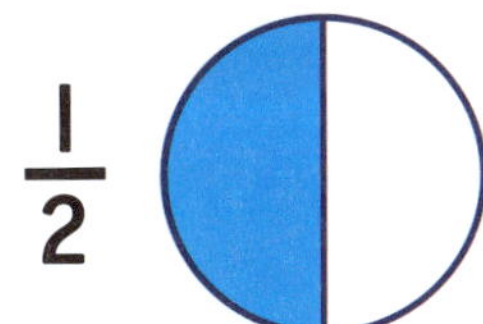 $\frac{2}{4}$ 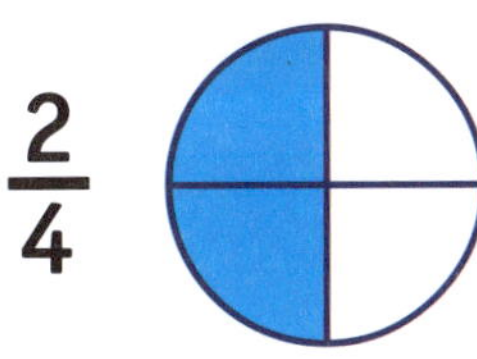

$\frac{1}{2}$ and $\frac{2}{4}$ are equivalent because they both represent one half of one whole.

1 whole										
$\frac{1}{2}$	$\frac{1}{2}$									halves
$\frac{1}{4}$	$\frac{1}{4}$	$\frac{1}{4}$	$\frac{1}{4}$							quarters
$\frac{1}{8}$	$\frac{1}{8}$	$\frac{1}{8}$	$\frac{1}{8}$	$\frac{1}{8}$	$\frac{1}{8}$	$\frac{1}{8}$	$\frac{1}{8}$			eighths
$\frac{1}{5}$	$\frac{1}{5}$	$\frac{1}{5}$	$\frac{1}{5}$	$\frac{1}{5}$						fifths
$\frac{1}{10}$	$\frac{1}{10}$	$\frac{1}{10}$	$\frac{1}{10}$	$\frac{1}{10}$	$\frac{1}{10}$	$\frac{1}{10}$	$\frac{1}{10}$	$\frac{1}{10}$	$\frac{1}{10}$	tenths

1 Use the diagram above to help you write equivalent fractions.

a $\frac{4}{8}$ = ______ b $\frac{6}{8}$ = ______ c $\frac{2}{10}$ = ______ d $\frac{4}{10}$ = ______

e $\frac{1}{2}$ = ______ f $\frac{4}{5}$ = ______ g 1 whole = ______ h $\frac{3}{5}$ = ______

2 Complete the equivalent fractions. eg $\frac{1}{2} \overset{\times 2}{=} \frac{2}{4}$ (×2)

a $\frac{3}{4} = \frac{\square}{8}$ b $\frac{2}{5} = \frac{\square}{10}$ c $\frac{1}{4} = \frac{\square}{8}$ d $\frac{1}{2} = \frac{\square}{10}$

e $\frac{3}{2} = \frac{\square}{8}$ f $\frac{2}{4} = \frac{\square}{8}$ g $\frac{4}{4} = \frac{\square}{8}$ h $\frac{4}{5} = \frac{\square}{10}$

i $\frac{3}{5} = \frac{\square}{10}$ j $\frac{2}{2} = \frac{\square}{8}$ k $\frac{2}{4} = \frac{\square}{10}$ l $\frac{1}{5} = \frac{\square}{10}$

Mastery Checklist I can:
- ☐ write fractions on a number line
- ☐ connect fractions with division
- ☐ identify and make equivalent fractions.

Unit 35 Adding fractions

Lowest terms

Find the highest common factor of both parts of the fraction. Divide.

$$\frac{6 \div 3}{9 \div 3} = \frac{2}{3}$$

1 Complete the table of equivalent fractions.

a	$\frac{1}{2}$	$\frac{}{4}$	$\frac{}{6}$	$\frac{}{8}$	$\frac{}{10}$	$\frac{}{12}$	$\frac{}{20}$	$\frac{}{100}$
b	$\frac{1}{2}$			$\frac{}{8}$		$\frac{}{12}$	$\frac{}{20}$	$\frac{}{100}$
c	$\frac{1}{2}$			$\frac{}{8}$		$\frac{}{12}$	$\frac{}{20}$	$\frac{}{100}$
d	$\frac{1}{2}$		$\frac{}{6}$			$\frac{}{12}$		
e	$\frac{1}{2}$				$\frac{}{10}$		$\frac{}{20}$	$\frac{}{100}$
f	$\frac{1}{2}$				$\frac{}{10}$		$\frac{}{20}$	$\frac{}{100}$
g	$\frac{1}{2}$				$\frac{}{10}$		$\frac{}{20}$	$\frac{}{100}$
h	$\frac{1}{2}$	$\frac{}{4}$	$\frac{}{6}$	$\frac{}{8}$	$\frac{}{10}$	$\frac{}{12}$	$\frac{}{20}$	$\frac{}{100}$

2 In the table above, circle the fraction in each row that expresses the equivalent in lowest terms.

3 Add.

a $\frac{1}{6} + \frac{1}{6} =$ ______ b $\frac{1}{10} + \frac{3}{10} =$ ______ c $\frac{5}{12} + \frac{1}{12} =$ ______

d $\frac{7}{12} + \frac{3}{12} =$ ______ e $\frac{1}{8} + \frac{3}{8} =$ ______ f $\frac{1}{8} + \frac{5}{8} =$ ______

g $\frac{1}{4} + \frac{1}{4} =$ ______ h $\frac{7}{8} + \frac{1}{8} =$ ______ i $\frac{2}{12} + \frac{4}{12} =$ ______

j $\frac{3}{6} + \frac{1}{6} =$ ______ k $\frac{1}{8} + \frac{1}{8} =$ ______ l $\frac{3}{10} + \frac{2}{10} =$ ______

m $\frac{7}{10} + \frac{1}{10} =$ ______ n $\frac{1}{4} + \frac{3}{4} =$ ______ o $\frac{2}{9} + \frac{4}{9} =$ ______

4 Illustrate the fraction additions with a diagram and then write the answer.

eg $\frac{4}{5} + \frac{3}{5} = \frac{7}{5}$

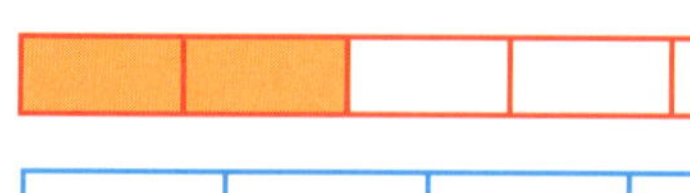

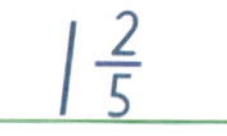

a $\frac{3}{4} + \frac{3}{4} =$ ______

b $\frac{5}{6} + \frac{5}{6} =$ ______

c $\frac{5}{8} + \frac{5}{8} =$ ______

d $\frac{7}{10} + \frac{7}{10} =$ ______

5 Explain how to teach your younger brother or sister that $\frac{7}{6}$ is the same as $1\frac{1}{6}$. Use a diagram if that will help.

______

Unit 35 Adding and subtracting fractions

1 The denominators are the same so subtract the numerators.

a $\frac{3}{4} - \frac{1}{4} =$ ______ b $\frac{5}{6} - \frac{1}{6} =$ ______

c $\frac{7}{8} - \frac{3}{8} =$ ______ d $\frac{9}{10} - \frac{3}{10} =$ ______

e $\frac{5}{8} - \frac{1}{8} =$ ______ f $\frac{7}{10} - \frac{3}{10} =$ ______

2 Draw diagrams to show the subtraction, then write the answer.

a $2 - \frac{1}{2} =$ ______ b $3 - \frac{1}{4} =$ ______ c $2 - \frac{1}{3} =$ ______

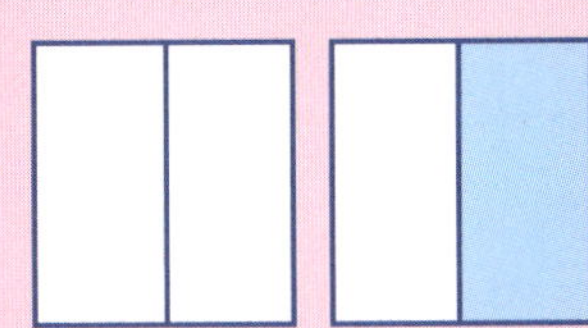

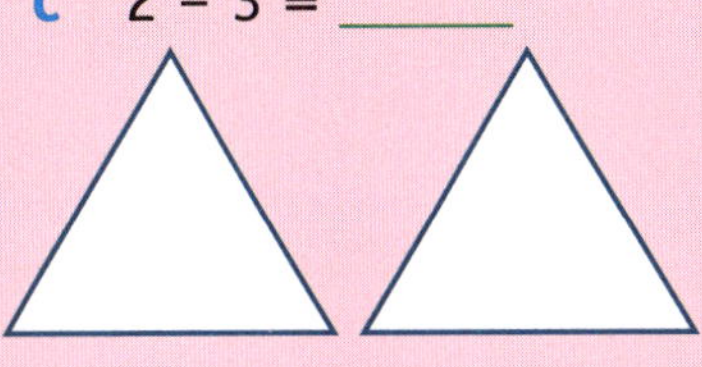

d $1 - \frac{2}{5} =$ ______ e $2 - \frac{1}{8} =$ ______ f $2 - \frac{1}{6} =$ ______

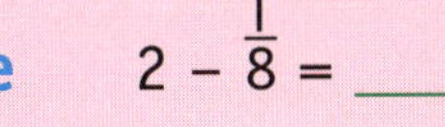
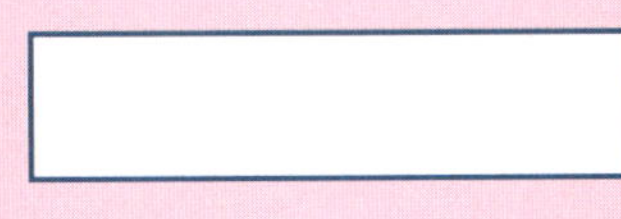

3 Use diagrams, eg $1\frac{1}{4} - \frac{3}{4} =$ $\frac{2}{4} = \frac{1}{2}$

a $1\frac{2}{5} - \frac{3}{5} =$ ______

b $1\frac{1}{3} - \frac{2}{3} =$ ______

c $1\frac{1}{5} - \frac{4}{5} =$ ______

d $1\frac{3}{10} - \frac{7}{10} =$ ______

4 a I had one and a half apples. My young brother ate three quarters of an apple from my bag. Now how much apple do I have to eat?

Number sentence: ______ Diagram: Answer: ______

b There were two chocolates on the table. Gran ate three fifths of one and I ate three fifths of the other. How much chocolate was left on the table?

Number sentence: ______ Diagram: Answer: ______

c Two pies sat on the shelf. Ping ate one and her cat ate $\frac{5}{6}$ of the other. How much pie was left?

Number sentence: ______ Diagram: 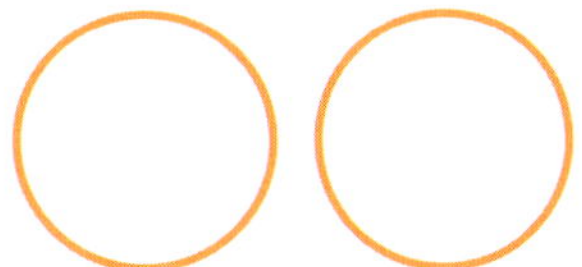 Answer: ______

Unit 35 Decimals to thousandths

	ones	•	tenths	hundredths	thousandths
a	3	.	2	4	1
b	1	.	3	6	8
c	4	.	1	3	9
d	0	.	7	2	0

1 Write each number in expanded notation.

a 3 + _______ + _______ + _______

b 1 + _______ + _______ + _______

c _______ + _______ + _______ + _______

d _______ + _______ + _______ + _______

2 True or false?

a 3·241 contains two hundred and forty one thousandths. _______

b 1·368 is the same as one thousand, three hundred and eight thousandths. _______

c 4·139 is made up of forty-one ones and thirty-nine thousandths. _______

d 0·720 is the same as seven hundred and twenty thousandths. _______

e Towards the right, numbers have values that are smaller. _______

f Towards the left, values of numbers decrease. _______

3 Write the decimal numbers in order from smallest to largest.

a 3·5, 4·2, 3·8, 4·7, 5 _______________

b 2·7, 2·68, 2·91, 2·74, 3·0 _______________

c 0·457, 0·475, 0·447, 0·435 _______________

d 8·058, 8·907, 8·790, 8·689 _______________

4 Place a number between the two decimal numbers given.

a 3·4 _______ 4·2

b 1·68 _______ 1·88

c 6·89 _______ 6·94

d 4·666 _______ 5

5 Write three decimal numbers that are found between the two numbers given.

a 3·718 _______ _______ _______ 4

b 6·809 _______ _______ _______ 6·9

c 10 _______ _______ _______ 10·165

Unit 35 Decimal patterns

Use a calculator.

1 a 7·6 × 10 = ______ b 9·3 × 10 = ______ c 8·2 × 10 = ______ d 1·6 × 10 = ______

e What happens? ______________________________

2 a 3·45 × 10 = ______ b 1·67 × 10 = ______ c 9·39 × 10 = ______ d 2·55 × 10 = ______

e What happens? ______________________________

3 a 1·3 × 100 = ______ b 9·2 × 100 = ______ c 7·5 × 100 = ______ d 4·1 × 100 = ______

e What happens? ______________________________

4 a 2·18 × 100 = ______ b 4·72 × 100 = ______ c 8·96 × 100 = ______ d 15·02 × 100 = ______

e What happens? ______________________________

5 a 8·2 × 1000 = ______ b 4·9 × 1000 = ______ c 6·5 × 1000 = ______ d 0·57 × 1000 = ______

e What happens? ______________________________

6 Try these without a calculator.

a 5·2 × 10 = ______ b 6·5 × 10 = ______ c 3·8 × 10 = ______ d 6·83 × 10 = ______

e 8·07 × 10 = ______ f 6·1 × 100 = ______ g 9·9 × 100 = ______ h 3·2 × 100 = ______

i 8·55 × 100 = ______ j 8·705 × 1000 = ______ k 7·572 × 1000 = ______

Use a calculator.

7 a 7·6 ÷ 10 = ______ b 1·5 ÷ 10 = ______ c 9·4 ÷ 10 = ______ d 3·8 ÷ 10 = ______

e What happens? ______________________________

8 a 564 ÷ 100 = ______ b 219 ÷ 100 = ______ c 728 ÷ 100 = ______ d 873 ÷ 100 = ______

e What happens? ______________________________

9 a 64·2 ÷ 1000 = ______ b 71·6 ÷ 1000 = ______ c 18 ÷ 1000 = ______ d 59 ÷ 1000 = ______

e What happens? ______________________________

10 Try these without a calculator.

a 69 ÷ 10 = ______ b 18 ÷ 10 = ______ c 93 ÷ 10 = ______ d 26 ÷ 10 = ______

e 122 ÷ 10 = ______ f 7·3 ÷ 10 = ______ g 8·7 ÷ 10 = ______ h 31·2 ÷ 10 = ______

i 89·1 ÷ 10 = ______ j 33 ÷ 10 = ______ k 213 ÷ 100 = ______ l 796 ÷ 100 = ______

m 406 ÷ 1000 = ______ n 558 ÷ 100 = ______ o 365 ÷ 1000 = ______ p 68 ÷ 1000 = ______

q 37 ÷ 100 = ______ r 12·3 ÷ 100 = ______ s 95 ÷ 100 = ______ t 722·1 ÷ 1000 = ______

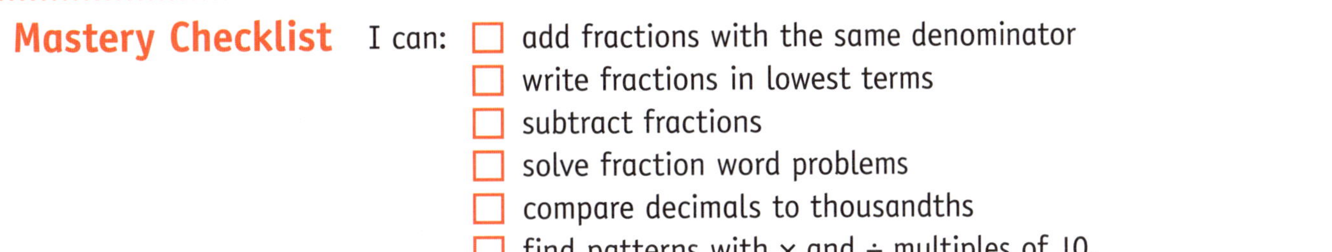

Mastery Checklist I can:
- ☐ add fractions with the same denominator
- ☐ write fractions in lowest terms
- ☐ subtract fractions
- ☐ solve fraction word problems
- ☐ compare decimals to thousandths
- ☐ find patterns with × and ÷ multiples of 10.

Unit 36 Timetable

Duration 

Location	Ferry A	Ferry B	Ferry C	Ferry D
Northside Wharf	1150	1215	1240	1305
University Gardens Wharf	1154	1219	1244	
Eastwood Wharf	1159	1224	1249	
Great Dome Hotel Wharf	1205	1230	1255	
Star Street Wharf	1214	1239	1304	
Westside Wharf	1219	1244	1309	
Kew Bridge Wharf	1231	1256	1321	
State Park Wharf	1235	1300	1325	
City Central Wharf	1240	1305	1330	

This is part of the timetable for the river ferries in a busy city.
Use am and pm notation to answer these questions.

1 When does:

a Ferry A leave Eastwood? ______________ b Ferry B leave State Park? ______________

c Ferry C leave Westside? ______________ d Ferry A leave Kew Bridge? ______________

2 How long does it take:

a Ferry A to travel from Westside to Kew Bridge? ______________

b Ferry C to travel from Westside to Kew Bridge? ______________

3 How long is the trip from:

a Northside to University Gardens? __________ b Great Dome Hotel to Star Street? __________

c Kew Bridge to City Central? __________ d Star Street to State Park? __________

e Eastwood to City Central? __________ f University Gardens to Kew Bridge? __________

g How long is the whole trip? __________ h How long would a return trip be? __________

4 Complete the timetable for Ferry D.

5 What is the longest time you have to wait for a ferry at:

a University Gardens? __________ b Great Dome Hotel? __________ c Kew Bridge? __________

6 Jerry has to be at City Central at twenty-five past one.

What ferry must he catch from Star Street? __________

Challenge! Work with a friend. Make up a transport timetable.
Write 8 questions about it. Make sure you know the answers.
Swap questions with another pair.

Unit 36 Length conversions

We use different units to measure different things.
There are one hundred centimetres in one metre.

100 cm = 1 m

165 cm = 1·65 m

1 Complete the table.

Centimetres	m and cm	Decimal metres
a 145 centimetres	1 m 45 cm	1·45 m
b	3 m 67 cm	
c		4·03 m
d 652 centimetres		
e	5 m 36 cm	
f		6·7 m
g		8·01 m
h 735 centimetres		
i	9 m 10 cm	
j		2·56 m
k	7 m 20 cm	
l 342 centimetres		
m		3·72 m
n	0 m 96 cm	
o 10 centimetres		
p		4·583 m

Unit 36 Perimeter

Work out the perimeter. First, convert to the same units.

1

2·7 m

1·3 m

Perimeter = ________ m

2

1·4 m

222 cm

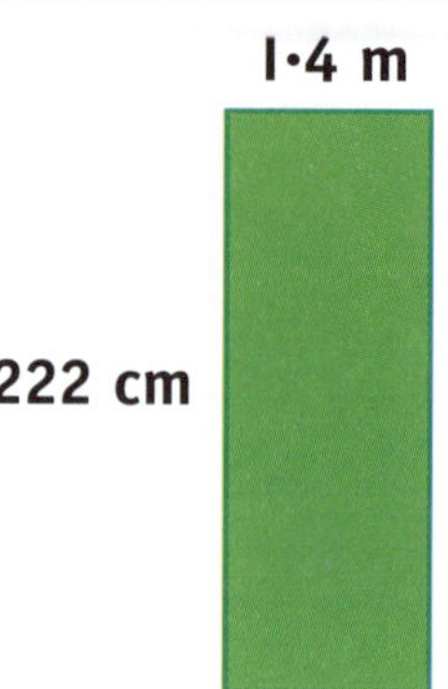

Perimeter = ________ m

3

510 mm

5·6 cm

Perimeter = ________ cm

4

6·3 m

1·5 m

720 cm

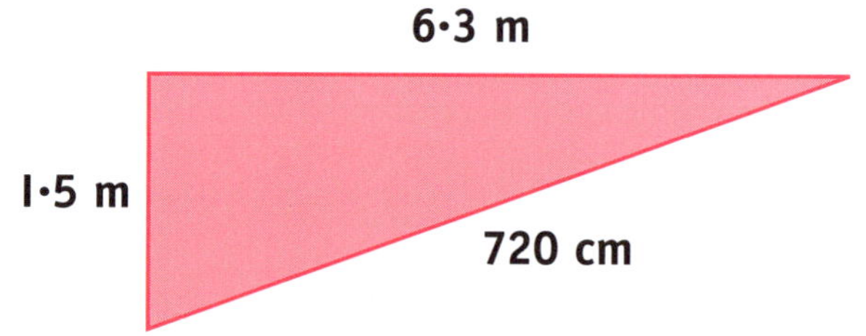

Perimeter = ________ cm

5

63 mm

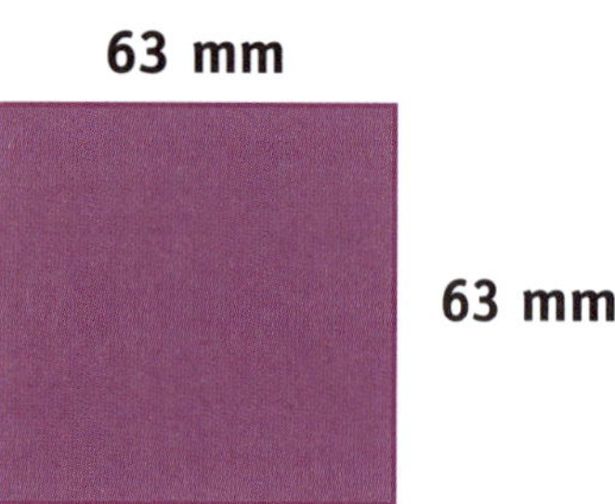

63 mm

Perimeter = ________ mm

6

34 mm

7·4 cm

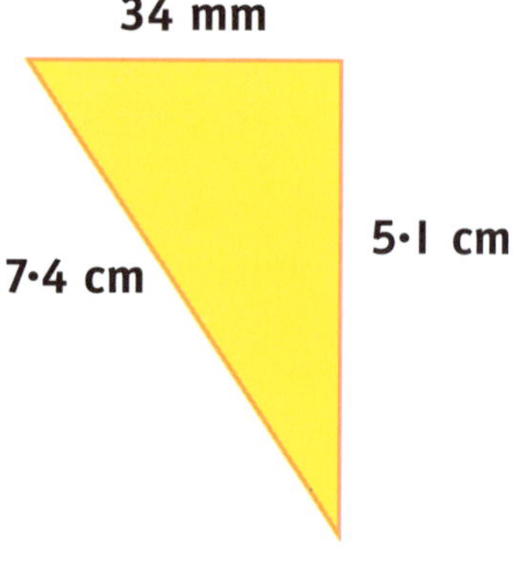

5·1 cm

Perimeter = ________ cm

AC9M5M02 Measurement **MA3-GM-02** Geometric measure A • Length: Measure lengths to find perimeters • Geometric measure B • Length: Connect decimal representations to the metric system

Unit 36 Mass

Mass can be measured in grams and kilograms.

1000 grams = 1 kg

3 kg 350 g is the same as 3·35 kg.

400 g is the same as 0·4 kg.

1 Write the masses in decimal kilograms.

a 2 kg 750 g = ________ kg
b 1 kg 250 g = ________ kg
c 4 kg 175 g = ________ kg
d 6 kg 260 g = ________ kg
e 8 kg 355 g = ________ kg
f 5 kg 475 g = ________ kg
g 7 kg 575 g = ________ kg
h 9 kg 140 g = ________ kg

2 Write the masses in grams.

a 2·36 kg = ________ g
b 8·85 kg = ________ g
c 6·7 kg = ________ g
d 3·5 kg = ________ g
e 9·94 kg = ________ g
f 4·34 kg = ________ g
g 7·21 kg = ________ g
h 1·12 kg = ________ g

3 Write the missing values. Pay attention to the units.

a 0·675 kg = ________ g
b 0·885 kg = ________ g
c 935 g = ________ kg
d 600 g = ________ kg
e 0·5 kg = ________ g
f 0·975 kg = ________ g
g 200 g = ________ kg
h 310 g = ________ kg
i 0·2 kg = ________ g
j 0·375 kg = ________ g
k 775 g = ________ kg
l 708 g = ________ kg
m 0·1 kg = ________ g
n 0·37 kg = ________ g
o 201 g = ________ kg
p 846 g = ________ kg

Mastery Checklist I can:

- ☐ use a timetable
- ☐ convert between centimetres and metres
- ☐ add to find the perimeter
- ☐ convert between grams and kilograms.

Unit 37 Equivalent number sentences

Equivalent number sentences have the same total.

Here, both sides equal 12:

$\underbrace{6 \times 2}_{12} = \underbrace{3 \times 4}_{12}$

Here, both sides equal 5:

$\underbrace{25 \div 5}_{5} = \underbrace{5 \times 1}_{5}$

1 Write the missing value in these equivalent number sentences.

a $63 \div 9 = 7 \times \square$

b $81 \div 9 = 3 \times \square$

c $7 \times 4 = \square \times 14$

d $66 \div \square = 3 \times 2$

e $100 \div 10 = 60 \div \square$

f $6 \times 6 = 12 \times \square$

g $144 \div 12 = 4 \times \square$

h $48 \div 6 = 72 \div \square$

i $8 \times 3 = \square \times 24$

j $\square \times 9 = 12 \times 3$

k $2 \times 9 = \square \times 6$

l $2 \times 8 = \square \times 4$

m $6 \times 7 = 21 \times \square$

n $100 \div 10 = 10 \times \square$

o $132 \div 11 = 6 \times \square$

p $72 \div \square = 88 \div 11$

q $5 \times 9 = 9 \times \square$

r $110 \div 11 = \square \div 10$

s $26 \div 2 = \square \times 1$

t $9 \times 9 = 810 \div \square$

u $6 \times \square = 12 \times 5$

v $32 \div 8 = \square \div 6$

2 Make these into equivalent number sentences.

a 77 ÷ 11 = 5 + 6

b ________ = 54 + 12

c 7 × 8 = ________

d ________ = 100 − 60

e ________ = 50 × 100

f 6 + 7 + 12 = ________

g 200 − 125 = ________

Unit 37 Area model for multiplication

Strategies

To use the area model, partition the numbers to help you multiply.

28 × 7

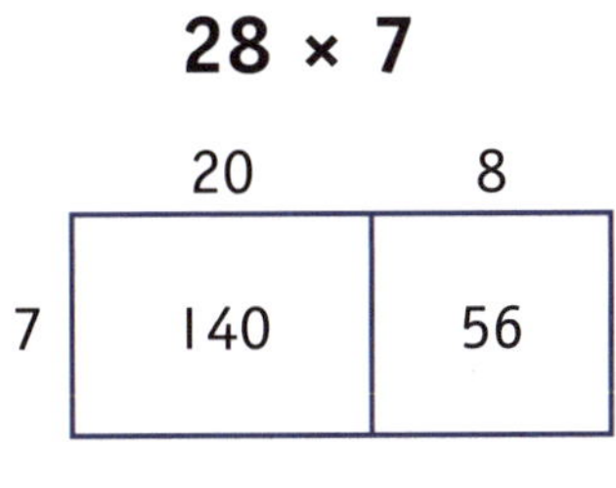

140 + 56 = 196

634 × 5

	600	30	4
5	3000	150	20

3000 + 150 = 20 = 3170

1 Fill in the area models to help you multiply.

a 35 × 6

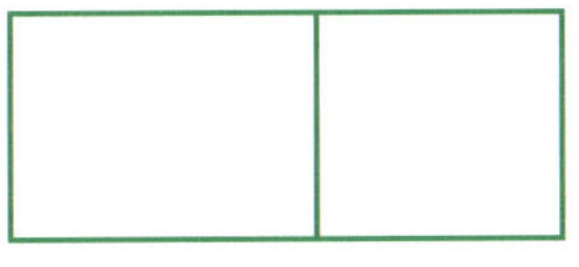

_______ + _______ = _______

b 64 × 7

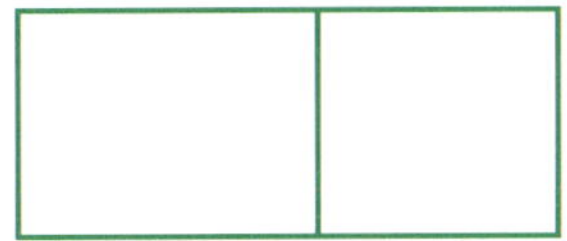

_______ + _______ = _______

c 94 × 4

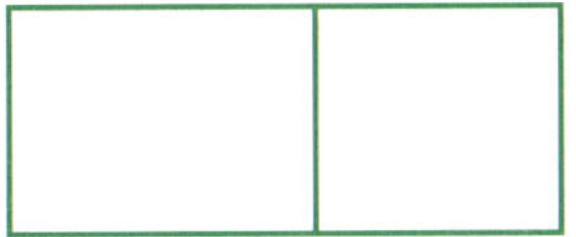

_______ + _______ = _______

d 46 × 5

_______ + _______ = _______

e 238 × 9

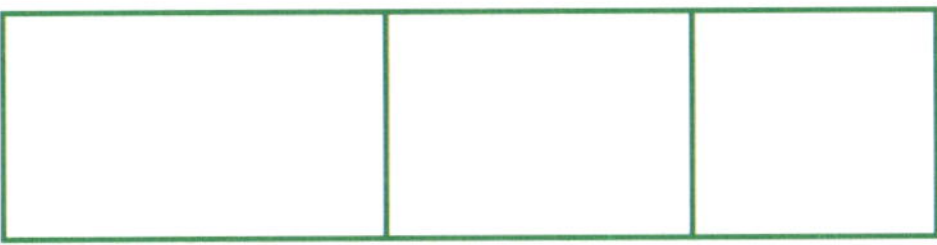

_______ + _______ + _______ = _______

f 177 × 3

_______ + _______ + _______ = _______

g 648 × 3

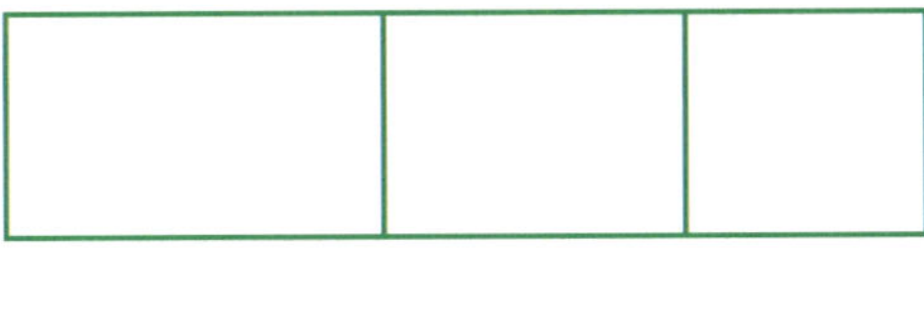

_______ + _______ + _______ = _______

h 984 × 6

_______ + _______ + _______ = _______

Unit 37 Multiply 2 digit × 2 digit numbers

Strategies

Use the area model

56 × 23

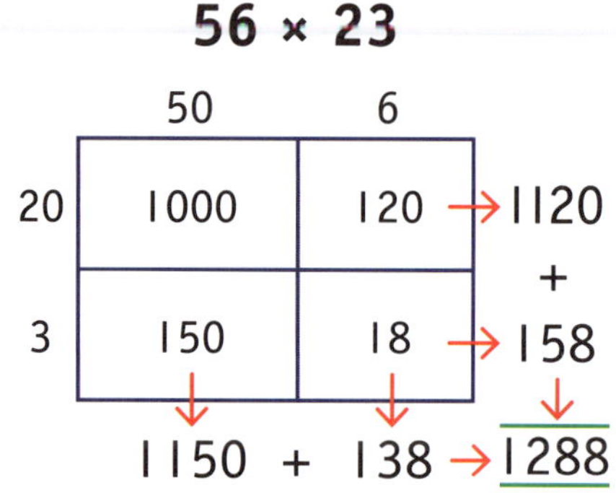

Use the algorithm

```
   1 1
    5 6
×   2 3
  1 6 8
+ 1 1 2 0
  1 2 8 8
```

1 Complete the multiplications using the area model and the algorithm.

a 29 × 47

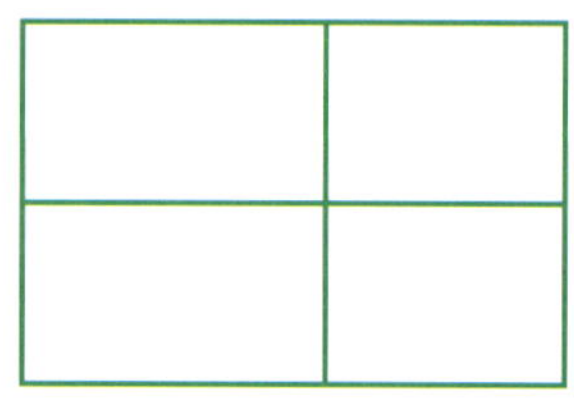

_____ + _____ = _____

```
    2 9
×   4 7
```

b 82 × 36

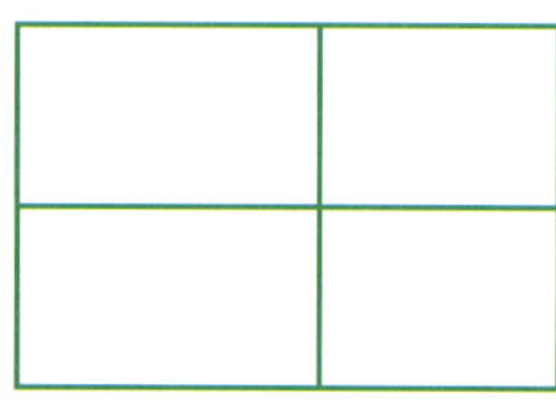

_____ + _____ = _____

```
    8 2
×   3 6
```

c 95 × 47

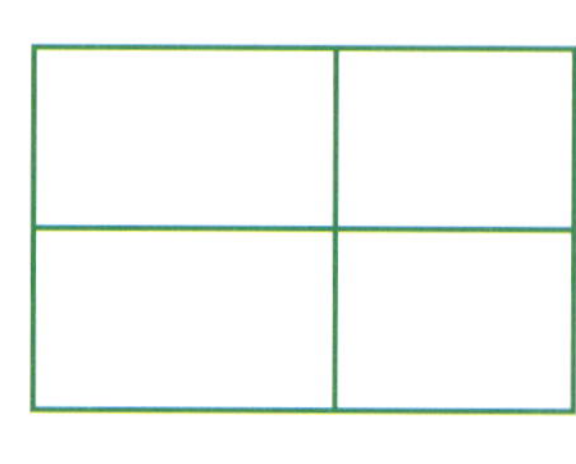

_____ + _____ = _____

```
    9 5
×   4 7
```

Unit 37 Multiply 3 digit × 2 digit numbers

Strategies

Use the area model

153 × 27

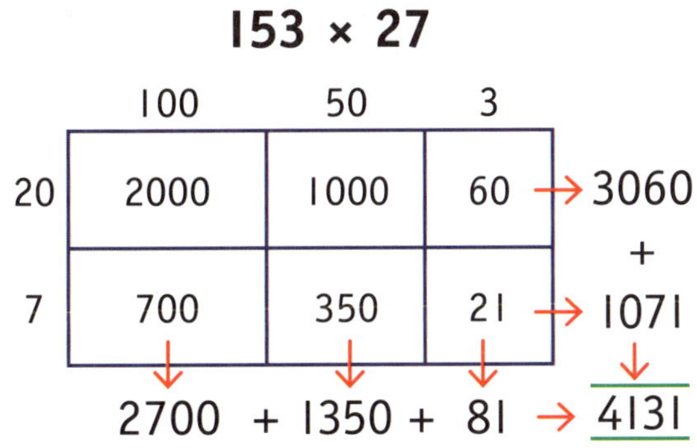

Use the algorithm

```
 ¹3 ¹²5 3
×     2 7
  1 0 7 1
+ 3₁0 6 0
  4 1 3 1
```

1 Complete the multiplications using the area model and the algorithm.

a 672 × 41

_____ + _____ + _____ = _____

```
  6 7 2
×   4 1
```

b 248 × 36

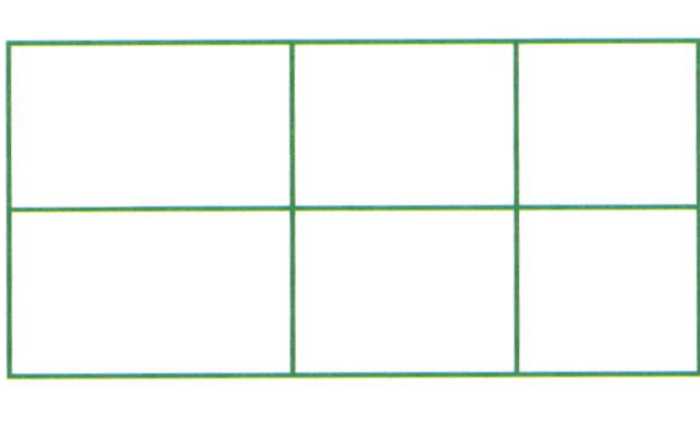

_____ + _____ + _____ = _____

```
  2 4 8
×   3 6
```

c 903 × 24

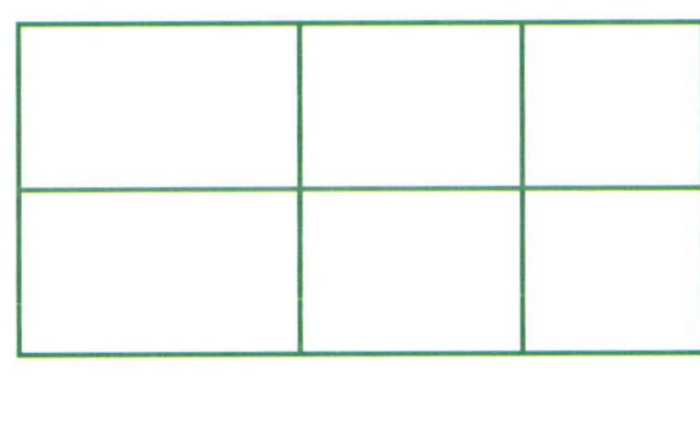

_____ + _____ + _____ = _____

```
  9 0 3
×   2 4
```

Mastery Checklist I can:

- ☐ use equivalence to find missing values
- ☐ use the area model to multiply
- ☐ use algorithms to multiply.

All the Fun of the Fair

Investigation 4

Games of skill are very popular at Fun Fairs. Make some of your own that will interest lots of people.

Target Try!

Look at the example in the box.

Now make up the rules for contestants.

Make rules for young children as well as older children.

Explain how a contestant can win a prize with the balls and targets.

Use +, −, × or ÷ to arrive at totals for prizes.

Here are some hints for your instructions:

- Make each instruction short and clear.
- Put the instructions in order.
- Test instructions on other people to be sure they understand them.
- Use spare paper if you have more than two game ideas.
- Add sketched illustrations if necessary.

Target Try

You can throw 3 balls at any one of the five targets.

Add up your scores from the targets and double that.

You win a prize if that total matches one in the prize list.

Instructions: Game 1

Instructions: Game 2

AC9M5N08 Number **MAO-WM-01** Working mathematically • choosing and applying mathematical techniques to solve problems • communicating thinking and reasoning coherently and clearly • **MA3-AR-01** Additive relations A • Apply efficient mental and written strategies to solve addition and subtraction problems • **MA3-MR-01** Multiplicative relations B • Select and apply strategies to solve problems involving multiplication and division with whole numbers

Dash of Darts

Make a game for 10-year-olds using darts and a board, working with a partner. Players win prizes for highest and lowest scores and the best strategy for working out the total. Use calculation instructions on the board. Explain how a person wins a prize.

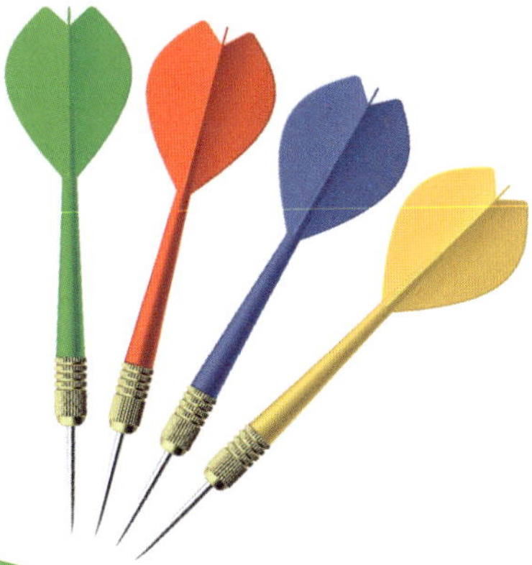

INSTRUCTIONS

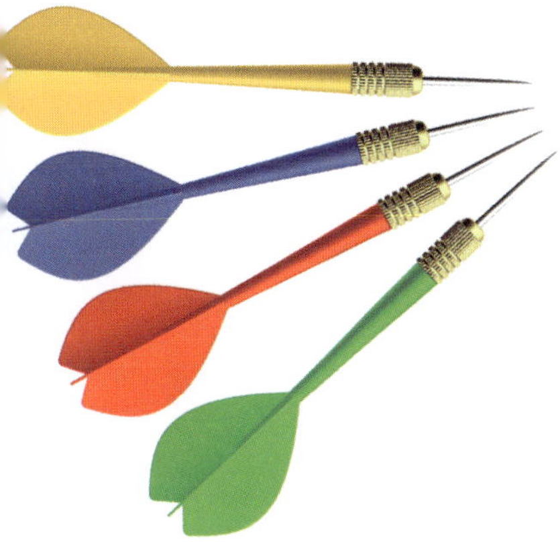

To carry out these tasks, I need to:

- ☐ use different strategies to make totals
- ☐ reason logically to make suitable prize totals
- ☐ write clear instructions
- ☐ work well with a partner.

I enjoyed this task!

Revision

1 What number is a factor of all these numbers?

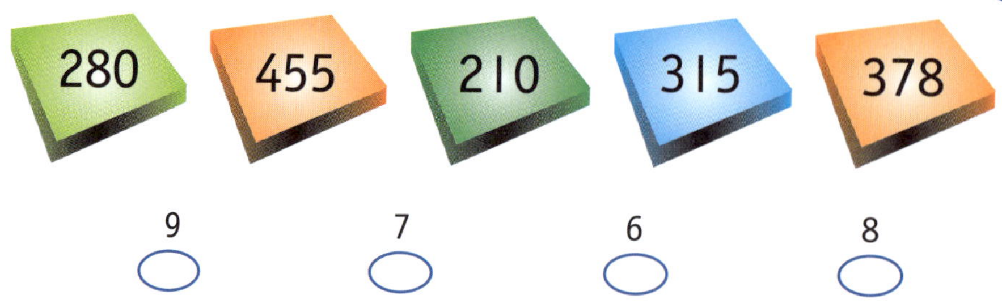

9 ◯ 7 ◯ 6 ◯ 8 ◯

2 Write the missing sign.

Write your answer in the box.

$$5 \times 3 = 45 \; \square \; 3$$

3 What is the quotient when 724 is divided by 5? ☐

4 Use multiplication to check the answer.

$$4\overline{)3\,4^{2}0}$$ with quotient 8 5

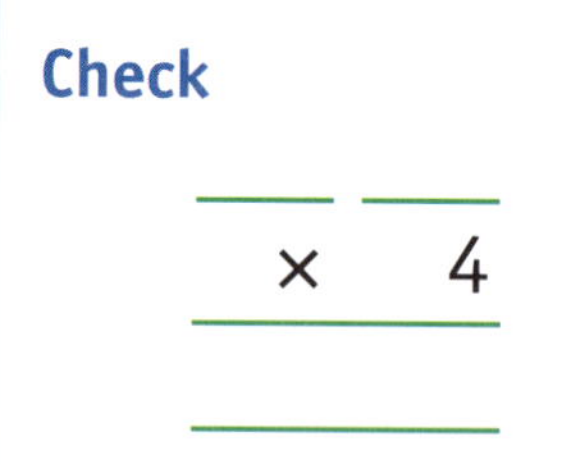

5 Darak divided 78 by a number and got 7·8 for the answer.

What number did he divide by? ☐

Write your answer in the box.

6 What is the average?

2, 4, 8, 7, 6, 9, 5, 5, 8

Average =

7 Write 4·859 in expanded notation.

4·859 =

8 Which diagram illustrates $\frac{7}{10} + \frac{4}{10}$?

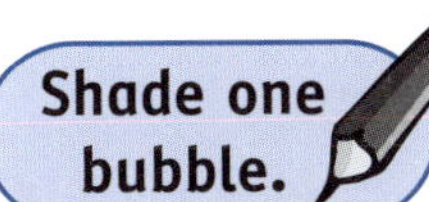

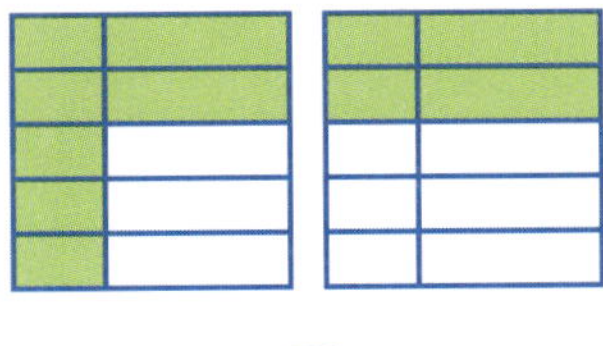

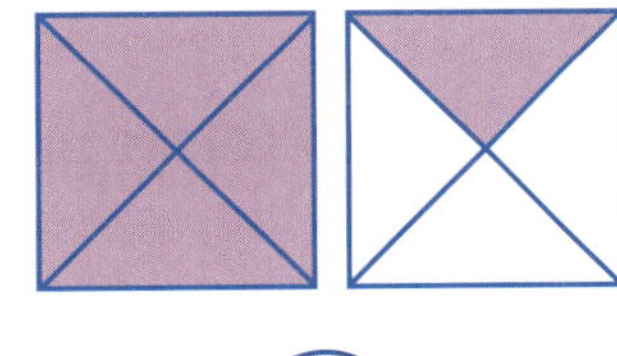

9 The probability of being born on the 30th February is

0·1 0 0·5 1·0

10 How many matchsticks for 8 shapes in this pattern?

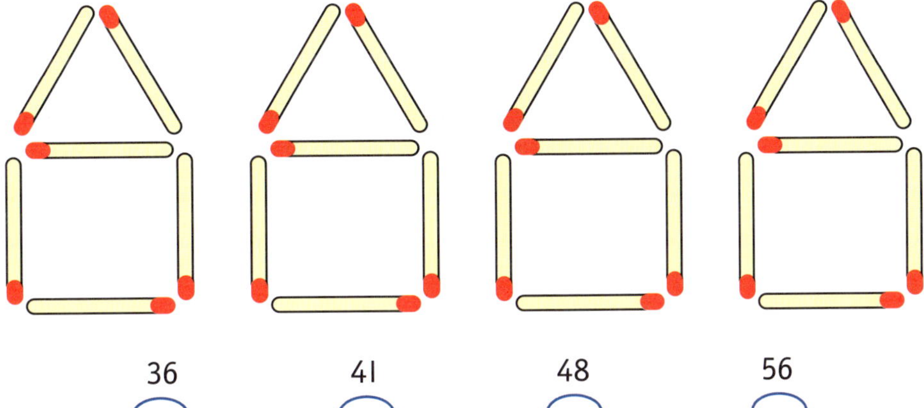

36 41 48 56

Unit 38 3D objects in real life

3D objects 

Match each item to a 3D object. Some might match to more than one.

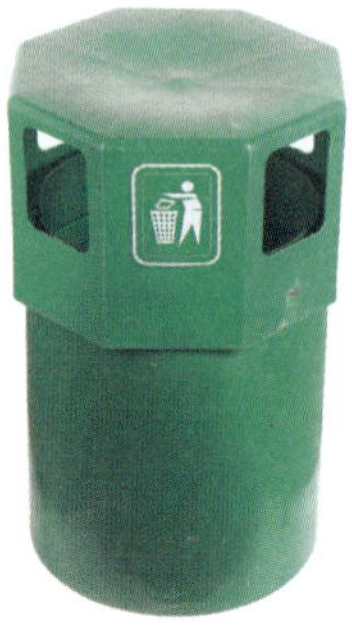

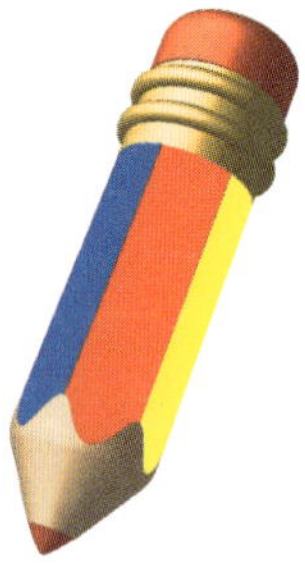

cube

cylinder

sphere

triangular prism

cone

rectangular prism

square pyramid

pentagonal prism

hexagonal prism

octagonal prism

Unit 38 Nets

3D objects

1 Draw and name the 3D objects you can make from these nets.

a

b

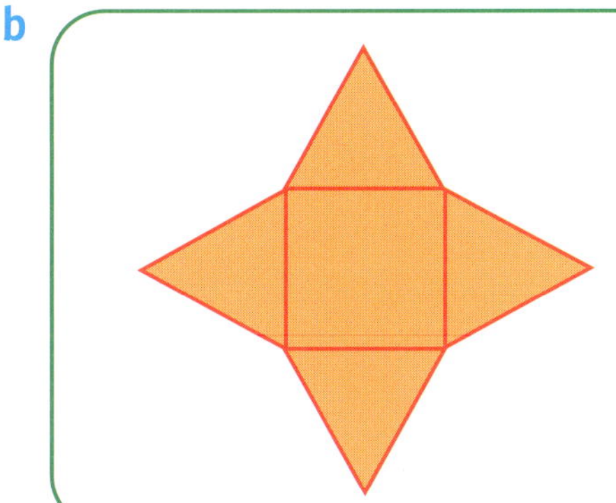

c

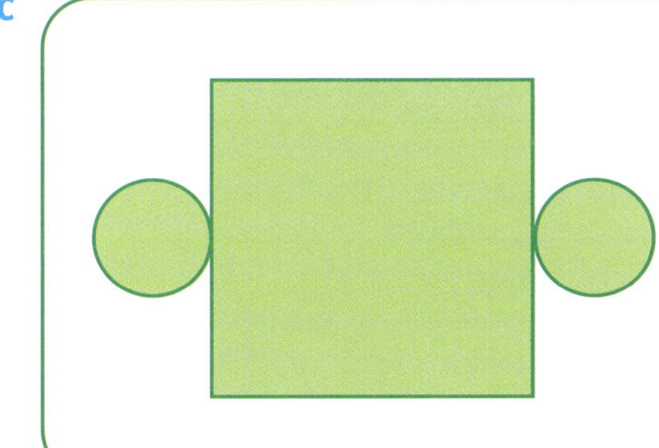

2 Draw a net for:

a a triangular pyramid.

b a triangular prism.

Trial and error

How many different nets can you make for a cube? Draw them.

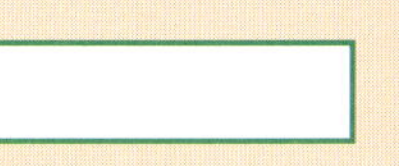

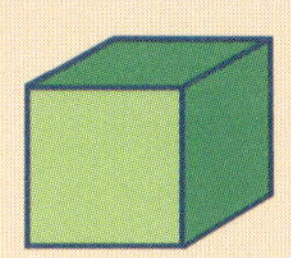

Unit 38 3D views

1 Draw the top, side and front views.

	Object	Top view	Side view	Front view
a	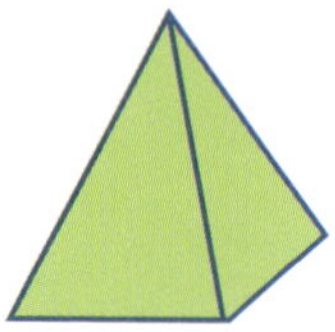			
b	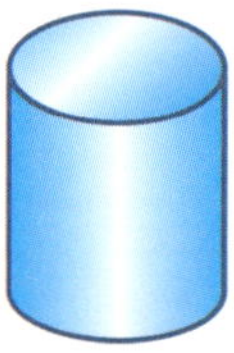			
c	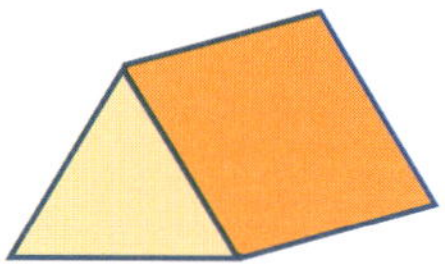			
d	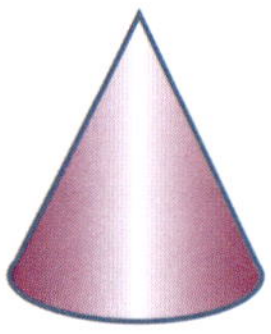			

2 Build each model using centimetre cubes. Then draw the top, side and front views.

	Object	Top view	Side view	Front view
a	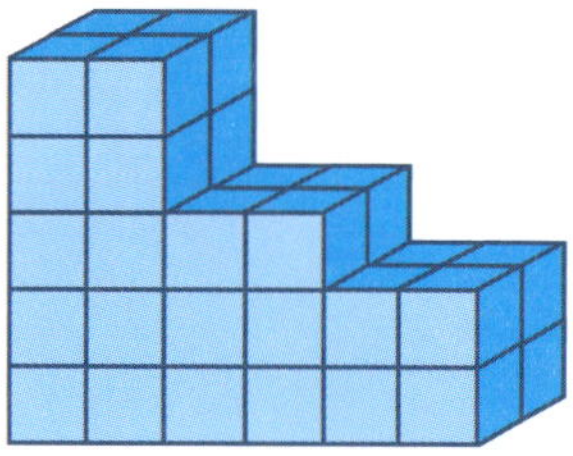			
b	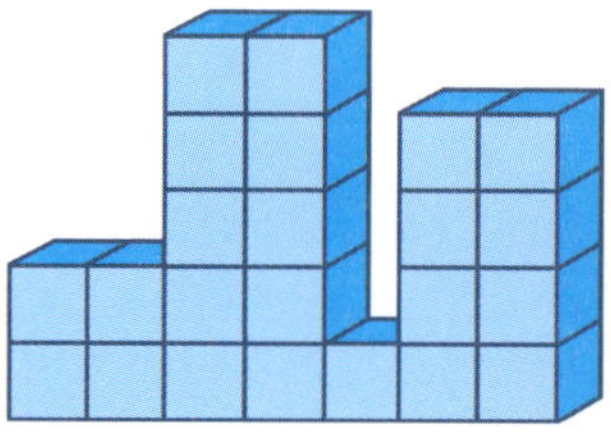			

Mastery Checklist I can:
- ☐ recognise 3D objects in the real world
- ☐ match 3D objects with their nets
- ☐ draw nets for 3D objects
- ☐ draw top views, side views and front views.

Unit 39 Transformations

1 Translate (slide) this shape three times.

2 Reflect (flip) this shape three times.

3 Rotate (turn) this shape three times.

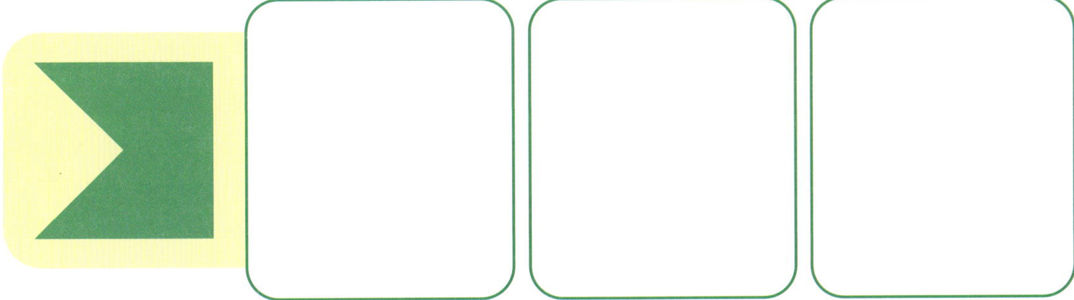

4 What has been used to transform these shapes?

a

b

c

d

Unit 39 More transformations

2D shapes

1 Reflect this shape on the red line.

2 Slide this shape to the right.

3 Turn this shape one quarter turn to the right.

Unit 39 Symmetry

1 For each shape, draw as many lines of symmetry as you can.
How many does each shape have?

A shape has symmetry if it can be folded exactly in half with no overlaps.

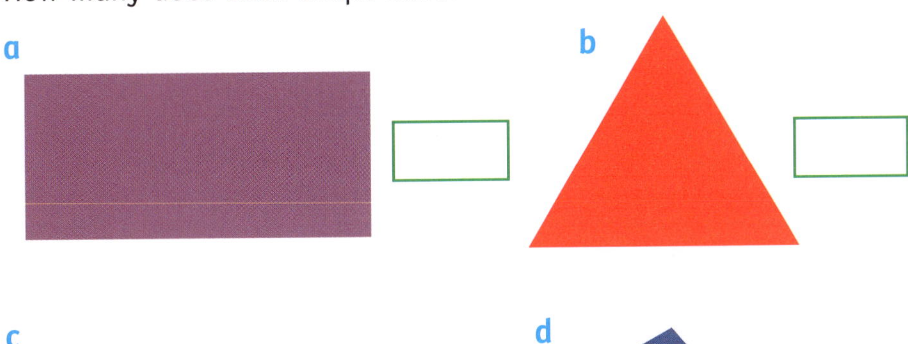

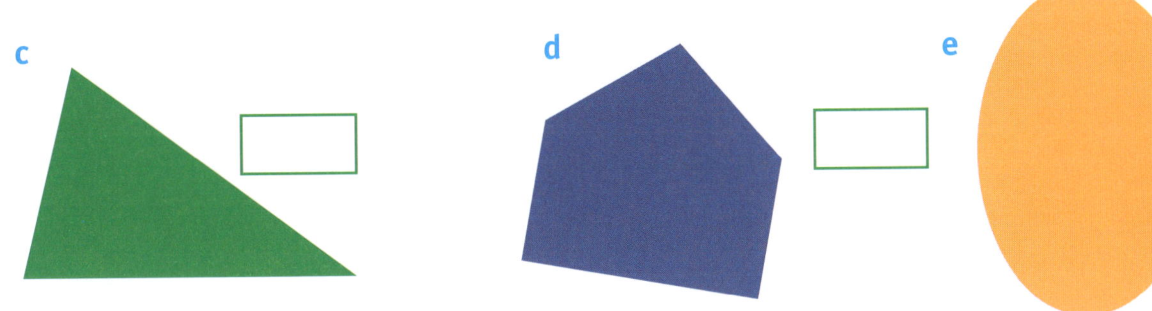

2 Make the shape on the left-hand side colourful.
Then make a symmetrical copy of it on the right-hand side.

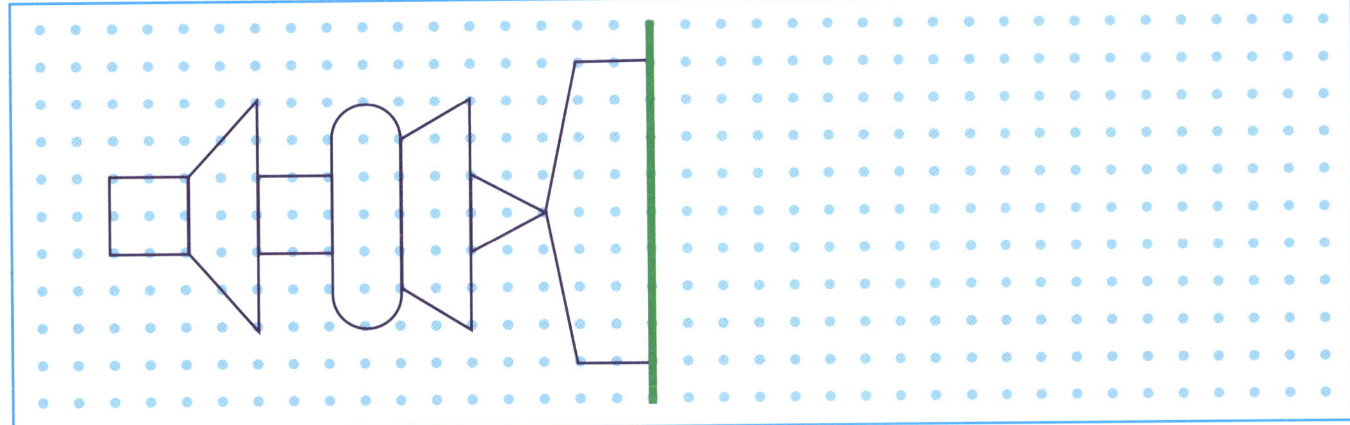

3 a Write 5 capital letters which have one line of symmetry.

b Draw in the line of symmetry.

4 Write 5 capital letters that have no lines of symmetry.

Unit 39 Rotational symmetry

1 Tick the quadrilaterals that have rotational symmetry.

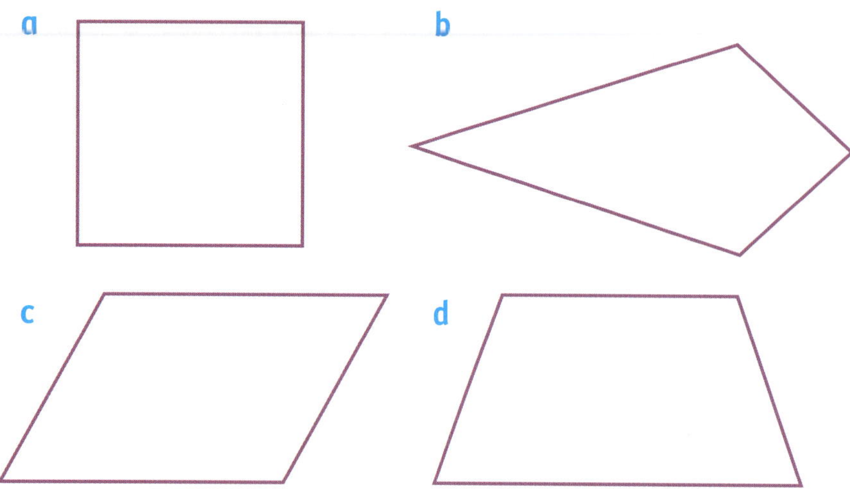

Rotational symmetry

A shape has rotational symmetry if a tracing of the shape matches the original as it rotates around its centre.

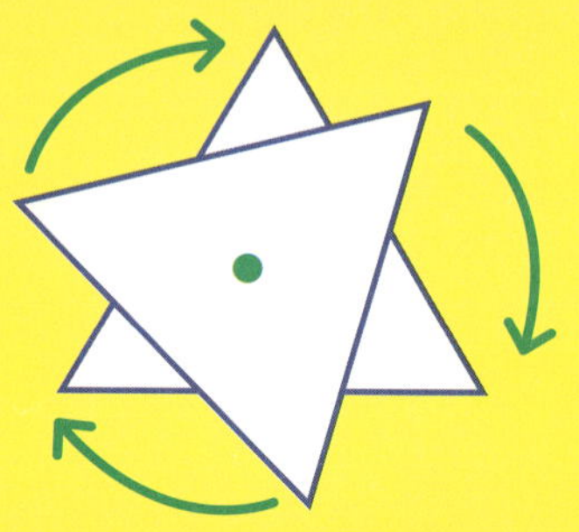

This equilateral triangle will match each time a corner sits on the top, so it has rotational symmetry.

2 Circle the shapes that have rotational symmetry.

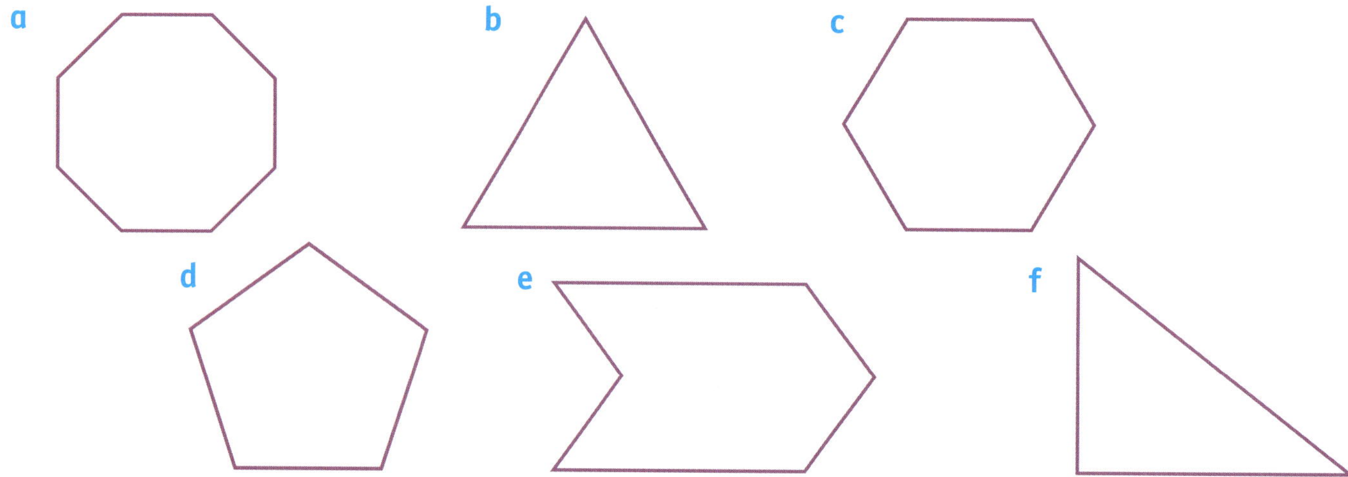

3 Draw this shape after it has been rotated:

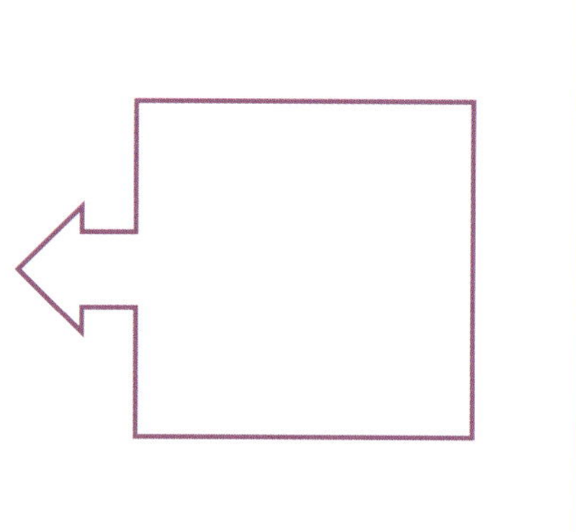

a a quarter-turn clockwise.

b a half-turn clockwise.

Space AC9M5SP03 describe and perform translations, reflections and rotations of shapes, using dynamic geometric software where appropriate; recognise what changes and what remains the same, and identify any symmetries

Unit 39 More rotational symmetry

1 Which shapes have rotational symmetry?

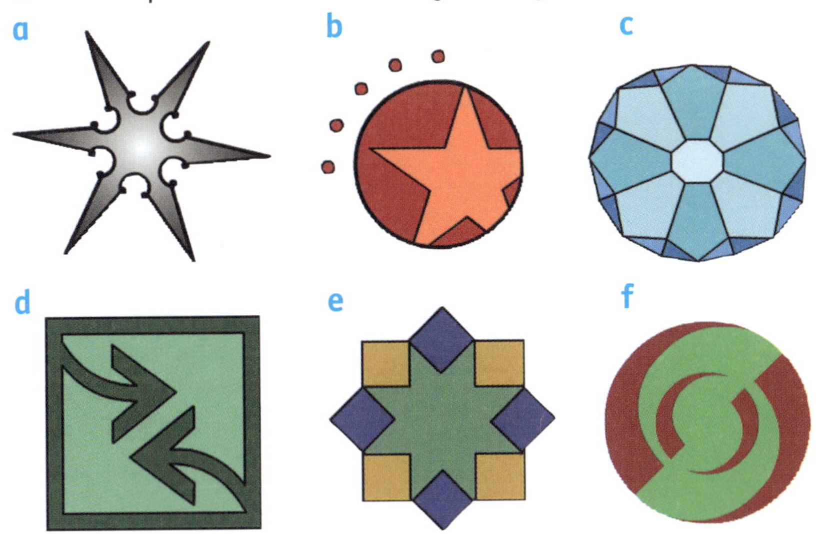

Order of rotational symmetry

An equilateral triangle has rotational symmetry to the order of 3 as it matches three times when turned on the central point.

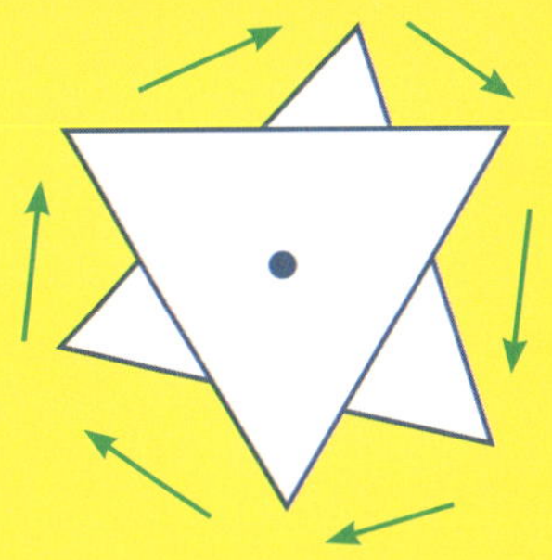

Trace the triangle. Pin the tracing on the original at the central point. Turn.

2 How many times do these shapes match as they make one complete turn?

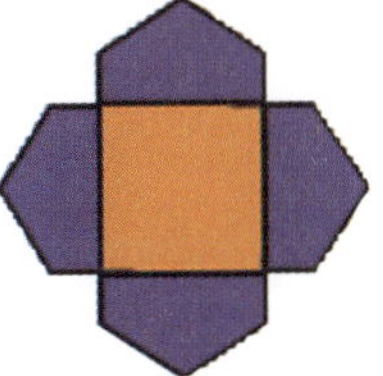

a ______ b ______ c ______ d ______

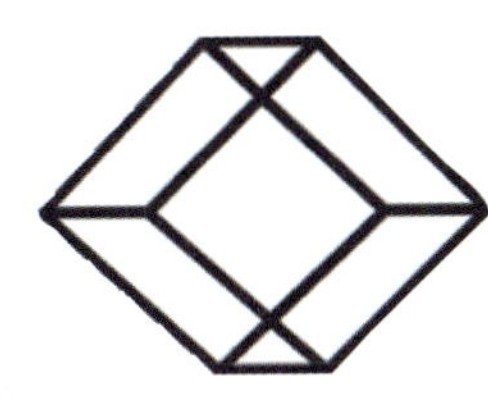

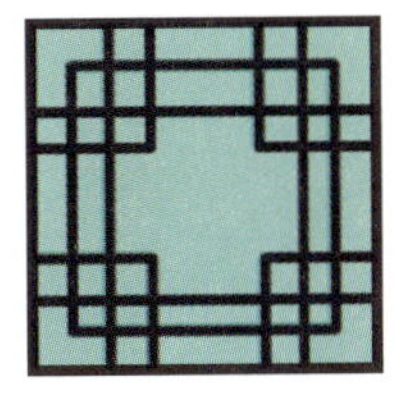

e ______ f ______ g ______ h ______

Challenge! Add to these shapes so that they have rotational symmetry.

eg

a

b

Mastery Checklist I can:

- ☐ identify types of transformations
- ☐ translate, reflect and rotate shapes
- ☐ find lines of symmetry
- ☐ find the order of rotational symmetry.

Unit 40 Predict probability

Marble Bingo

chance experiment

Work in a group of three.

You need an opaque bag with these marbles inside.

Counters or centicubes can be used if they are the right colours.

Take it in turns to pick out one marble and then replace it.

1 Colour your Bingo card circles to make it most likely for you to win. You must use the three colours at least once each.

2 Colour your friends' cards to make it likely for them to lose. You must use the three colours.

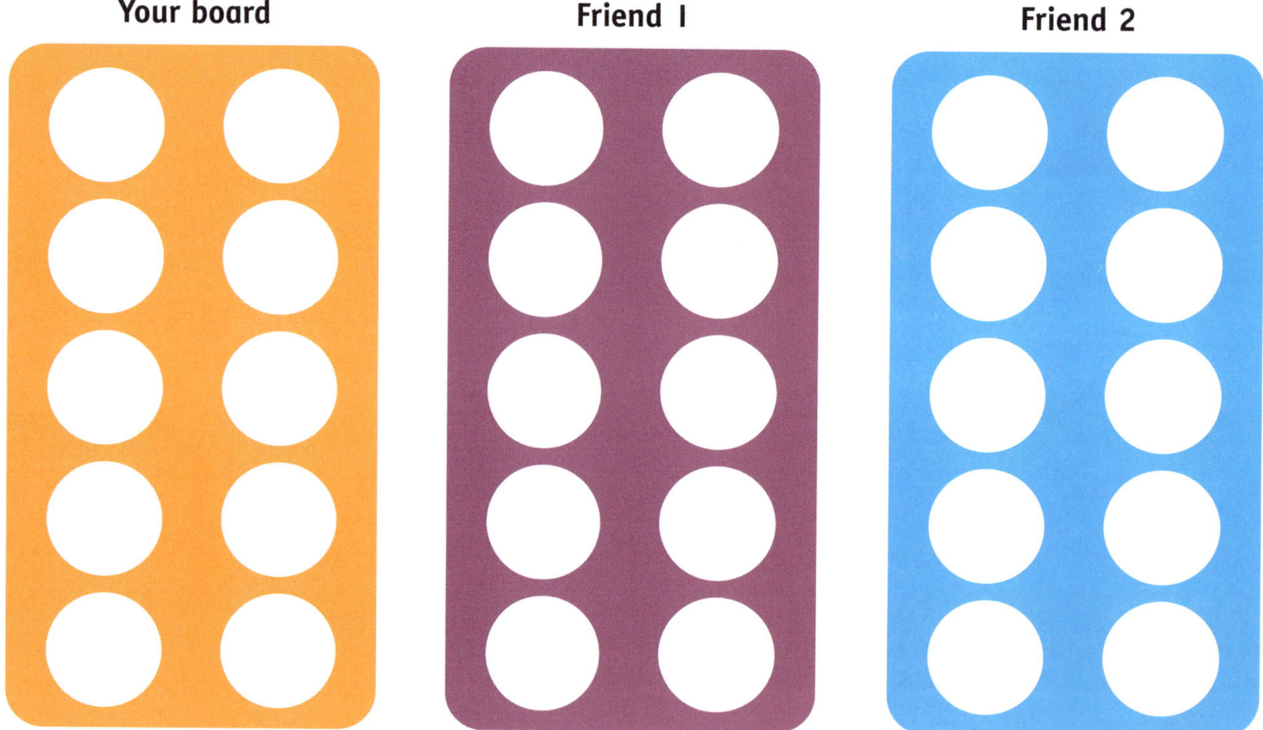

3 Using numerical values only, predict the probability of each of your friends winning the game.

Friend 1 ________ Friend 2 ________

4 Using numerical values, predict the probability of you winning the game. ________

5 Take it in turns to pick out marbles. As each marble is picked, tick one circle of that colour on each board and then replace the marble in the bag.

6 The first card with all the circles ticked is the winner.

7 Discuss what has happened.

Unit 40 Calculate probability

Chance

1 a Colour the spinner yellow, orange and pink.
Colour it so that yellow is most likely to come up.

b Write the probability of spinning each colour.

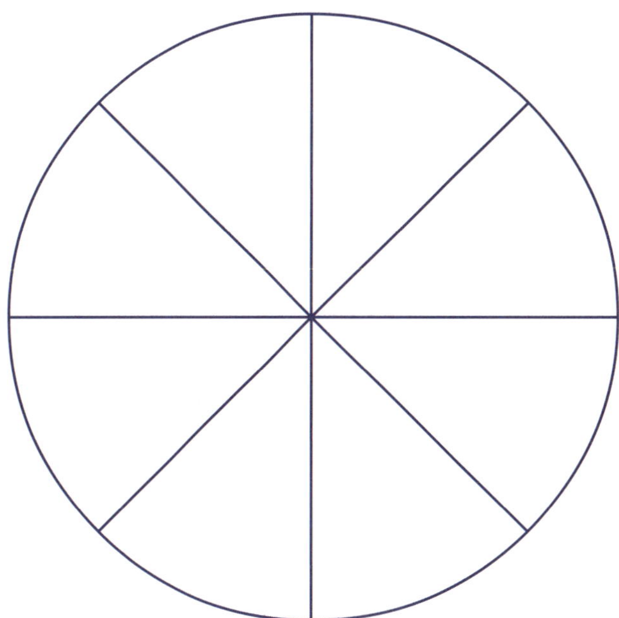

yellow $\frac{\square}{8}$ which is a ______ out of 8 chance of spinning yellow.

orange $\frac{\square}{8}$ which is a ______ out of 8 chance of spinning orange.

pink $\frac{\square}{8}$ which is a ______ out of 8 chance of spinning pink.

2 a Colour the counters in the bag so that a red counter is twice as likely to get drawn out of the bag than a green counter.

b Write the probability of choosing counters of each colour.

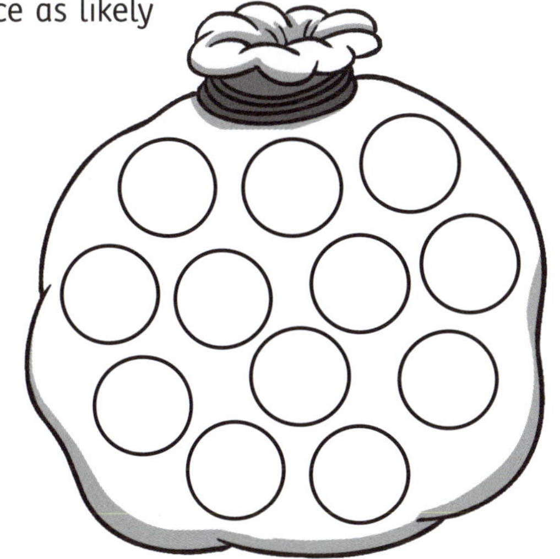

red counter $\frac{\square}{12}$ which is a ______ out of 12 chance of choosing red

green counter $\frac{\square}{12}$ which is a ______ out of 12 chance of choosing green

3 Write the missing numbers.

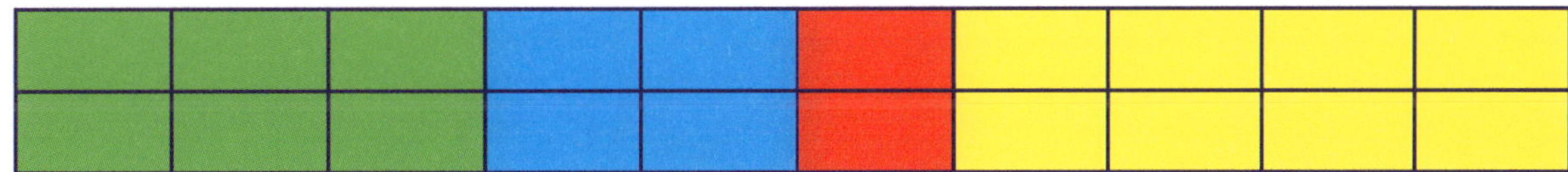

a There is a ________ out of 10 chance of landing on red.

b There is a ________% chance of landing on blue.

c ________ is the least likely colour to land on.

d There is a ________ in 10 chance of landing on yellow.

e There is a ________ in 10 chance of landing on blue.

Unit 40 Animals on the mend

Graphs 2

The Vet nurse drew dot plots to record how many animals spent the night in the Vet's hospital.

Wednesday

Cats	● ● ● ●
Dogs	● ●
Birds	●

Thursday

Cats	● ●
Dogs	● ● ●
Birds	● ●

Friday

Cats	● ●
Dogs	●
Birds	●

1 a What type of graph is this? ____________

b Why was it chosen for this information? ____________

____

2 Write a title for the graph.

3 How many animals were in hospital on:

a Wednesday? ________ b Thursday? ________ c Friday? ________

4 What is the average number of animals in hospital over the three nights? ________

5 Give one reason why fewer animals stayed in hospital on Friday night. ____________

____

6 Why would a Vet nurse keep a graph like this? ____________

____

7 Suggest two other types of information a Vet or Vet nurse might collect. Name the best type of graph to display it.

a ____________

b ____________

Unit 40 Graphs

Pierre drew a graph of the meals he served last week at his cafe.

1 How many meals did he serve:

a on Saturday? ___________

b on Tuesday? ___________

c on Monday? ___________

d on Thursday? ___________

e during the whole week? ___________

Sun.	
Mon.	
Tues.	
Wed.	
Thur.	
Fri.	
Sat.	

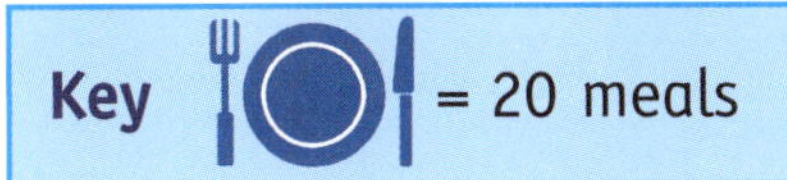

2 a Give a reason why no meals were served on Sunday. ___________________

____

b He wants to close on another day too. Which day would you suggest and why?

____

____

____

____

3 a Draw Pierre's information on a column graph.

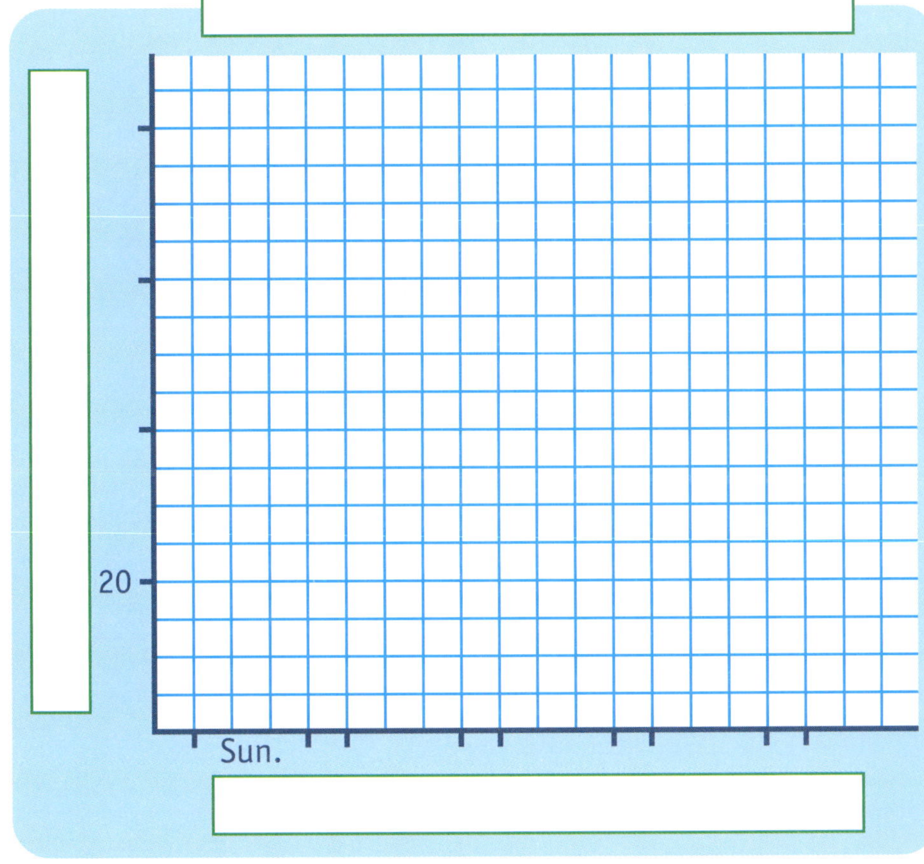

b Write the title.

c Label the axes.

d Which graph do you prefer?

____

Why? ___________________

____

____

____

____

Unit 40 My graph

You are to survey 20 people about the places they visited for entertainment in the last month, eg theatre, restaurant, concert etc. They can choose more than one.

1 Choose five types of entertainment you want to survey. Write them in the table.

Entertainment	Tally	Total

2 Use tally marks to gather the information.

3 Work out the totals.

4 Draw a graph to show the information. It can be a picture graph, column graph or dot plot. Remember a title and labels on the axes.

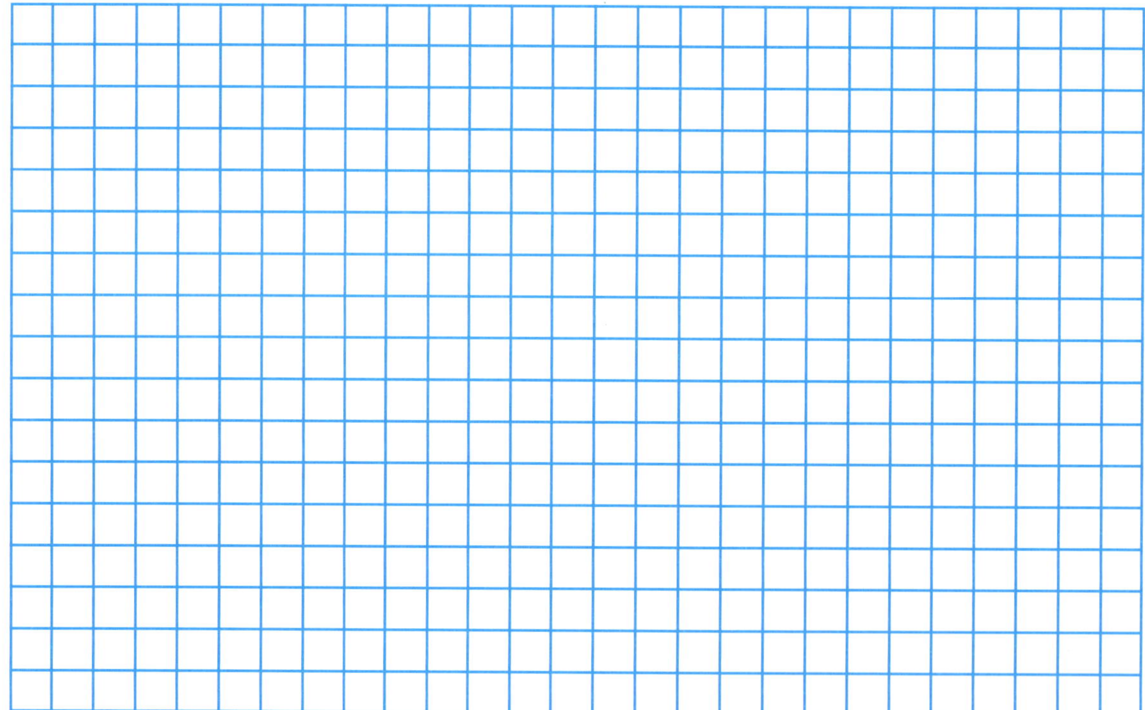

5 Who might use this information? ______________________

Why? ____

____

6 Were your choices of entertainment good ones? ____________

Why? ____

____

Unit 40 Spreadsheets

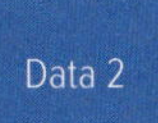

A spreadsheet has data organised into rows and columns.

Shark's Soccer Club Expenses

	A	B	C	D	
1	Date	Item	Cost	Balance	
2	3 May	Opening	–	$8500	
3	5 May	Registrations	$500	$8000	D3 = D2 – C3
4	10 May	Bought goals	$450	$7550	D4 = D3 – C4
5	16 May	Bought balls	$300	$7250	D5 = D4 – C5
6	18 May	Bought jerseys	$1200	$6050	D6 = D5 – C6

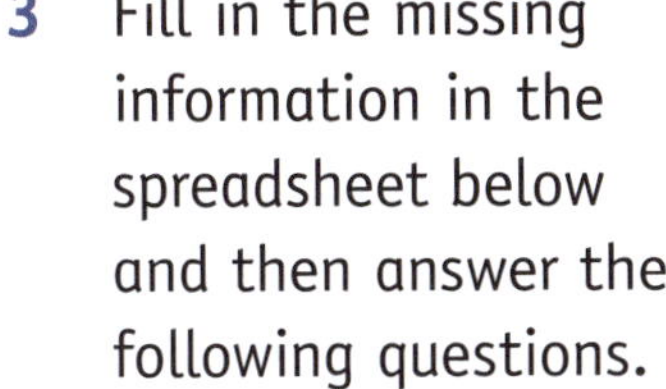

1 Use the spreadsheet above to answer the questions.

a What was the largest cost? ____________

b The smallest cost was paid on ___ May.

c Goals were bought on ___ May.

2 What was the balance on:

a 5 May? ____________ b 16 May? ____________ c 18 May? ____________

3 Fill in the missing information in the spreadsheet below and then answer the following questions.

	A	B	C	
1	Date	Deposit	Subtotal	
2	6 Jul	$4000	$4000	C2 = B2
3	9 Jul	$1200		C3 = C2 + B3
4	13 Jul	$3420		C4 = C3 + B4
5	28 Jul	$1225		C5 = C4 + B5
6	29 Jul	$1800		C6 = C5 + B6

a What is the subtotal for C4? ____________

b How much money was deposited on 13 July? ____________

c How much money was deposited in total over 28–29 July? ____________

d How many deposits were made in July? _____

Mastery Checklist I can:

- ☐ predict the probability of winning a game
- ☐ use fractions and percentages to describe probability
- ☐ interpret a dot plot
- ☐ draw a column graph
- ☐ choose the best type of graph to present data
- ☐ interpret spreadsheets.

Revision Term 4

1 Check your answers by multiplying. p 155

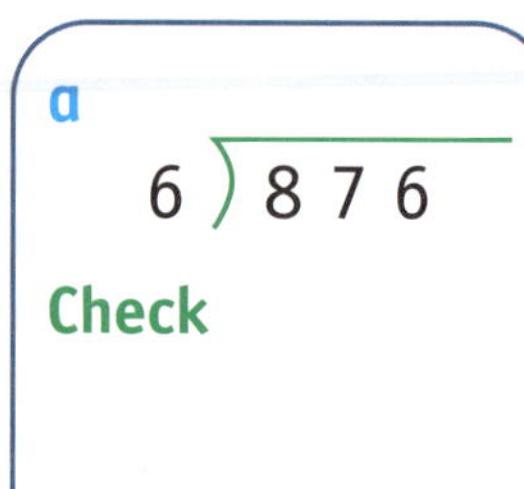

a $6\overline{)876}$

Check

b $5\overline{)940}$

Check

2 a 387 + 6 914 + 84 = ________ p 159

b 5 097 + 9 + 2 315 871 = ________

Working

3 Jan had \$10. She bought a sandwich for \$5.85 and a drink for \$1.45. How much does she have left? ________ p 160

4 At the fair Pony Rides cost \$3.15, the Jumping Castle costs \$2.45 and the Merry-go-round costs \$1.95. p 161

What is the cost of:

a 6 children on the Pony Rides? ________

b 4 children on the Jumping Castle? ________

c 8 children on the Merry-go-round? ________

5 Large plants cost \$5.50 each and small plants cost \$4.40 each. p 161
I bought 3 for \$13.20.
Did I buy large plants or small?

____

6 Find the average of these sets of scores. p 162

a 9, 11, 7, 5, 13, 9 ________

b 7, 5, 6, 16, 4, 8, 8, 10 ________

7 Prove with a diagram that p 168
$\frac{5}{8} + \frac{7}{8} = 1\frac{1}{2}$

8 Draw diagrams to show: p 169

a $2 - \frac{2}{5} =$ ____

b $1\frac{1}{3} - \frac{2}{3} =$ ____

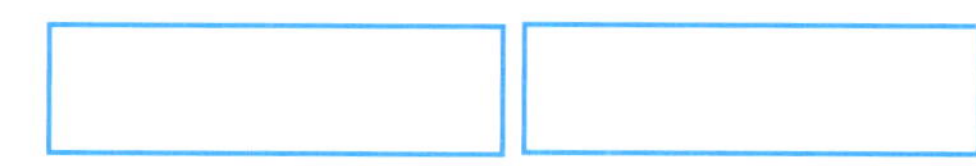

9 True or false?

a 4·72 is the same as 472 hundredths. p 170

____

b 2·075 is 2 tenths and 5 thousandths.

____

10 a 8·3 × 10 = ________ p 171

b 6·29 × 100 = ________

c 28 ÷ 10 = ________

d 257 ÷ 100 = ________

11 This is part of a timetable for school buses leaving Getty High School. p 172

Bus	Destination	Time		
747	Sanville	3:18	3:25	3:40
575	Downtown	3:20	3:30	3:45
707	Farmly	3:18	3:32	3:45
929	Beachside	3:15	3:25	3:42

Revision Term 4

p 172

a How many minutes between the first bus and the last bus?

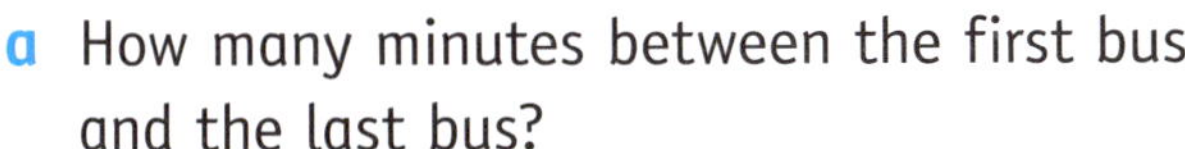

____

b If the Sanville trip is 42 minutes, at what time will the 3:18 bus finish the trip?

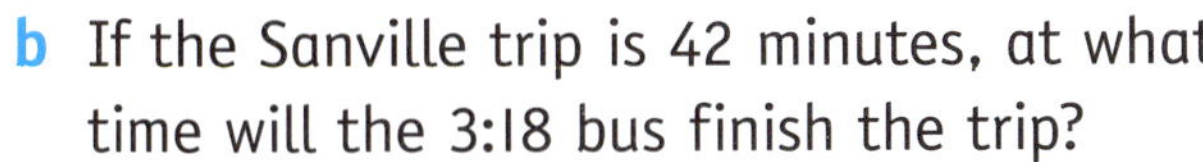

____

c Why is it unnecessary to write am or pm on this timetable?

____

d Which two buses leave seventeen minutes apart?

____

12 Complete the length conversions. p 173

a 1 m 89 cm = ______________ m

b 678 cm = ______________ m

c ______________ cm = 4·87 m

d ______________ cm = 10 m 2 cm

13 Use the area model to multiply. p 179

809 × 67

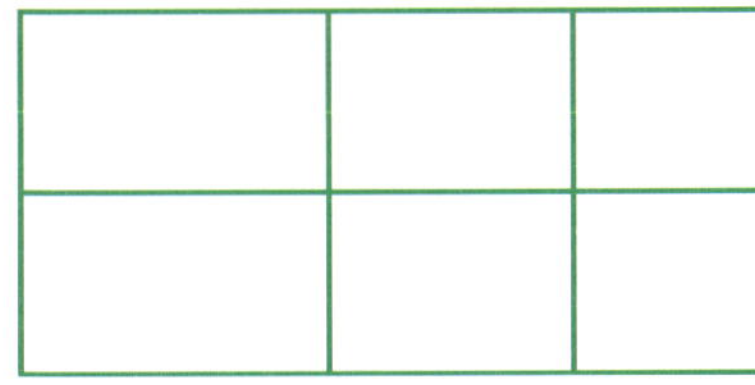

______ + ______ + ______ = ______

14 What 3D object can be made from this net? p 185

____

15 Draw a net for these 3D objects. p 185

a

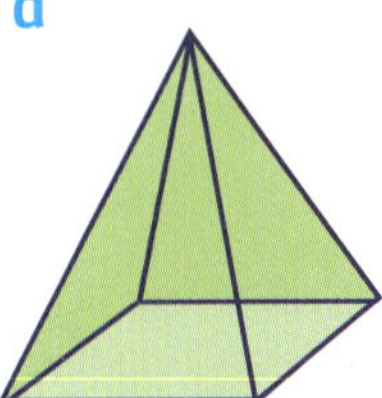

b

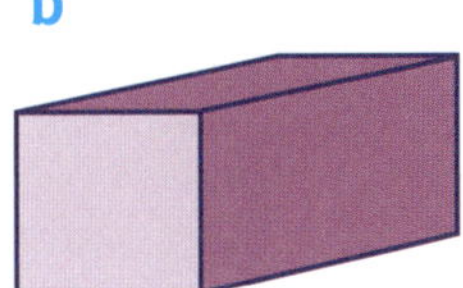

16 Draw the top view, side view and front view. p 186

side view

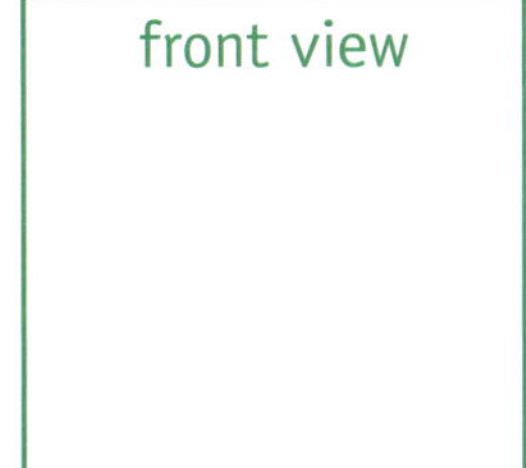

17 Draw the transformations. p 187

a Translate.

b Rotate 90° clockwise.

c Reflect.

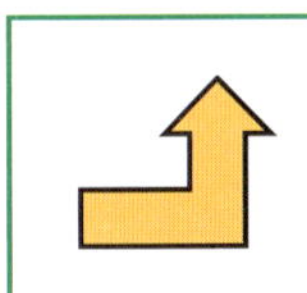  

Revision Term 4

18 Does this shape have rotational symmetry? p 190

______

19 Predict the probability, between 0 and 1, that: p 192

a you will turn 18 this year. ______

b the sun will send out heat. ______

c you'll flip heads the next time you flip a coin. ______

20 In a bag there are 3 green jelly beans, 4 red jelly beans and 1 yellow jelly bean. On the number line, order the probability of: p 193

a picking a red one.

b picking a black one.

21 The Scout group tallied the seasons of their birthdays. p 194

Season	Tally	Total
Summer	𝍸 𝍸 𝍷	
Autumn	𝍸 𝍷𝍷	
Winter	𝍸 𝍸	
Spring	𝍸	

a Complete the total column.

b Draw a dot plot to show this information. Remember the title and labels.

c How many in the Scout group? ______

d Put a cross beside the questions that are not answered by this graph.

How many birthdays in July? ______

How many summer birthdays are there? ______

Are more birthdays in summer than winter? ______

e Can you find the total number of Scouts in the survey from the dot plot? ______